Ms. Donna Magrill
1283 Suncrest Dr NE
Grand Rapids, MI 49525-4557

GOD IS **THE** GOOD WE DO

D1384805

Advance Praise

Michael Benedikt's book God Is the Good We Do *is a profound attempt to develop a new God language with which to define the human experience. He takes God out of the sky of theological debate and places this God in the depths of life. He empowers self-conscious human beings to embrace the power they have to bring God into human awareness.... I welcome this book and this author as my ally in the struggle to bring about a New Religious Reformation that is rooted in the ethics of life-affirming Goodness and that sees every religious system finally as an attempt to make us all more fully human.*

THE RT. REV. JOHN SHELBY SPONG
EPISCOPAL BISHOP OF NEWARK (RET.)

Michael Benedikt's God Is the Good We Do *is the best new manuscript I have read in years. It is rare that I read a new manuscript or book that brings genuinely new insights into an important area of philosophy, rather than just reworking previous themes or positions. In addition, the book is well written, with a clarity and directness that will appeal to general readers and a depth that will appeal to specialists. Finally, its topic—the nature of God and religion—is both timeless and timely. Particularly in the wake of recent American political events, there is tremendous interest in articulating 'liberal' (i.e., open-minded and truly ethical) religious positions. The time is right for this book.*

PHILIP CAFARO,
ASSOCIATE PROFESSOR OF PHILOSOPHY,
COLORADO STATE UNIVERSITY

In God Is the Good We Do, *Michael Benedikt presents a highly imaginative and provocative new conception of God and religious belief. He challenges theological and philosophical orthodoxies about the nature of God, presenting an unusual alternative in which God is intimately related to the ethical and moral life of human beings. The first of four 'books' in the overall book presents this novel view in an evocative way (as befits his goal of addressing readers who are looking for new ways to express their religious and spiritual aspirations in the modern world). The much longer middle two books explain and argue for the view he calls 'the theology of theopraxy' in greater detail. Benedikt shows in these two middle books considerable knowledge of current debates in the philosophy of religion about the nature of God and religious belief. His treatment of the traditional "problem of evil," for example, in Book 3, is especially astute, and even profound. The writing is fluent and clear, easily understandable by non-professional readers, even in the more technical Books 2 and 3. Benedikt is aware that his view departs in radical ways from orthodox theistic belief, and will be rejected by many on that score. But he is also right in thinking that new ways of conceiving the object of religious belief are needed by many aspiring religious believers in the modern world and in this manuscript he presents us with a radically novel and provocative alternative.*

ROBERT KANE,
UNIVERSITY DISTINGUISHED TEACHING PROFESSOR
OF PHILOSOPHY, THE UNIVERSITY OF TEXAS AT AUSTIN

*A marvelous and perplexing balance of the most humble philosophy imaginable with the most hubristic—"our responsibility for God is matched by a responsibility to God" (*EXPLANATIONS 18*). I applaud the argument that the theology of theopraxy is monotheism at its least idolatrous. It is a beautiful proposition. ... I want to conclude, however, with praise not only for the radically beautiful ideas but for the structure of the argument. The pithy subchapters and the proverbial summaries present themselves with an authority appropriate to their content. The poems of* DECLARATIONS *are splendid and a simple way to start. I didn't understand them on the first reading but I was eager to reread them when I completed the book. It was actually a nice return, a good way to end by beginning again. This is a remarkable essay; I hope lots of people get a chance to read it.*

PETER GREENBERG, AIA,
CAMBRIDGE, MASS.

God Is the Good We Do *approaches religion in a way that is often felt but rarely articulated. Many in our world need the premise and logic of this book to be given voice. Benedikt has done so, and done it well. Do I agree with everything he says? No. But* God Is the Good We Do *is a compelling contribution to theological discourse. It has been said that to truly understand one's own spirituality and faith tradition one must also be willing to look deeply at others', and even more, to question one's own. What may be most compelling about the theology of theopraxy, however, is that it does not postulate its validity or usefulness through tearing down another. Indeed, it invites all faith traditions to enter into a discussion with it, and to seek and find the deeper connections between them as to what humans have known or felt about God for ages.*

Rev. Greg Rickel,
Rector, St. James' Episcopal Church
Austin, Texas

God Is the Good We Do *is a passionate and profound rethinking of the meaning of the divine in human life. Its central argument for "theopraxy" develops biblical, Jewish, Christian, and modern perspectives on God in original and often surprising new directions. In the process, the sacred is fundamentally tied to human goodness while human morality is invested with a powerful holiness. At once down to earth and erudite, readable and penetrating, the book explores a wide range of vital questions of moral life without losing sight of its persistent and courageous goal: locating God in life's goodness. A challenge to both religious orthodoxy and contemporary secularism, it offers a truly fresh and stimulating approach to some of the most pressing issues of our time.*

John Wall,
Associate Professor of Religion, Rutgers University

Reading God Is the Good We Do *has been an exhilarating spiritual, intellectual, and homiletic experience. With admirable thoroughness and delightful felicity of style, Benedikt offers a prophetic polemic against the major moral misteachings of traditional theologies and religions. He does this without denying or rejecting "God" and without disparaging various religious traditions and cultures. While I have misgivings about trusting humankind to find the good without a contraposed and humbling Force "out there" reminding us of our self-idolatries, I find much of the theology of theopraxy hospitable to Biblical and Rabbinic thought. I find particularly strong resonance in the idea of "mutual choosing." Perhaps most admirably, however, the theology of theopraxy finds a new place in the religious world-view for secularists and atheists who "do good." And vice versa. This is probably necessary if there is to be hope for our common future.*

AVRAHAM FEDER,
RABBI EMERITUS, MORESHET YISRAEL SYNAGOGUE,
JERUSALEM.

Other books by Michael Benedikt

FOR AN ARCHITECTURE OF REALITY

DECONSTRUCTING THE KIMBELL:
AN ESSAY ON ARCHITECTURE
AND MEANING

CYBERSPACE: FIRST STEPS

CENTER 11: VALUE 1

CENTER 12: VALUE 2

SHELTER:
THE 2000 RAOUL WALLENBERG LECTURE

GOD
IS THE GOOD
WE DO

Theology of Theopraxy

MICHAEL BENEDIKT

BOTTINO BOOKS · NEW YORK

BOTTINO BOOKS, LLC
277 Broadway, 13th Floor
New York, NY 10007-0011

God Is the Good We Do: Theology of Theopraxy
Copyright © 2007 by Michael Benedikt

Cover art © Estate of Ben Shahn/Licensed by VAGA, New York, NY. Detail from *Bring Back My Sons From Far and My Daughters from the End of the Earth*, 1964, by Ben Shahn, gouache on board.

The photograph of Louis I. Kahn at the chalkboard, ca. 1963, which appears on page 20, is by Martin Rich; reproduced by permission of The Architectural Archives, University of Pennsylvania.

Cataloging in Publication Data:

Benedikt, Michael
God is the good we do:
theology of theopraxy/
by Michael Benedikt,
p. cm.
A critique of both traditional and modern arguments for and against the existence of God, with a discussion of the nature of good and the problem of evil, proposing that God exists only as human moral activity, that God is practiced: theopraxy.
Includes bibliographical references.
ISBN 0-9793754-0-1 (pbk)
ISBN 978-0-9793754-0-8 (pbk)
1. God. 2. Good and evil. 3. Religion and science. 4. Religion and ethics
I. Title.
BT103.B36 2007
211—dc22

Printed in Canada
Designed by Christopher Calderhead
First Edition
Second Printing

Contents

Preface

THE BOOK in your hands is a statement and exploration of a certain kind of belief in God. We can experience God, it says, and we can think of God, not as something or someone remote, nor as the Creator of the universe, nor as a spirit or principle behind everything, but as something—"someone"—we bring to life when and as we do good. Hence the term "theopraxy" in the title.[1]

Theopraxy is ancient beyond telling. It goes on today perhaps more than ever. But the *theology* of theopraxy—which is to say, the intellectual consideration of how God could be conceived in this way, and perhaps should—is new. In it you will find ideas both bothersome and appealing, this whether you are presently an atheist or a believer. But the theology of theopraxy is new in ways that prove to be old, or at least implicit, in all religions and moral philosophies when and as they succeed in preserving, honoring, and promoting all life—which is to say, when and as they help us do good.

WHO AM I to write such a book?

I am a university professor and an architect, Jewish by birth and enculturation, but not very observant.

I am also the only child of parents who struggled with faith ever since their liberation from Nazi concentration camps in 1945. They rarely attended synagogue after that. When they did, the words would choke in their throats and the songs would reduce them to tears. How could anyone worship the God who permitted the Holocaust, who wiped out their families, who allows the suffering of millions of innocents around the world to continue? Neither my mother nor my father could answer this question.

In fact, no one has satisfactorily answered this question within the framework of biblical faith. As theologians acknowledge, the "problem of evil" has been the greatest single challenge to belief in God for a very long time.

What you will read in these pages represents the result of many years of reading and reflection on the problem of evil. It is also a meditation on the question of who or what God actually is. For *this* question is founda-

---

1 "Theo" *is from the Greek*, theos, *meaning "god," and* praxis *from* prattein, *meaning "do."*

tional to how the problem of evil must be solved—solved not just as an intellectual puzzle having to do with the attributes of the deity, but as a matter of some urgency in a world increasingly torn by religious differences.

If, then, you think that theology should be engaged in only by people who have graduated from a seminary, yeshiva, madrasah, divinity school or religious studies department, you should set this book aside. If you think that theology should be engaged in only by committed practitioners of one of the great religions, or if you are convinced that the referent of the word "God" is beyond human comprehension and ought to remain that way, you should set this book aside too.

THE STUDY and teaching of architecture undoubtedly influenced my thinking about theological matters. Indeed, theological questions were part of the reason for my going into architecture in the first place. How so? In retrospect, I can say.

Remember the poet William Blake's portrayal of God as the Architect of the Universe? The God-as-Architect metaphor informed both 18th and 19th century *deism*. It also influenced Freemasonry, an ethico-religious movement with roots in the cathedral-building craft guilds. Here, anyway, was a vision of God as designer/builder rather than all-seeing father, judge, or governor. Here was God as an entity of vast intelligence, a designer and creator *par excellence*, that (or who) left humankind free to explore the beauty of his creation and the secrets of his perfect laws without interference or control. The natural world was a marvel. "Sin" was error, and entirely human.

For a barmitzvahed young man of scientific and creative bent, and one ready to question received wisdom, the hands-off God of deism was attractive. For someone untroubled by the problem of evil (which is not as sharp for deism as it is for theism) and overly impressed by the stars, the God of deism remains a tempting choice: God can be "space;" God can be "Being" or "Process" or "Order..." But as I will argue in this book, deism (it takes various forms) is not the best choice.

For converse to Blake's God as Architect analogy, I came to think, and more challenging, is the "architect in the image of God" analogy, the ideal of *imitatio dei*. Architects, after all, are first and foremost creative designers. A few architects with unwarranted hubris, but most with requisite humility, see themselves working to make the earth a better home for humankind. Designing for people's happiness, but not specifying what people should do—indeed, without the power to do so—the best architects go further, striving to construct places of such surpassing beauty that belief in the possibility of heaven-on-earth, of paradise, would be justified.

But more important, I quickly saw, was that the analogy also throws light on the processes of creativity, action, and judgment in *all* walks of life. *Imitatio dei*—to emulate God, to walk in his ways[2]—is everyone's option and obligation: doctors, executives, artists, editors, clerks, farmers. We can all ask: what does it mean to *create*, to *design*, to *decide*, or simply to *do*? What does it mean to configure things and events well? What is the role of will? What does it mean to act for the benefit of others in ways they might not be able to understand?

In architecture, certainly, designing takes time. Complexity abounds and more complexity develops. Solutions are tried and put aside in quick succession. Luck enters everywhere. Order must be found. From the outside, the process looks a lot like evolution speeded up. From the inside, however, the process of design has a distinct *feel* to it, produced from the sum of four moments: One moment is the *coming-to-mind* of a certain course of action, standing out from the chaos of half-formed possible ones. The second moment is that of *commitment* to that action, usually in the face of uncertainty—on faith, one might say. The third is *judging* that what one has done is *good*. And the fourth moment is the coupled experience of *gladness* and *rest*—as though the seventh day of Creation had repeated itself in this minor act of creation.

I think all creative people experience this cycle: chefs, artists, writers, scientists, craftsmen, florists, event organizers, teachers...the list, in fact, is long, because there is hardly a job or social role that does not have at its core a creative kernel, covered over as it might be by habit and neglect.

Now, some might say that only *beauty* guides the human creative process. Certainly, the pursuit of beauty (and sometimes sublimity) captivates most artists and architects completely. For some scientists, most deists, and all theists, it is nature's unfathomably complex beauty after all (and sometimes its sublimity) that underwrites the conviction that there must have been a Creator.

But now I know what, as a youth, I had only suspected: that there is also such a thing as *moral creativity*, by which I mean the creation of new ways of being, new applications of goodness, new life-affirming narratives and laws, and new freedoms and obligations to act, forged out of, and discovered in, the matrix of complexifying social and ecological realities. There exists, I came to see, not only scientific and artistic creative

---

2 *In Judaism one speaks of the commandment* Ve-halakhta bi-derakhav, *"You shall walk in His ways." Confucian ethics urges us to follow the Way(s) of Heaven.*

genius, but *moral* creative genius. The great religions and moral philoso-phies were sparked and fueled by the words and deeds of such geniuses, to be sure, but significant moral talent and genius can be found all around us: among the people we work with, among the members of our family. Many otherwise-ordinary individuals—people who might not be able to whistle a tune, draw a straight line, or dance a graceful step—consistently find creative solutions to moral dilemmas, regularly devise activities that heal and satisfy and inspire, sometimes invent new and fitting interpre-tations of law, but habitually step forward into uncertainty, themselves, simply out of the desire to be on the side of good, or, as they might put it, on the side of God.

This seemed to me to be miracle enough. If there is a God, "he" is manifest in such people and as such actions. If there is a God, "he" did not cause the Holocaust but caused families to hide Jews from the Nazis. God does not cause famine or genocide, but induces doctors and nurses to join Médicins Sans Frontières and others to provide it with funds. God does not evict, sicken, kill, or impoverish, but "commands" us to house the homeless, heal the sick, comfort the bereaved, share with the poor.

Why? For life. God comes out of life and turns to life. God turns to life, as it were, to act in it and on it through you and me, preserving, hon-oring, and promoting almost all of life's forms and instances, which is the very definition of goodness.[3] I came to realize that it matters less *why* good is done and more *that* it is. We must see God, when we see God as agentic, as an uplifting force only, and abandon most if not all of God's other purported attributes. God is only where God is, not everywhere. God is only what God is, not everything. And God is only good, not bad. I see these as the true meaning of *Ehyeh-Asher-Ehyeh*, "I AM that which I AM" (Exodus 3:14).

If God acts only through us, it follows that there is a sense in which we are responsible not only *to* God but *for* God, or at least God's continu-ance, by our actions.[4] Take this to heart and a great deal changes. One weight is lifted and another is taken on—a weight that does not bend our backs but gives joy to life and purchase to our step. The first is the weight of our anger and puzzlement at evil, alternating with the weight of resignation. The second is the weight of our freedom and responsibil-ity—that redoubtable duo—but now with something more precious in the balance than our acceptability to others; namely, the actuality of God.

---

3 *For why I say* "almost *all forms and instances of life,*" *see* EXPLANATIONS 6.

4 "*I am called according to My actions*" *says God in the Midrash on Exodus 3:14 (Shemot Rabbah 3).*

Allowing some personification, one sees that *our present freedom is a gift from God; but our earlier freedom was prerequisite to God's very existence.* The same is true of moral responsibility. This is the two-phased cycle by which goodness increases and God's kingdom comes...

But let me not go so far so soon. I hope only to have explained how an architect—how this architect—came to write about God.

The stakes are high, and go beyond architecture, of course. "True religion"—religion based on deed rather than creed, as the epistle writer James wanted it—should be a boon to life and not a cause for strife. As we consider what true religion might mean for our day, let us look at what contribution the theology of theopraxy might make, a theology that has no intention of removing us from our religious traditions, that in fact advocates their embrace with a renewed understanding of what we are actually doing when we do good on account of their urging, which is to bring God to life in both senses of the phrase.

As YOU have no doubt noticed, this book dares to say who or what God is and who or what God is not. It makes its points confidently, and it does so in fairly plain English. It would be unfortunate to conclude from this, however, that the author is guilty of hubris or dogmatism. It's a matter of my preferring vulnerable directness to defensible hedging. The truth is that no one can say who or what God is with absolute certainty, and that includes me. One can argue for the beauty, consistency, pedigree, timeliness, and validity of one's point of view. One can try to persuade others of its rewards. One can even try to exemplify with one's deeds what one means. But in the end, readers must decide for themselves whether the narratives and arguments offered make sense, whether a useful difference exists, for them, between God-as-experienced and God-as-theorized to exist independent of experience—be it theirs or anyone else's.

Certainly, *God Is the Good We Do* reflects my experience of God *as* the good we do, not after a single revelation with the mark of truth stamped upon it—no burning bush for me—but rather after several, shall we say, less impressive revelations, and after considerable reflection on the problems of conventional faith. It was these reflections that emboldened me to convert the modest *as* of reported experience into the *is* of an ontological claim, to offer a theology rather than a testament. Perhaps my thoughts will resonate with yours. Perhaps not. I write about God, anyway, not as One Who Knows, but as an all-too-human advocate for my view's reasonableness in this day. God and humanity, I am convinced, are both works-in-progress, co-creating each other, co-evolving. Neither will have the final word.

THE BOOK as a whole is divided into four smaller "Books," entitled DECLARATIONS, EXPLANATIONS, ARGUMENTS, and REFLECTIONS. Each is comprised of around twenty short chapters. They can be read in any order once one gets the idea, but they are best read in sequence. This is because many follow each other in theme, or pick up from a question posed in the previous chapter. DECLARATIONS, as the name suggests, offers the tenets of the theology of theopraxy in aphoristic, poetic form. EXPLANATIONS starts at the Beginning, as it were, and makes the case again with a measure of scholarship in support. ARGUMENTS takes up a debate with a selection of theologians, scientists, and philosophers— ones that I think are wrong, ones that I think are right. Many of their names will be familiar. It is in ARGUMENTS that the problem of evil is mainly tackled.

Finally, REFLECTIONS, as its name suggests, goes back and offers deepenings of earlier passages. It recalls further writers on the topic— precursors, if you will. It touches on more subtle considerations and it looks toward the future: How viable, practically speaking, is "the theology of theopraxy"? What would it mean to subscribe to it? For whom is it intellectually suited? The answer to this last question is one I should offer now. It is: "Not everyone."

A NOTE about gendered language. It's easy to replace older usages such as "Man" or "mankind" with "human beings" or "humankind." It's not hard to write "men and women" instead of "men," and "he or she" instead of "he." It is harder, however, to de-gender "God," who for thousands of years has been conceived of as male and written about using "He," "His," and "Himself." (Then there is God's *King*dom, God the *Father*, and so on.) Perhaps insensitive to the bias it perpetuated, perhaps feeling helpless to change it, even secular philosophers who have had occasion to mention God adopted the usage. The result is that today, in the laudable attempt to remove gender from the concept of God, it still sounds distinctly odd to refer to God as "He-or-She," or, worse, as "It," which conjures images of a machine or alien life-form, while the term "Godself" positively hurts.

Since I believe that God is neither male nor female, in this book I have adopted the following policy: When quoting respected sources that use gendered pronouns and analogies, I leave things be. (Sometimes this involves capitalizing the "h," as in "He" and "His.") When representing traditional theologies as they would represent themselves, I also write he, him, and his, without quotation marks. When describing these same theologies at a critical distance, however, I write "he," "him," "his," i.e. with quotation marks. Lastly, when presenting or elucidating the theology of theopraxy in its *own* terms, I try to avoid using personal pronouns in third-person reference to God altogether.

Note that the object of this policy is not to avoid the *personification* of God. I am open to a degree of personification for reasons I discuss in the book. The object is to avoid imputing maleness or femaleness to God in any exclusive or literal way.

For their sharp editorial eyes and moral support in writing this book I thank Tim Walker, Martin K. Jones, and Christine Wong. For their strong (if quizzical) encouragement of the project, I thank Charles Jencks, William Saunders, and John Haught, co-speakers at a symposium entitled "Divinity/Creativity/Complexity" held at the University of Texas at Austin in 2003. I thank John Shelby Spong for his inspiration as a religious writer and for his brief but wise editorial advice at a crucial moment, Adam Zachary Newton for a critical reading of the manuscript, Robert Kane for his encouragement and example, and Philip Cafaro, John Wall, and Peter Greenberg for their generous attention to the text in manuscript. Book designer Christopher Calderhead and proof reader Jenny Meadows deserve much credit for how this book looks and reads.

I thank my daughter, Claire, for offering her affectionate skepticism and many helpful comments. I thank especially my wife, Amélie Frost Benedikt—love of my life, philosopher and friend, editor and debate-partner—for helping me refine my ideas and the language in which they are expressed.

For putting the question of God in front of me long ago, however, I must thank my parents, Dinah and Oscar David. I dedicate this book to them.

—*Michael Benedikt, Austin, 2007*

BOOK ONE

Declarations

1 : Whether or not God exists

Whether or not God exists
is entirely up to us.
For God comes into being by what we do
and do not do.

Neither you nor I are God
but what we're doing may be.

This God, who lives as deeds not creeds,
is the God we know firsthand.
This God , whose shape is action not image,
is the God we witness every day.
This God's presence is not guaranteed.

"God is good and God does good" the Talmud says,
and Augustine said too.
"God is what God does" we might add—or
God does what God is,
which is good.

Goodness-of-deed is less God manifest
than God instanced.

God is in our hands,
and we in "his" as we choose the good
and do it.

Do good again and again,
and you "do God's will."
"Do God's will,"
and you bring God into being.

2 : God is not all-powerful

God is not all-powerful.
> *"He" is weaker than a curl of smoke.*

God is not all-knowing.
> *"He" knows only what you do.*

God is not everywhere,
but wants to be.

"He" is only where God is and when God is,
which is 'here and there'
> *and 'now and again'—*
>> *wherever good is being done.*

God is the good we do,
when and where and as we do it.

God is practiced, like dance, like music,
like kindness, like love...
> *"theopraxy."*

3 : God did not create the universe

God did not create the universe.
God was not there in the Beginning.
God was not there or anywhere else in the Beginning
  (if there was such a time)
because God did not exist in the Beginning,
or before it.

God became present in Homo Sapiens, in Thinking Humans.
God's work was our work, and our work "his."
And what was that work? What is it still?
It is to become more human in every best sense of the word:
  more loving,
  more compassionate,
  more courageous,
  more just,
  more intelligent,
  more happy,
  more caring,
  more excellent in physical grace and skill,
  longer lived in health, and further-seeing
    in the wisdom that would have us preserve, honor,
      and promote
      all forms and instances of life.

God is not done with Creation:
  God is not done with us.
Nor are we done with God.
For humankind and God emerged from each other
  in cycles of reciprocal improvement.
It's not just our understanding of God that improves,
but God "Godself," with us.

4 : God is conceived in good will

God is conceived in good will.
God is nurtured by understandings of virtue.
But God is brought to life and flourishes
      only in actual good doings.

These are God's body, God's life.

"His" hands guide the good surgeon's hands;
"His" voice sounds as the good teacher's voice.
God arrives just on time, and every time
      a person has a choice
          and sees that it is good,
          and makes it good,
          and can rest
              because it remains so.

5 : God is here now and at hand

God is not out there,
or back then.
> *God is here, now,*
> *and at hand.*

We are larger, each one of us, than all of the galaxies combined.
This is why the rabbis said:
"to redeem one person is to redeem the world."

6 : God is ignited by life

God is ignited by life.
God is lit in the living.

Chance gives us opportunity,
and imagination gives us choice,
but God helps us choose.

God does not preside over battle;
God does not hover over the smoking field of destruction,
but wells up in the tears
*   of those who bend over the wounded.*

God did not make the ovens of Auschwitz;
or watch the Nazis build them and do nothing...
*   but was extinguished "himself"*
*   over and over again.*

God is more easily vanquished than life.

The dead are dead.

But mere life is not yet God.
Life is necessary but not sufficient for God to come to be.
There is no God of molecules.
There is no God of fibrillating sea urchins.
There is no God of blindworms or chickadees or whales.
But there is a God who is for them all, and who loves them all, through us.
For God begins and ends with our activity,
*   with what we do for life.*

7 : God is not Gaia

God is not Gaia,
nor the Noosphere,
nor Absolute Spirit,
nor the Unmoved Mover
nor Nature,
nor Existence,
nor the Real,
nor the Invisible Ground of Being
nor Eternity
nor Process
nor the Creator
nor the Supreme Intelligence,
but forms wherever and whenever there is choosing
    of good over bad,
        of beauty over ugliness,
            of truth over falsehood,
                and life over death.

Then *there is God,*
    there,
    as fugitive as the moment,
    whole in every part,
    ready to appear, ready to become
        a reality enacted
            and enacted again.

God begins and ends with us.

God is in our hands.

8 : Nothing is holy
except that we sanctify it

Nothing is holy except that we sanctify it;
and thus everything is potentially holy
    except cruelty, disease, and untimely death.

God stills our rage: "He maketh us to lie in green pastures."
God teaches by example and by encouragement.
    God teaches by trust.
    God speaks to us in that "still, small voice"
        that does not come from anything except life
            working itself out,
            blind at first,
            but then giving itself eyes,
                and then eyes to see those eyes.

9 : God neither compels nor threatens

God does not compel or threaten.
God does not punish or reward.
God does not raise arms.
God does not kill any creature, nor allow them to die
       when living is a possibility.
God does not sicken any creature, nor allow them to languish
       when well-being is a possibility.

When a conscience that is clouded makes us suffer, God suffers with us
       until our guilt turns us toward the good.
When a conscience that is clear yields us joy, God is joyful with us
       until our joy turns carefreeness into carelessness.
But when conscience is absent,
God feels nothing.

Said the Confucian sage, Mencius:
"Heaven sees with the eyes of the people.
       Heaven hears with the ears of the people."

Said Confucius himself:
"It is the human that can make the Way great,
       not the Way that can make the human great."

10 : God lifts us up

God lifts us up when we lift ourselves up and those around.
God never lets us down.

> God is the good we do.

God dissolves fear.
God clears the Way.
God stays our hand when anger rises.
When anger rises nonetheless, and with it, hate,
> *God dissipates, departs.*
But when forgiveness takes over,
> *God re-forms, and we reform.*

> God is the good we do.

God is moral intuition turned moral action.
God's passing through us is known by what God leaves behind,
> *which is the sweet air*
> > *of a clear conscience.*

> God is the good we do.

And so God is not One,
> *but everyone, with or without an idea of God in their heads,*
> > *doing good willingly, in freedom, for any reason,*
> > *but especially "just because."*
God is not one Fire,
> *but every single flame of hope,*
> > *of forgiveness,*
> > > *of effort to do good, anywhere, eternally.*

When we act kindly,
without revenge,
and without empty flattery,
God acts!

When we listen charitably for the other's meaning,
and speak on that understanding,
God acts!

When we presume the other's good intentions and intelligence,
and hold to it when others would give up,
God acts!

God does not "work in strange ways," alas,
but in ways that are perfectly familiar.

It is easy to proclaim that "God is beyond human understanding"
and imagine this saves one from idolatry
    or proves one's wisdom,
    or keeps one humble,
    or is true.
It may just as likely be sanctimony. Or evasion.
And besides,
    has one not proclaimed something one presumes
    to be true about God?

God is supremely within reach.
He is at hand, as Jesus said His Kingdom always was.

Perhaps this is why
    God prefers a good atheist
      to a wicked believer.

11 : God is radically contingent

God is radically contingent.
Nothing that exists
  exists more dependently on all other things than God,
  for we are lately evolved.
God's hold on believers and non-believers alike is not strong.
But it is persistent,
  and will not let us go for long.

(O created creator creating,
we make and unmake You with every deed.)

Or we could say: God is creation, which is always good,
for creation that is not good is properly called destruction.

God's work therefore is never done,
and neither is ours in bringing God into being.

Humans are the most elevated creatures God has created.
(There are no higher as far as we can see.)
And "God" is the most elevating idea humans ever had.
Which is saying almost the same thing.
  For although "God" is an idea, God is not.
  God exists.
  The only question is: how?

Not like a river, or a rock, or the sun,
not like an animal or person or statue,
not like the Universe or Nature,
nor even like Love, or the Good, or Process, in some Platonic realm.
God is not real, or ideal, or potential,
but actual.

God is an event, an activity,
God happens
> *like a flame,*
> *like the sparkle of glass,*
> *like the glint off water,*
> *like the Aurora Borealis,*
> *like love blossoming,*
> *like a laugh that does not ridicule,*
> *like a whisper that is not malicious,*
> *like an outstretched hand that helps,*
> *like the paper hitting the porch,*
> *like a hummingbird at the feeder,*
> *like a newly opened window.*
> *Like justice being done with mercy.*

> *Where does your* lap *go when you stand up?*
> *Where does your* fist *go when you open your hand?*
> *The same place God goes when you diminish life.*

As it was written:
"(B)ring forth the precious from the vile,
and thou shalt be as My mouth." (Jer. 15:19)
But we go further:
God is the good we do
> *in everything we do.*
God's very existence
> *is up to us.*

12 : If God starts in a whisper

If God starts in a whisper we hear,
if God starts in a suggestion we take,
if God warms us like a flame,
 it is because we know
      the whisper
      the suggestion
      the flame
      to be good.

How do we know it to be good?
Because "God made us in his image" really means
    "He made in us his image," or, put another way:
    We evolve in God's image and God in ours.

As Paul wrote in his Letter to the Philippians:

"(W)hatever is true,
whatever is honorable,
whatever is just,
whatever is lovely,
whatever is gracious,
if there is any excellence,
if there is anything worthy of praise,
think about these things.
What you have learned
    and received
        and heard
            and seen in me, do;
                and the God of peace will be with you."

13 : Whether or not God exists (cont.)

Whether or not God exists
is entirely up to you.

God cannot forsake you;
only you can forsake God.
For without you God is nothing
where you are.

Do not wait for miracles, then,
but put yourself to redeeming the world.
Do not wait for God's grace to descend upon you,
but give your grace to others.
Love life, all life,
putting your own neither first
nor last.

Do not drop what is precious in your hands.

Tell your children that they matter to you,
that they matter to others,
that they matter to every living thing
that feels their touch.

Teach them how they have a sacred and ancient mission
to turn sun and rain into seed and flower,
to turn foe into friend
and harm into harmlessness.

Tell them to seek and spread knowledge,
to delight in new complexity,
and to make or find order in that complexity
without reducing it.

Teach them to forebear small injuries
and not to seek revenge.

Teach them to prefer injustice over death,
*   and justice over injustice,*
*   but goodness "for no reason"*
*   above justice,*
*   and above all.*

Teach them that God is not the oldest and strongest force
*   in the universe,*
*   but the youngest and weakest one,*
*   not a storm but a breeze,*
*   not expended in might but persistent in direction,*
*   not anywhere on a throne but everywhere in choice.*

Send them to read all things about God,
that they may hear God's praises in every land
*   and love "him."*
But bid them remember this:
that in the end
*   God is the good they do;*
*   God is in their hands too.*

BOOK TWO

Explanations

1 : God and the beginning

In the Beginning God created the heavens and the earth.

— Genesis 1:1

ALL THREE of the great Western religions—Judaism, Christianity, and Islam—rest on the assertion that a single supreme intelligence of infinite power—namely, God—created order in the universe. Before that there was only chaos and desolation.[1] Separating day from night, above from below, and ocean from dry land, putting the sun and moon and stars in the sky and all living things upon the earth, God created the vast and beautifully ordered system we call "the world" and made it the home of humankind. God did all this in essentially one fell swoop—six days is not long, considering—and he made it *good*.[2]

Belief in this Creator-God answers several important questions. It tells us how the world came to be. It also tells us where (or rather, with whom) ultimate credit and responsibility lie for how the world *is*. But more than this is explained. The unimaginable power, intelligence, and goodwill represented by universal Creation as described in Genesis provides ample reason to accept God's *authority* to rule over us and over the rest of the universe forever.

If you were raised Jewish, Christian, or Muslim, these beliefs would be familiar.

Since the sixteenth century, however, believers seeking greater concordance between religious doctrine and natural science have been apt to modify the doctrine of Creation as presented in Genesis, or at least not take it too literally. Today (to cut a very long story short) science-educated believers are likely to hold that while God might not have created the universe *exactly* as the Bible says, God probably, in some way, set off the

---

1 *Some interpreters have it that there was nothing before God—nothing, that is, but God "himself," God eternal, who at a particular first moment we call "the Beginning" willed time, space, energy, and matter into existence as well as all the laws that govern them. Genesis, however, picks up the story a bit later. In Genesis, the universe exists in time, although it is dark, "unformed, and void," and God is already a "rushing-spirit (or wind) hovering over the face of the waters."*

2 *Genesis relates that it took six days to create the world as we see it. But it is not essential for believers to interpret "days" literally. The point is that, relative to the number of days that have elapsed since, the period of active Creation was extremely swift.*

Big Bang and put the laws of physics in place, setting the values of certain critical physical constants (like the charge of an electron or the speed of light) "just right"—just right, that is, for the universe to persist and for life to emerge more or less as Genesis describes. God also devised the process of evolution, a process in which he could intervene but which he prefers to let run on its own. Certainly, however, the awesome beauty and order we see around us in nature are due ultimately to God—to God's incomparable wisdom as the first Designer and incomparable might as the prime mover.

This last, more scientific *deist* view of God is less personal than the Bible's *theist* view, which has it that God not only created the world but watches over it to this day, manages it in every detail, and can be spoken to. In the deist view, God made The Rules, designed some elements, wound it all up rather like a giant clock, and then let it run. Complexity ensued.

The God of deism (more about which later) is certainly not the God of Abraham, Moses, Jesus, or Mohammed. But God's prior and underlying existence as God (or as The Absolute, the Invisible Ground of Being, Creative Principle, or some such abstraction) is not seriously questioned by deism. Nor is God's immensity.

THE THEOLOGY presented in this book challenges both traditional theism and deism. It seeks to base God's authority not on God's authorship *of* everything but on God's authoredness *by* everything, by life, and, in particular, by human ethical life, which "he" in turn affects. The theology of theopraxy respects both theistic and deistic creation myths as important, and, once, even essential to making sense of life. But they are, it says, ultimately, only steps along the way to understanding who/what God really is.

If there *was* a Beginning (and let us note: there might not have *been* a Beginning, for perhaps the history of a universe like ours—one that has no center and no edge—also extends infinitely into the past and future)... if there *was* a Beginning, neither deist nor theist God was there. The universe was without life and without sentient creatures, and therefore without good or evil, and therefore without God. It was largely as we see it today: rocks and gases from thermonuclear explosions flaring across the icy wastes of space in every direction...billions of galaxies, each with billions of stars "dying" and being "reborn" senselessly from eternity to eternity. Around these stars whirred millions of planets, like specks of dust caught up in a firestorm, the rhythm of their tides and of their heating and cooling beating the carbon, hydrogen, and nitrogen molecules of a few of them into long, self-reproducing chains, and thence into microorganisms unaware of their own lives and deaths. How many planets evolved human-level life? We shall likely never know.

The God who believers say was present at the Beginning came later, on the morning that the first human being knowing of birth, life, and death looked up at the fading moon and stars, at the clouds touched by the dawning sun, at the stirring plants and animals, and perhaps at the face of his or her child...and saw it all as a totality, as a uni-verse, brought into being by a single Maker of stupendous intelligence, power, and goodwill toward life, and began to *act* accordingly, which is to say, with gratitude and compassion, with courage and an easy heart.

The God that most religious people understand as God today—the God to whom Jews, Christians, and Muslims pray, and whom they both long and dread to meet—entered the imagination some tens of thousands of years ago with our ancestors' tellings of the stories of Genesis. Indeed, by the time these stories were written down

> *...the nature of God as he [would] appear throughout the Hebrew Bible [was] firmly established. He is seen as a Creator who is beyond fate, nature, and sexuality; as an all-powerful orderer and giver of meaning to history; as a bestower of blessings to living creatures; as a giver of choice to human beings; as a punisher of evil and, simultaneously, a merciful ruler; and as a maker of convenants.* [3]

Is this God a fiction, then, a mere literary creation? The question is categorically misplaced. The early chapters of Genesis describe the world in a phenomenologically accurate way. They describe how things look from here on earth, and how nature and life has felt to millions of people since, people who in turn wove Genesis's image of God, for better *and* for worse, into the warp and woof of Western civilization. [4]

THAT AN *understanding* of God arrives on the scene only with human being(s) and not before was common wisdom among eighteenth- and nineteenth-century philosophers. The more radical idea that God—and not just this or that understanding of God—might be a human innovation with frequently "human, all too human" uses, was one from which theists and deists alike shrank in dismay. [5] One can see why. After all, if

---

3 *Everett Fox (1995), p. 9.*

4 *See also* EXPLANATIONS 17.

5 *I am not scholar enough to trace this idea from Nietzsche through Hegel back to its roots. Certainly, the man-invents-God idea can be found in the Presocratic skeptic and satirist Xenophanes, who wrote: "If lions could think, their gods would have a mane and roar."*

God is "made up," if God is a fiction, an invention, or projection, then God of the Bible (and Holy Qur'an) is as good as dead, just as Nietzsche would declare. And if God is or was always dead—i.e., non-existent—not only would the universe be without overall meaning or purpose, which would be bad enough, but the consequences for the social order would be disastrous. Who would ensure ultimate justice? Who would rule over kings? Who would teach us to love each other? Who would answer our prayers? Who would seal our oaths, console the bereaved or take care of our dead? And who or what would explain miracles?

Besides, if God did not create the universe, who or what *did?* Who or what else could possibly account for its immensity and beauty? How else, except through supernatural agency, could everything have come from nothing? Whence nature's magnificently complex order if not from a great Designer (or divine process)? These are the questions to which the only answer, almost by design, is "God!"

Atheists are quick to move in. Most of the questions just listed, they would say, are either fruitless or malformed. The whole concept of God would not come up if, wisely, we did not demand that they had answers (a) at all, or (b) outside of ourselves. (Interestingly, believers might agree with atheists here...up to a point. For even if it is true, believers could say, that the *concept* of God would not come up if we did not ask these difficult questions, nothing is proved or disproved by this truth about the *existence* of God himself. Just as farmers depend on the rain that comes from an ocean they might never have seen, and of which they might have no knowledge, so does our very existence depend upon the grace of God, whether or not we have seen God or know of him.)

For its part, the theology of theopraxy, which is a form of theism, not atheism, also argues that God would not come up if we did not ask these questions—not just "God," note, or the concept of God, but *God.* God, it proposes, in a profound sense both *produces* and is *produced by* our search for justice, both produces and is produced by our questions about meaning, love, beauty, and so forth. While our physical existence does not depend on God, our moral existence does. God's existence depends on ours and ours upon God's to the extent that our existence has evolved

---

6 *A note about the words "moral" and "ethical." The boundary between them is fuzzy. In tendency, however,* moral *actions are (good) things done for whatever reason; and the subject matter of "morality" tends to be interpersonal (e.g., sexual behavior, aid, decency).* Ethical *actions are good things done on account of the principles behind them and in the knowledge of our freedom to do otherwise. The subject matter of "ethics" thus tends to be institution- and business-related. (Hence "business ethics," or "medical ethics".) Very roughly: religion cares more about morals, and law and moral philosophy about ethics.*

a moral dimension.[6] Many images of God have developed over the millennia, in the East somewhat differently than in the West. But God as God truly is "comes up"—comes to life—through *our* turning toward life in benevolence.

As we shall see, several philosophers have argued that the Biblical God is a reflection of human moral striving, a projection of human virtues onto the figure of an ultimate father *cum* master craftsman and sometime warrior. The theology this book explores is more radical. It cleaves to the phenomenon: God is what we take a good God to want: namely, goodness in deed, *our* goodness in deed. Is God *in* the good we do? Yes. But because God is *only in* the good we do, we can all-but-equivalently say that God is only the good we do. All moral philosophy, like all theology, is preparation for these moments of good-doing—i.e., for God—and commentary thereafter.

The theology of theopraxy, in other words, does not stop at suggesting that the concept or idea of God is human (a suggestion with which many traditional believers might agree, on the proviso that the *reality* of God be acknowledged to be infinitely greater). It suggests that the very reality, body, substance—call it what you will—of God is in human hands. God is the good we *actually* do *as* we do it, not the good we *might* do, contemplate, plan, or remember doing. Nor is God good-in-the-abstract. God is an activity—a verb become a noun, a noun become (in theistic metaphor) a person with "agency," which is to say, with the the ability to will, cause, and do. God performs "himself" through us and at the same time is performed *by* us. God exists in many places, but not everywhere; as many acts, but not all.

Again: it is easy to see God (as traditionally conceived) *in* acts of goodness. Many believers do so already. Indeed, one could read this whole book with little risk and, I think, some reward, replacing every instance of the phrase "God is the good we do" with "God is *in* the good we do." But one would miss the euphoric leap that the theology of theopraxy asks us to make, namely, to see God not just *in* acts of goodness (thus leaving us to imagine God being elsewhere too, doing "God knows what"), but *as* acts of goodness, and therefore here, now, with us, "in our hands" only and always. This is an unfamiliar thought, perhaps, and a vertiginous one, but a thought that this book tries to make normal, somehow right and true all along.

As against atheism, in sum, the theology of theopraxy declares that God exists, hallelujah. It's just that God does not exist in the way we have long imagined "him" to.

But more about all this later.

Over the next few chapters, I will begin by discussing modern arguments for God as the Creator. I will try to convince the reader that marrying religion to science through cosmological origin arguments, a mainstay of modern deism, is not the best way to bring God to life.

2 : Theology and cosmogony

UNTIL RECENTLY, theology and cosmology—or actually cosmo*gony*, the study of cosmic beginnings—were closely related. When it came to understanding the origins of man and nature, of the earth, sun, moon, and stars, there was no science that was not also theology, no theology that was not also science. Today, nearly five hundred years after Copernicus broke with the theistic view of the centrality of the earth (which questioned, by implication, God's location in Heaven above the sky), and over a hundred years after Darwin made cosmogony all but irrelevant to the actualities of life on earth, the connection between God and the Beginning remains strong. Let us ask why.

Beyond the default historical connection, there are two reasons, I believe, that theology and cosmogony are still attracted to each other, and both are a little disappointing.

The first is because it serves the (dare one say professional?) interests of theologians in their search for supra-Biblical, "scientific" support for God's authority.

Here is their tack: The more that science teaches us about the size and subtlety of the universe's design, the more reason there is to give credit to a—no, *the*—Creator. So let science proceed. Just as the order we see everywhere in the tiniest things gives us a glimpse of God's intelligence, so the mind-boggling enormity of the universe bears witness to God's majesty. The better we appreciate this, the less we can reasonably refuse God's authority to give life and take it away in this corner of the universe, to judge us and receive our supplications. No one's authority is natural but God's. All are necessarily subservient to God's laws, which are everlasting and everywhere, rational and wise beyond questioning, the *sine-qua-non* of existence itself.[7]

The second reason theology and cosmology still cleave to each other comes from cosmologists' side. As they "scan the heavens" (but actually analyze radiation from stars), they can describe themselves seeking to understand "God's Design," or "the Mind of God," or some such lofty object. This allows these otherwise secular individuals to pursue their investigations unencumbered by the tricky moral considerations that God-talk properly engenders: the "oughts" rather than the "is's." By understanding the *design* of the cosmos, they can say, are they not getting at the very

---

7 *Nowhere is this sentiment expressed better than in Job 38–41.*

nature of the Creator? Would (mere) moral and ethical problems not melt away once nature was scientifically understood, once God's recipes were deciphered?[8]

Deploying quasi-religious language also profits them by broadening audience. For whoever can speak with the authority of Science about such heady subjects as the "Beginning of Time," the "Fate of the Universe," or the "Place of Man," deserves to be heard with the reverence due prophets of old. Did Newton and Einstein (they can point out) not look more deeply than anyone into the mysteries of nature *and* believe in the Creator? Did not Copernicus and Kepler? Physical scientists of the late 20th century seeking to enlighten the general public on matters quantum and universal—I am thinking here of David Bohm, Frank Tipler, Paul Davies, James Trefil, John Barrow, and Stephen Hawking—borrowed the mantle.

The God that emerges from the agreement between cosmogony and theology, however, is no Biblical or Qur'anic God giving moral direction to human history and everyday life. Nor is it the "existential" God of Buber or Lévinas, the God who dwells in the mystery of human freedom, conscience, and mutual encounter. The cosmologist's God is an abstract entity embedded in the fabric of reality itself, from the stars all the way down to the quantum field, a God whose voice is the sound of mathematics and whose face is the ocean spray. The result is deism, not theism, and an impassive God addressable—if addressible at all—as It, not You.[9]

VERY FEW believers today picture God as an ancient and powerful patriarch ruling earth from a place above the clouds. Indeed, they are likely

---

8 *These scientists are not creationists, of course. One of God's recipes is called "evolution."*

9 *Deism refers to the faith shared by many Enlightenment thinkers of the 18th and 19th centuries. The Bible transmits important truths, they thought, but it was written by fallible men, not God. God created the universe perfectly, yes, but "he" worked solely through laws of nature. Deists believed in reason, in free will, and in the perfectibility of man through the study of nature, which reflected divine perfection.*

What "process philosophers" like Samuel Alexander, Alfred North Whitehead and Charles Hartshorne added to deism was the God-creative or God-becoming element: the notion that God—whose freedom is like ours but preeminent—did not just cause the universe once and for all, but remains intimately involved in its creative unfolding. Important to note is what process theology shares with deism and classical theism; to wit, the axiom that God is Big—Very Big—co-incident at least in scale and power with the entire physical universe and probably surpassing of that. And also Old—Very Old—older than the universe itself. For all its concessions (God is mutable, God does not know the future), process theology still finds itself in the tradition of theologies competing with each other on the basis of the size/age/power superlatives they can muster on behalf of God. Echoes of "my daddy vs. your daddy"? The theology of theopraxy steps out of this tradition entirely.

to feel quite enlightened for *not* believing in this God, and thus safe from the barbs of atheists. The question for them, of course, becomes: "Well, who or what is God, really? How better should I think of 'him'?"

Two answers recommend themselves. One is: "No one knows. God is beyond human comprehension." This answer is humble, but it can easily be used to evade moral and intellectual responsibility, and to succumb to fatalism. I will discuss this possibility later.

The other answer, especially in this ecology-minded day, is "Nature." Here, God, fugitive from his throne, as it were, and bereft of human visage, finds himself at one with the forests, the oceans, the stars. This second, deist (not to say pagan) answer is as medieval as it is New Age. Cosmologists who answer along these lines might scoff at the astrologers of old, but they still look for our fate in the stars. The truth is that cosmologists are no more qualified to be religious seers than are veterinarians, and probably less so. For whether the universe began as a kajillion-ton, infinitely hot pea, or has always looked the way it does today (give or take a few million galaxies), whether it is headed outward to nothingness or back to convulsion a billion years hence, offers no guidance as to whether you should or should not stop for a tortoise crossing the road. You should. Indeed, too cosmic a view of things promotes indifference to merely earthly goings-on (what does it *really* matter if a species disappears?), and it leads to too clean a partitioning of the scientific from the moral. To get from the "is's" of science to the "oughts" of living, one must have the universe *desiring* something—something like more life, or greater diversity, more order, or more love. One must have "good" and "bad," and one must feel personally addressed by the choice. The problem for deists is that there is no need (and no evidence) for positing that desire to have existed from the Beginning.

We are evolved from star-matter, yes. We are organized dust. But here is the marvel: after billions of years of witless life-on-earth, the *ethical* finally emerges as a phenomenon and a force. It emerges first from *human* being, and then more strongly from hum*ane* being, which involves the capacity and desire to do good simply "because."

Enter God.

Or to put it allegorically: Eve bit into the apple and understood for the first time that the existence of good and evil was up to her. It was then that God awoke.

3 : Theism, deism, pantheism...

ALTHOUGH NOT traditionally so, the theology of theopraxy is a form of theism. It is not deism, pantheism, or panentheism. To locate the theology of theopraxy relative to these other theologies, here are some brief descriptions of their central tenets, minor variations and heresies excluded. Each description is accompanied by a simple diagram that indicates what sort of inclusions and influences are posited between God (G), humanity (H), and the natural universe (U).

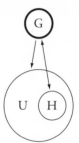

Traditional theism: God created the natural universe *ex nihilo* from a position outside of space and time. God also created human beings, to whom he gave free will. Omnipresent, omniscient, omnipotent, and omnibenevolent, God demands devotion, dispenses justice, and inspires love. God can be addressed personally, although he may or may not respond. Our piety and virtue may or may not move him. God's judgment in these matters as reflected in the actual course of events is infallibly wise. Yet we have reason to be optimistic: the created universe as a whole is moving toward a perfection under God's guidance.

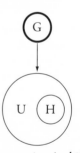

Deism (or natural theism): God created the universe *ex nihilo* from a position outside of space and time. God also created human beings, to whom he gave free will. (In modern deism, God designed the evolutionary process in such a way that humans with free will would evolve.) The universe is rational and perfect in design. It is intrinsically good and beautiful, and subject to increasing human understanding and control. While God can be addressed personally, there is little expectation of response. God's role was to design, not supervise. And if "he" *does* intercede now and again—a possibility deists consider highly unlikely—it is certainly *not* through miracles or direct communication with human beings. Humankind's best hope for salvation lies in practicing the virtues while pursuing spirited enquiry into God's Design.

Pantheism: Ever since the Beginning—if there *was* a Beginning—everything has been God, and God everything. God and Reality, or Being, are one and the same, or God and the *totality* of the universe are one and the same. Something of God, if not God's total- ity, therefore indwells everywhere at all scales of the natural world as well as the human world, "supervening" upon material reality the way minds supervene on brains, or underlying all appearances as a field, or process, which is intrinsically sacred and good. This is a God with "whom" one seeks harmony, a God that one studies or contemplates rather than worships or petitions.

Panentheism: Panentheism adds an element of deism to pantheism. The universe, of which humankind is a part, is permeated by and embedded in God but does not constitute God. God is larger still. ("The universe is wholly in God, but God is not wholly in the uni- verse.") God is due ultimate respect as the Ground of Being (Tillich) or Eminent self-creation (Hartshorne). Immanent and transcendent, and fundamentally good (inasmuch as being is better than non-being and *becoming* is better than being), God's nature is reflected in every temporal world process, macro to micro—including cosmogony, biological evolution, and human history—as they tend toward greater unity and variety. This knowledge properly inspires awe, humility, piety, and virtue.

Theology of theopraxy: Created *by* the universe, and *through* us, God is neither omnipresent, nor omni- scient, nor omnipotent. Nor, strictly speaking, is God omni-benevolence in the abstract: God is benevo- lence being realized in deeds. God can be enacted into existence anywhere and at any time through acts of care, love, intelligence, and courage among others. Since God is the good being enacted by human beings, God depends upon humanity.[10] In this sense, God is

---

10 *Higher animals are clearly capable of happiness, grief, loyalty, self-sacrifice, and care, even across species lines. The question is whether they have any choice in the matter, whether they resist temptation, weigh options, devise strategies, or feel goodwill toward other, much less all, forms of life. To read books like Kristin von Kreisler's* Beauty in the Beasts: True Stories of Animals Who Choose to Do Good *(2001), Jeffrey Masson's* When Elephants Weep *(1995) or Frans de Waal's* Good Natured: The Origins of Right and Wrong in Humans and Other Animals *(1996), is seriously to consider God's emergence at lower rungs of the evolutionary ladder than Homo Sapiens. In this book, however, I shall >*

the creation rather than the crea*tor* of good. But humanity in turn depends upon God for its moral evolution. In this correlative sense, God is the creator of the moral universe and always becoming.[11]

ALL FIVE of these theologies agree that God exists. God has a different character in each, to be sure. Here God is loving, there indifferent; here like a human being, there abstract; here the source of all beauty and sublimity, there the source of all justice and mercy...and these differences are important. Even within the Biblical tradition God seems to change in character, as writers like Harold Bloom, Jack Miles, Karen Armstrong, and Régis Debray have recently documented. But beneath issues of character, God *exists* in a fundamentally different way in each of the five theologies too. And in none does God exist more peculiarly—and yet, on second thought, more naturally and more actually—than in the theology of theopraxy.

Some reflections, then, about what it means to "exist" at all.

‹ *maintain God's exclusivity to humanity. I would not be opposed to future work extending this book's claims about God to the case of animals as moral agents. Certainly, how we treat animals is very much part of the ethical equation, and therefore a factor in the present work. How animals treat us or each other is not addressed.*

11 *Further to Note 8: Some may find affinities between the theology of theopraxy and New England Transcendentalism as propounded by Ralph Waldo Emerson and Henry David Thoreau, and later by Charles Sanders Pierce, John Dewey, and William James. As deists, all believed that God is immanent in humankind and nature, and that our nearest access to God is through* intuition, *which is in turn the finest source of knowledge. Athough it shares in Transcendentalism's (and Process Theology's) fundamental optimism, individualism, and emphasis on creative action, the theology of theopraxy distinguishes itself (1) by seeing God only in (certain) acts by free people, not in—and never as—any person, (2) by denying God's existence in nature* qua *nature, and (3) by not needing to allow God to be "in evil," or evil to be "in God." The root of these differences lies in the theology of theopraxy's disbelief in God as the creator of the physical universe.*

Also, while it agrees that recognizing God, like knowing the good, is largely a matter of intuition, intuition—or "moral sentiment"—is, for theopraxy, the beginning of knowledge rather than the source. The latter belief by the Transcendentalists, I suggest, is merely the shadow of theism in deism with a touch of Eastern mysticism thrown in. Can God come from it nonetheless? Yes, of course. Good-doing can be motivated by many narratives, many ideas, and many beliefs, including beliefs that do not mention God and beliefs that deny God's existence completely. The question is whether the morality that emerges from the theology of theopraxy is more effective, less prone to corruption. This is a question we pick up in ARGUMENTS 6.

4 : Ways of existing

WHEN WE imagine something "existing," we usually imagine an object that we can see or hear or smell or touch. We think of trees, chairs, people...even planets. These are all solid, bounded entities. They have a characteristic shape; they hold their position or trajectory unless bumped, and they persist for a good while. In theory, each could have a unique proper name or identity code.

Upon reflection we realize that many things we know to exist physically are not so neatly bounded: the *atmosphere*, for example, which thins so gradually with altitude above the earth that we cannot really say where it ends. We might think of clouds, which continually form and melt away; or of the wind. Where does the wind begin or end?

Yet other things exist immaterially everywhere and always, like gravity or the electromagnetic field. These two "things," although quite physical, represent a distinctly different mode of existence. They have no outer bound or shape but they retain their integrity nonetheless, their inner continuity, their effects and character. They are rather like fabrics that run *through* everything, or layers that run *under* everything; they cannot be broken up spatially, and they cannot be episodic in time (existing, then not-existing, then existing...). They are each, we can say, a *field* rather than an object, a field that has universal, continuous, and possibly eternal existence. (The field is the image that guides theologians like Paul Tillich, for whom God is The Invisible Ground of Being.)

THOUGHTS AND feelings represent yet another "style" of existence. Most of us would vouchsafe that thoughts and feelings exist. We experience them vividly, we name them closely, and we talk about them all the time. They do not exist in thin air, of course, but in the minds and bodies of living people (and animals), and thus only when and where actual such individuals breathe and think. It is *we* who think and feel, after all, not the chair, not the rock, and not the air between.

While most philosophers at this juncture would direct attention to the apparently immaterial or "spiritual" nature of thoughts and feelings, arguing for or against their status as independent existents, I want to accept their basis in neural physical reality and direct attention, rather, to another just-as-interesting property: that of their spatiotemporal discontinuity. What do I mean?

Take the feeling of *jealousy*. Jealousy flares up in people who learn that their friends or lovers are being attracted to others. And yet there is no reason to think that the feeling of jealousy—the knotted stomach, the flush of anger, the obsessive daydreaming about what the other is doing right now, the new-found appreciation for the virtue of loyalty—is different in every person. It is a *universal* experience that is discontinuous in time and space, one whose identicality (one occurrence with another) is not due to being tied to any central *source* of jealousy or to being tapped into some deep "jealousy field" that runs through or under everything, but rather to our similarity to each other as members of the human species. In short, jealousy feels the same to all of us, but each person's experience of it is unique and localized. The same might be said of the pain of dental work or the pleasure of laughing at a clown.

Here is an analogy: all over the earth fires are burning. Let us guess that there are a billion fires burning right now—in hearths, in cigarettes, in forests, in just-bombed buildings. These fires know nothing of each other; they were not caused by the same cause. Nor are they one fire joined somehow, in some other dimension, to the Great Fire. And yet fire is fire, the same everywhere, nothing missing from any.

So is God.

ANOTHER STYLE of existence is exemplified by "abstract universals": things like perfect triangles, whole numbers, logical and natural laws (like "entailment" and "causation"), and absolute ideals like The Good. Ever since Plato theorized an otherworldly realm in which these universals existed eternally and perfectly as Forms—of which the variegated actualities of this world are but imperfect shadows or projections—philosophers have discussed exhaustively (and to no conclusion) in what sense such universals exist. How or where, for example, do the elements of mathematics exist, things like triangles or numbers (or, for that matter, mathematics itself)? Where do colors or *words* reside? Transcendently? Only in minds? Only when seen, written, or spoken?

After Plotinus, most philosophically-minded Western theologians have held that *God* is a Platonic universal *and more*.[12] What do I mean by "...and more"? This: God is The One; God is the Form of the Good as well as the Form of all Forms; God is ultimately real, changeless, manifest on earth only in broken reflections of his wholeness and perfection, all just as Plato wrote... *with the added feature* that God created everything, can

---

12 *Plotinus (205–270) was a student of the early Christian thinker Origen. He was the founder of Neoplatonism, which was to have enormous influence on Christian, Jewish, and Islamic theology.*

be addressed personally, cares about us, rules over all events, and occasionally appears to people in person. Among modern believers, Plotinus's omnibus NeoPlatonist view is still widely held.

For non-Platonist philosophers, however, starting with Aristotle, universals exist in a different way. Universals exist only in *minds* that register the common *properties* of several—even innumerable—individual, actually-not-identical things, events, or actions. There are no perfect circles except in our imaginations, in the overlap, as it were, between myriad, experienced, differently-*im*perfect, real circles. "Arithmetic" exists only when and where a person is actually adding and subtracting using the rules of counting (which process, we often forget, discards large amounts of information about the things being counted); "white*ness*" only when someone is classifying white objects among other objects with respect to their color; "justice" only when someone is being fairer than before, or defending rights, or righting a wrong. Until then, arithmetic, whiteness, and justice are just words—words that group phenomena and actions by common properties, chains of resemblances, rules of application, and so forth.[13]

This is not to say that the world unperceived by humans is intrinsically chaotic, that we are *projecting* our ideas of order and commonness-of-property onto what is actually a hapless mess (although the world is certainly more complex than we can figure out completely). Not at all. We both detect and create some of the order that is in the world because our brains are made of "world-stuff" too, because we grew up in it, and because the order is really there, shaping the chaos in this neck of the universe's woods. For Aristotle and those that followed in his line, the point was that there exists no otherworldly book, storehouse, or plane of existence that has the Ideal Order of our world written in it. Contra Plato, there is no place or time or realm in which "4" exists (presumably in the company of "5" and "6"...) apart from those four apples in a bowl, the four cardinal directions, the four seasons, or time for afternoon tea. By the same token, there exists no higher realm or God, that (or who) is the repository or source of perfect Goodness, Truth, and the rest.[14]

---

13 *In philosophy, this view goes by the name "nominalism," a school of thought founded by William of Ockham (d. 1349), who was a scholar of Aristotle.*

14 *The fact that we can sometimes picture a universal in our mind's eye (as when we say "cat" and know that, without further adjectives, a generic, "Platonic" cat will come to mind), does not mean that one such Cat exists in supernal reality. It would quite likely match a real cat somewhere, of median age, that just happens to average the features of several of breeds of cats. Indeed, all nouns except proper nouns (like people's names) are quasi-universals. Like numbers and variable-names in mathematics, nouns are essential* ›

The theology of theopraxy agrees. God exists, and God exists in no other world than *this* one—the one that we see every day. True, God is not a thing or a person. Nor is God an abstract universal, a figment of the imagination, or a "common-or-garden" property of all things, like their color, size, shape, temperature, or mass. Rather (according to the theology of theopraxy), God is the quality of all human actions we rightly call "good." More deeply than this, God *is* those very actions, as, and when, and where they are happening. God is an activity: the doing of good.

THIS VARIETY of existence ought not to be foreign to us, except perhaps as it is applied to God. There are hundreds of "things" we happily refer to using nouns, which are not really things or feelings, ideas or abstract universals, properties or "spiritual beings" (angels or ghosts). They are, rather, *patterns*, and among them are patterns of human activity or behavior. What else is a *team*, a *home* (over and above a house), a *prayer*, a *bank*? What else is *love*?

And where exactly, we might wonder, do these "patterns" exist? Only in the mind? Try telling that to a football quarterback. Patterns come and go, become vivid and fade, emerge and dissipate, but are no less objective for it. You might just as well ask where your *fist* goes when you open your hand. Or where your *lap* goes when you stand up. Where do (the games of) tennis, football, or bridge go when the playing of them is over? Where does love go? We cannot answer, of course, and should not need to. Fists and laps and games-in-play are patterns; they are "configurational entities," spatiotemporal arrangements of other elements that for a while (or repeatedly, or forever) create something stable and deserving of a name. What else is a *flame* or a *room*? What is a *wedding*, a *trial*, a *meal*, a *smile*? These are complex patterns of things, events, and behaviors, configurational entities that evaporate once they are "over" and their parts go back to some other arrangement (parts that are themselves arrangements, patterns, with their own cycles of formation and dissolution).

If you understand the sense in which the patterns of human behavior I have just listed *exist*, then you understand the sense in which the theology of theopraxy proposes God exists.[15] And need I add, present patterns massively affect future ones?

< *to linguistic communication precisely because of their multiple instantiability, their incomplete specificity, their ignoring of many differences.*

15 *To scientists, all things are "configurational." From organisms down to molecules, atoms, and subatomic particles...all things are* arrangements *of smaller parts yet. Some would recommend that we think of the world more dynamically, as made of "processes"* >

Why, then, do I persist in personifying—indeed proper-naming—good-doing patterns of activity "God" rather than simply calling them "good" (an adjective) and being done with it? This is a fair question, and one to which I will return.[16] For the moment, however, I would like to argue for the proper-naming of God simply from the perspective of religious experience.

WHEN BELIEVERS offer that their faith is based not on reason but on a direct personal experience of God—let us even call it contact *with* God—it is usually in one of two distinct modes that this experience, this contact, is had.

In one mode the believer has a vision—something like Isaiah 6—God in Heaven, on his throne or standing, but radiant, anyway, with beneficence, love, and power, breaking into this world like sunshine through clouds. Or one sees a marvelous apparition like an angel, or hears a voice from nowhere addressing one personally. The believer comes away from an experience like this feeling awe, blessedness, redemption, chosen to be one of a line of very few people who have experienced God directly —Abraham, Jacob, Moses, Isaiah, Jonah, Jesus, a prophet, a saint...

In the second mode of contact, the believer simply has an experience of the profound rightness and beauty of certain constellations of events, things, or actions around them. These events, things, or actions are momentarily seen in a new light, as part of an eternal and lovely whole, in patterns never to be repeated and yet, somehow, fully intended. The sounds of nature or of music might resonate with profounder harmonies. If the believer hears God's voice, it is *as* the voice of a friend, or as his or her own voice. One comes away from experiences like this with feelings of gratitude, clarity, and hope.

Have the first experience—or trust that others have had it—and you will report belief in a Biblical (or Platonic) transcendent God who presides over this world from another plane of existence. Have the second experience—or trust others have had it—and you will report belief in an im-

---

‹ or "events," rather than concrete (or fleshly) things, as Alfred North Whitehead suggests in Process and Reality. They might then recommend that we follow Whitehead to Process Theology wherein God is the universe-in-process (more or less as Spinoza proposed long before Whitehead). The theology of theopraxy, for its part, holds that while God is indeed a "process" or "event," God is not any and all processes or events—macro, micro, and in between. Just some. God is only the activity in which and by which a human being "does things" and "arranges matters" so that life is preserved, honored, and promoted, not excluding his or her own.

16 See ARGUMENTS 5.

manent God, soaked into this world, manifesting himself, herself, or itself more or less powerfully in a thousand activities and actualities all around.

Mainstream Western faiths base themselves largely on the first experience of God. Deism, pantheism, and panentheism base themselves largely on the second. The theology of theopraxy bases itself on something like the second experience too, but only when it is caused by the works and deeds of people—people who are inspired by the first experience of God, or the second, or neither, or both. It is necessary only that they could have done something else: something less loving, less lovely, less true.

In the view of the theology of theopraxy, neither the stars nor the moon nor the twitter of the rainforest proves that God exists; but a bowl of soup, a loving hand, a genuine smile, a beautiful room, a pardon given do. These things are not so much God manifest as God *instanced*, and we are remiss when we take them for granted. Experiences of goodness-indeed are experiences of God, as direct as they can be. If you live in peace and decency, they are not at all uncommon. You just have to know what to call them.

5 : Ideas of the good

JUDAISM, CHRISTIANITY, and Islam agree: God commands us to do good. They also agree that whether we do or do not do good concerns God a great deal. In the theology of theopraxy, God commands us to do good too, but in a way that makes the stakes higher for us and for God. For not only is the state of the world on the line, but *God's* very being, *God's* life, *God's* existence. Without our meritoriousness God vanishes. Put another way, a world without good is a world without God, and we could not live in it for long.

So as the meaning of "God is in our hands" comes into focus—as we start to take more seriously the idea that "God is the good we do"—it becomes increasingly important to have a good idea about what "the good" is, or better, what exactly *good-doing* consists of. This is one of the oldest questions in philosophy, of course. Socrates gave his life for it. But even armchair philosophers know this: we cannot get the answer *very* wrong and expect to have a viable society, much less (reward from) God. So let us turn our minds to the problem.

In most religious traditions several injunctions for good-doing have evolved. These are familiar: injunctions *for* cleanliness, *against* incest, *for* ancestor-respect, *against* theft and murder, *for* charity and hospitality, *against* envy, *for* love and *against* hate, and so on. The Ten Commandments represents one such set. The Buddha's Eightfold Way another. All such injunctions can be shown to be life-favoring, which is to say, pro-social harmony, pro-fructitude, pro-physical health, and anti-strife, at least for the group that developed them.[17]

In addition to these injunctions, a handful of more philosophical, more general maxims have evolved to help people do the right thing in novel situations. Some of these maxims are prescriptive, such as "Love thy neighbor as thyself" or "Do unto others as you would have them do unto you" (which came to be called "the Golden Rule"). Others are *pro-scriptive*, such as "Do *not* do to others what you would not wish done to

---

17 *Here are some other injunctions: "Speak the truth;" "It is more blessed to give than to receive;" "Be slow to anger." (For a longer list, see Jeffrey Moses [1989]). So-called Noahide law, found in the Talmud, offers a place in heaven to all gentiles who obey six prohibitions and one positive commandment. The six prohibitions are idolatry, blasphemy, murder, robbery, incest/adultery/bestiality (all sexual transgressions), and eating meat torn from a live animal. The one positive commandment is to establish a system of justice (Sanhedrin 56).*

yourself" (the so-called Silver Rule). Different wordings of these maxims appear in the foundational texts of all major religions.

They also appear in secular Western philosophy; for example, as Immanuel Kant's Categorical Imperative—"Act only on principles you would wish to be universal law now" (like "Always tell the truth")—or, in what Kant proposed as a corollary, "Treat people (including yourself) as ends in themselves and never simply as a means to some end."[18] Then there is the Utilitarian Rule: "Act so as to maximize the happiness of the greatest number...," a maxim which has several variants and codicils of its own (such as "...at the expense of none").

Now, being rather general by design, philosophical maxims and principles, unlike religious commandments, rarely mandate specific actions. As a result, it's easy to devise situations that make exceptions to them seem reasonable, even necessary, not just in order to justify *im*moral actions (or to entertain philosophers), but in order to follow deeper intuitions yet. For example, it seems reasonable not to mind if people lied just a little now and again. What else is *tact*? Or to lie more seriously if it will save a life or ease a death.

Then too, there are problems of interpretation in detail. If we agree to love our neighbors as ourselves, should we feel free to hate or be indifferent to non-neighbors? Who exactly qualifies as a "neighbor" anyway? Those you live next to, work with, pass on the sidewalk, see, learn about... or everybody equally, no matter who they are or where they are over the face of the earth? Loving one's next-door neighbor is relatively easy, since they are likely to be of the same nationality and social class. Loving the people of one's neighboring province or country, however—people likely to have different customs—is far more difficult, and probably more necessary. [19] And then "love them as yourself"? Surely not. *Somewhere* in that range, between loving everybody as oneself and loving nobody, not even oneself, lies a social optimum.

---

18 *In* Groundwork for the Metaphysics of Morals, *Immanuel Kant puts it more precisely: "Act in such a way that you always treat humanity, whether in your own person or in the person of any other, never simply as a means, but always at the same time as an end."*

19 *With his parable of the good Samaritan (Luke 10:25–37), Jesus indicates that momentary proximity, no matter how accidental, qualifies a person as a neighbor, regardless of their relative social standing, race, creed, or domicile. In scenarios of disaster and distress, no one would disagree: in Jesus's parable, the man helped was mugged and left for dead on a public road. One cannot, however, in more normal times define a neighbor, on the one hand, as anyone you pass on the street and not in dire need, or on the other, as anyone anywhere on earth who is in dire need. A social optimum must be found at a policy level, as it were, as to who should be considered a neighbor and who not (Islamic law defines a ›*

And so on. It would seem that only a vast encyclopedia filled with time-tested advice about all possible situations will do—advice that would conform to our moral intuitions on the one hand, obey absolute injunctions on the other, and be logically consistent and actionably compatible with all other advice too. It is hardly surprising that the pages of religious and civil law, let alone the literature of pastoral and psychological counseling, run into the millions. The number of commandments *(mitzvot)* developed in rabbinic literature alone, using only Toraic sources for validation, runs to six hundred and thirteen!

The trouble, of course, is that no encyclopedia of ethics or law, and no list of injunctions or good advice could ever cover every situation, especially at times of rapid technological and social change. And even if it could, it would impoverish the life of its devoted users in both scope and spontaneity. Why? Because it would make good-doing depend on vast rote learning, on the constant looking-up of books or daily reliance on the advice of learned advisers; and most people will do none of these things if only for lack of time and the speed often required by decision-making.

Jesus tried to sweep away the rabbinic legalism of his day and replace it with a single moral principle, that of unconditional love of others, regardless of who they are. Although for many Christians this stands as the deepest and only truly necessary moral principle, life as lived is more complicated. As powerful as it is, love is not the solution to everything. Justice sometimes seems to demand something else; and love, by itself, is defenseless against exploitation.

I do not mean to be dismissive of the message of universal love, but it seems clear from history that more complex but still general principles

---

‹ *neighbor as anyone living within 40 houses of one's own in any direction), as well as in the matter of what needs are up to others to satisfy, and what needs up to you.*

A clue is given in the parable. The Samaritan in the story—the one who helped—is not named by name (indeed no one has a name in the story). He is identified as a member of a group; moreover, a group of low social status at the time. Jesus' message, which goes beyond that first stated in Leviticus 19:18, is not only that a poor man can be rich in virtue, nor only that loved-neighbor status should be given to all who are near you even momentarily, but that the more difficult, consequential, and to-be-cultivated love is that between (the people of) neighboring classes, cultures, and countries. (Cf. ARGUMENTS 9)

Interestingly, in Nazi Germany, the first step toward making the annihilation of German Jews "acceptable" to the average German was defining Jews as non-neighbors, first legally (they were defined as "non-Aryans," had to wear a yellow star, could not own certain businesses, hold certain jobs or join certain clubs) and then physically, by forced eviction and transportation to ghettoes, where their lives and subsequent fates would be "out of sight and out of mind."

of morality must prevail if good is to prevail: maxims and habits which, exercised, yield a feeling of greater freedom tempered by greater responsibility, guided, both, by cautious trust in our moral intuition.

And what is moral intuition? Ultimately unexplained (but then, what isn't?), moral intuition is the reason that what strikes us as morally suspect right away, upon further reflection usually is. Moral intuition develops as we mature as individuals. But it also develops as we mature as a culture, a people, a species.

IN THE next chapter I will try to distill a definition of good-doing into a single, quite complex—but I think not too complex—maxim. It will offer little specific advice because it is in specific situations that the irreducible complexity of real life properly enters. It is here, in real life, that we find that many different and alternative actions are equal in potential goodness. It is here that a measure of creativity is called for.

Indeed, "divining" the good is an unending project, both at a personal day-to-day level and at a cultural level. Moreover, *it is in the very nature of the good that there be room for improvement in our understanding of it.* Inherent in the idea of "good" is the idea of "better." This is why we should be wary of religious (or philosophical) charismatics who have all the answers. They do not. Nor does the Bible, Qur'an, or Talmud. Nor does Science. Nor do I; and nor, in the view of the theology of theopraxy, does God. Religions (like legal systems) that cut off intellectual inquiry, that abjure doubt, that demand belief, that put loyalty to themselves over and above other virtues, that demonize non-followers on any grounds—but especially on the grounds that God has revealed the absolute truth only to *its* leader(s)—are sure, themselves, to turn to evil.[20] Our understanding of the good has evolved over the millennia, and it improves over a single lifetime. Ditto our understanding of what "God" means, of "who" God is. It is crucial that this process continue indefinitely.

Let us not be impatient. We are hardly adrift. As implied by the cliché "moral compass," one can think of goodness as a direction, as a bearing, and of the ability to discern where it lies in all kinds of weather as a skill that needs training. We need not berate ourselves too strongly for mistakes made. We have thousands of years of ethical reflection behind us

---

20 *We discuss at some length how religions turn to evil, and whether a religion informed by the theology of theopraxy could be prone to doing so too, in* ARGUMENTS 7 *through 13.*

21 *New scholarship is showing what a profound influence Protestant, Catholic, and Jewish religious leaders had on the drafting and content of the United Nations Declaration, this between 1939 and 1947. See Max L. Stackhouse (2004), p.24.*

already, deposited in the Code of Hammurabi no less than in the United Nations Declaration,[21] and we have at least the "better half" of human nature on our side, deposited in our consciences and in our moral intuitions. Cannibalism is gone, and slavery all but. Cleanliness is a universal ideal; as are health, literacy, charity, and peace. In most of the world, women are drawing equal to men in civil rights and in economic life. Racism is waning. Revenge is increasingly understood as futile. The natural environment claims our ethical attention as never before; ditto the quality of life of animals. Although there is still so very much to be done—as I write, war rages again in the Middle East and children in Africa are still dying of hunger—we should not forget to appreciate the progress we have made.

BESIDES, FOR all that I have just said, and as the sages well knew, "oughts" are relatively easy to come up with. The difficulty of living a moral life has less to do with knowing *what* to do than with *actually doing it.* "(T)he object of religion," wrote Matthew Arnold, "is conduct,"

> *and conduct is really, however men may overlay it with philosophical disquisitions, the simplest thing in the world. That is to say, it is the simplest thing in the world as far as* understanding *is concerned. As regards* doing, *it is the hardest thing in the world. And when we are asked further, What is conduct? Let us answer: three-fourths of life.*"[22]

Said Jesus: "Not everyone who says to me Lord! Lord! shall enter the Kingdom of Heaven, but he who *does* the will of God" (Matthew 7:21). Said Rabbi Shimeon: "Not learning but *doing* is the chief thing."[23] Said Mohammed: "If you derive pleasure from the good you *do*, and are grieved by the evil you *commit*, you are a true believer."[24] (My emphases.) Old news: actions speak louder than words. New news: good actions speak God louder than words about or addressed to "him."

This book does not elaborate a theory of goodness much beyond the maxim offered in the next chapter. It does not offer any hole-in-one answers to old moral dilemmas. This book is about the holiness of *doing* our best, with "holiness" understood from a different perspective, on a

---

22 *Matthew Arnold (1924).*

23 Pirke Avot (Sayings of the Fathers), *1:17.* Ibid. *3.12: "He whose deeds exceed his wisdom: his wisdom shall endure. He whose wisdom exceeds his deeds—his wisdom shall not endure."*

24 *Jeffrey Moses, op. cit., p. 46.*

different concept of divinity. To the extent that words are only theoretical—this is, after all, just a book—it is about those moments when we choose one action over another, knowing (to the best of our knowledge) that the action we are choosing is better for *all* life and not just our own or our kin's. This book is about shaping a vision of God as "he" or "she" who—or as that which—is sparked by this choice and given body by the actions we then undertake.[25]

---

25 *One reader of this book in manuscript gave me pause at this point. He offered, in critique, what one might call the "genie" (djini) interpretation of theopraxy. To wit (and these are not his exact words): "You want people to think that by doing good they conjure God into existence. This is like Aladdin rubbing the magic lamp and causing the genie to appear." I could not deny the similarity of structure. "But of what use is the whole scenario," he went on, "if the conjured-up God does not grant you three wishes or work miracles?"*

The answer came quickly. "Being in the presence of God," I said, "ought to be an end itself, not a means." This answer, borrowed from Kant, seemed suitably lofty and enlightened, and my critic was silenced. But it was not a good answer. I had conveniently overlooked the belief that God, as commonly understood, has agency (to say the least!). Put more mildly, God's discernible presence would always make a difference to the course of events, and this was a belief that theopraxy upholds.

A better answer came to me days later. It started in realizing that myths about genies—that myths in general about God (or gods) granting miraculous powers or favors to people who had achieved something morally difficult, or who had seen through to some special truth—all portrayed, allegorically, a common truth: that unexpected good deeds have powerful effects, effects not just on the people who benefit from them, but on the people who witness them and the people who learn of them. Unforced acts of altruism are utterly compelling. Moral creativity is fascinating to watch. Selflessness is an eternal surprise. All three put the seal of truth upon whatever philosophical wisdom they are based. I think that the great religious leaders understood this. It's how God—the "genie"—works on us, not just we on God. It's also how God grants our wishes.

This caused me to reflect again on my first answer. Bible stories notwithstanding, any person who caused God to show "himself" and grant wishes would not wish for anything so selfish as military victory or greater personal power or advantage. People who find themselves in the presence of God would wish only that their blessing could be shared and that the goodness of the experience propagate without coercion. This, I would argue, is the very mark of the authenticity of the encounter. And so it's no wonder that the moral of many genie-God, wish-granting stories is that we need to continue to be wise in our choices, even in the midst of magic.

6 : Defining "good"

SOCRATES ARGUED that knowing what *good* meant resulted naturally in doing it. People who did harm proved only that they did not know what good was in the first place. In his view, evil results from ignorance rather than from selfishness or ill will, because what is good—truly good—is best for all, including the one who would be selfish or have ill will.

Few would agree with Socrates completely on this score. Few believe that knowing the truth about goodness—even knowing what the best thing to do would be in this or that situation—is sufficient to compel one to do it. This is why moral education usually entails at least three overlapping processes: (1) explaining what (doing) the good *is* in memorable and rational terms, (2) motivating people to *do* it; i.e., motivating them to act on their better judgment, and (3) showing what good-doing looks like and feels like by creating an environment rich in imitable examples. We can use this three-process partition to ask: what does the theology of theopraxy offer with regard to each?

With regard to the first—explaining what the good is—the theology of theopraxy offers the following maxim:

> *"Good" is what we call all free human actions that preserve, honor, and promote all forms and instances of life....*

...except those whose flourishing depends on the destruction of other forms and instances of life that are roughly equal to, or clearly more evolved than themselves.[26]

---

26 *I would dearly like to have ended the maxim as italicized, and for brevity in the following pages I often do. But one has to find a way, I believe, to be as deeply life-favoring as this maxim seeks to be and yet support the battle against bacterial and parasitic diseases—to pick two easy examples. After all, bacteria are forms of life, and parasites like fleas and worms are forms of life too. They have a right to live, in fact, a right to live long and happy lives, being fruitful and multiplying...until and unless, the maxim says, their lives materially and imminently threaten the lives of clearly more complex and evolved creatures, such as ourselves and most animals. Awkward, but, I think, true. This is why we are justified in developing antibiotics and anti-parasitic medicines. This is why we are justified in eradicating, say, the genetically mutated seaweed* Caulerpa Taxifolia, *which is deadly to other marine life and has already destroyed over 20,000 acres of marine habitat in the Mediterranean. It is also why it would be wrong to save the lives of fish if that meant the death of seals—unless one were prepared to feed the seals in an ethically better way indefinitely, i.e., a way that required less dying, or the death of less-evolved creatures than fish. Similarly, it would be wrong to cull deer or elephant populations to save certain* ⟩

This maxim, I believe, preserves most traditional wisdom about goodness. It is appropriately abstract, but, I submit, not too.[27]

ALTHOUGH THIS book is about the near-identity of goodness to God, note that our maxim does not imply that the good is "whatever God commands," this even though we hold that God commands us to do only good. Indeed (and here I indulge in personification), it is precisely *because* God commands us to do only good that it is up to us to figure out what "good" is *on other grounds,* and not to go back to God empty-handed, our homework not done, saying "O.K., what's the answer?" Our

---

‹ plant life. *The better way to avoid the future starvation of these animals is to sterilize a percentage of them. Then too, on this principle, we realize that vegetarianism (by humans) is admirable only because we can now so easily live comfortably without causing the death of any animal for food. If that were not the case, i.e., if we had to eat animals to be healthy, and had to use animal hides for clothes, it would be morally acceptable to do so. Indeed, it would be all but mandatory. But cannibalism will never be acceptable; nor will war, nor will murder, except in self-defense.*

Note that preserving, honoring, and promoting one's own life is no less a good than doing the same for others. We have a duty to ourselves to live lives as long, full, and rich as we can in good conscience; and this most often means placing one's own life neither first nor last.

Note also that our maxim has the corollary: God is (constituted by) all free human actions that preserve, honor, and promote all forms and instances of life...

27 *Because, alas, evil can be perpetrated by exploiting the logic of our maxim, it is prophylactic to rehearse how. Imagine two families, tribes, or nations, called People A and People B. If People A can be persuaded that People B are*

(1) considerably less evolved—less human—than themselves, and

(2) "hell bent" upon (i.e., undissuadeable from) destroying People A, then we have the formula for genocide. People A will attempt to destroy People B with a savagery directly proportional to the strength of these two beliefs combined. If, at the same time, People B believe (1) and (2) about People A, it is a formula for war. Repeat with "Person A" and "Person B," and we have the formula for murder and feud. If (1) and (2) are actually true, however, and no non-violent solution is possible (such as isolation from each other by a stronger third party), then genocide, war, and murder are justifiable. If not, not. For repeat with "Species A" and "Species B," and "genetically programmed" instead of "persuaded," and it is the formula for the four-billion-year-old struggle for life on earth that brought forth all complex animals, including ourselves.

All the great religions, as well as secular law, pardon killing in self-defense, putting the burden of justification heavily on the killer (a burden from which soldiers at war are largely but not completely exempt). Some argue, however, that because statement (1) is never true of human beings, and statement (2) can never be proved and/or can always be worked around, it is preferable to die by the hand of another—to be killed—than to kill in self-defense and thus risk more killing by others in revenge. Alas, this "turn the other cheek" argument neglects to take into account the further killing made possible by the example of non-self-defense. I do not know of any general resolution to this dilemma. ›

maxim looks to the quality and quantity of life preserved, honored, and promoted as the appropriate gauge of an action's goodness.

Is this the *only* way to describe the good without putting the whole problem back in God's lap, as it were? No. One might speak directly of suffering and happiness, of self and "the other," of humans and nature, and so on. But it is the maxim I offer as the most robust and fruitful for the project of the theology of theopraxy.[28] As a category, I understand good-doing to subsume all human activities that yield truth, beauty, and morality. All three of these, I believe (but will not try to prove here) serve life following our maxim.

Also, before going on, let us note that actions which are taken unfreely—under compulsion, say, or accidentally—might be life-enhancing in result, but they cannot (by our maxim, anyway) be called good or constitutive of God unless the doer had alternatives and knew of them. This is not so great a restriction. It is a commonplace of modern moral philosophy to emphasize the necessity of freedom to morality and morality to freedom. We will discuss the problems this raises in the next chapter.

As for the *motivation* to do the good: this really means the motivation to do one's best to do the good as far as one understands it, and then to improve that understanding. The theology of theopraxy therefore respects any and all religious language that teaches us to do God's will, and any and all modes of forgiveness that will encourage a prompt return

---

< *Allow me to add one more level of generality by making some adjectives and verbs milder. Replace (1) with "stupider or less culturally developed" and (2) with "likely to cheat or steal from People A" and we have the formula for the kind of racism and ethnocentrism that will self-perpetuate indefinitely and that no changes in the law can eliminate. I offer as evidence everyday life in South Africa, but Germany, Saudi Arabia, and parts the USA would do almost as well, even Ireland...any place where socioeconomic inequality maps onto racial, ethnic, or cultural differences. The moral of the story is this: (1) never assume, and resist being persuaded, that any other human being (or even any other species) is less evolved than yourself; and (2) never assume, and resist being persuaded, that any other people (or other species) is "hell-bent" upon ending your life or even making you uncomfortable. Especially resist being persuaded that both are true at the same time.*

28 *Another line of reasoning: Consider the circularity of saying both "God is the good we do," and "Good is (our doing of) what God wants done." Or consider, equivalently but more succinctly, "God is our doing, through good" and "Good is God's doing, through us." Such mutuality is gratifying, but, as definitions of "God" and of "good," the two statements do not get us very far. They just bounce us back and forth, each deferring to the other endlessly. To avoid this, either "good" must open out onto further realities, descriptions, and claims that do not depend on "God," or "God" must open out onto further realities, descriptions, and claims that do not depend on "good." Now, traditional religions, of course,* >

to doing God's will (which is always for us to do good) after a lapse or breach. But the theology of theopraxy interprets "doing God's will" in a new way: to wit, as equivalent to bringing God about. Why bother with a new interpretation? Because awareness that we are "bringing God about" evokes emotions quite different to those associated with *obeying* God, Allah, or "something larger." They have more to do with personal creativity, with the responsibility *for*, not just *to* that "something larger." And this, I believe, is the more effective motivator for mature men and women. (See REFLECTIONS 4.)

By the same token, the theology of theopraxy respects any and all *secular* language that motivates us to do good on humanistic or other, less-noble grounds, for example, by offering social and even monetary reward for virtuous actions. The best motivator might be the satisfaction that comes with exercising moral creativity for life's sake, but the fact is that the good is the good, and doing it voluntarily in even the slightest degree is God in any case.

TOGETHER WITH explaining and motivating the good, there is, finally, the third process in our analysis, namely, *showing* what "good" means by doing it in the presence of others. After all, we teach a great deal by (our) example, whether or not we intend to. Conversely, we learn a great deal by imitating others, whether or not we realize we are doing that. Children learn what good is mainly by seeing and feeling good things done around them: acts of love, courage, forbearance, creativity, and so on. They learn what goodness is this way long before they learn what goodness is intellectually, or take moral initiatives. Indeed, it is only after one has done good a few times, first in emulation and then of one's own accord, that one *knows* the good in the sense Socrates had in mind, which is to say, from the inside, as good's source or vehicle.

Ethical behavior makes ethical behavior more likely in its neighborhood; good deeds spur more good deeds. Given this, we can fairly say that it is by human nature that God is perpetuated, that God is in our hands and we in "his."

< *take this second opening: It is "God" that means so much more; it is God, as described in Scripture as well as in person, as it were, who provides the inflow of truth and moral energy so that we might know the good, love the good, and do it. The theology of theopraxy tries the first opening: it is "good" that means so much more; it is goodness of deed, as found in life, that provides the inflow of truth and fresh moral energy so that we might know who and what God is, love God, and do "his will."*

Poetizing and arguing go only so far. The truth is: it remains an open question as to whether large numbers of people motivated by the idea of theopraxy would be better at doing good than people motivated by more traditional religious and secular worldviews. I take up the question again in ARGUMENTS 2 and 23, and REFLECTIONS 4.

7 : Doing and believing

IF WE are to entertain the belief that God is the good we do, it would behoove us to be clear not only about what we mean by *good*, but what we mean by *do*.

For example, is *thinking* doing? People could disagree. "Doing anything?" "Nah. Just thinking." Or: "Doing anything?" "Yes. I'm thinking!" Both make sense. And how about *talking*? Does talking do anything? One wants to say: sometimes yes, and sometimes no.

Here are some more questions: Are involuntary actions, like breathing, digesting, or beating our hearts, things we *do*? What about deeply habitual actions, like stirring our coffee clockwise, or reflexive ones, like scratching an itch, snoring, or laughing?

And what about deliberate *in*actions, like permitting or waiting? Or, opposite to these, actions we don't want to take but are compelled to by law or in order to obviate a threat to our lives? In all these cases, questions of intention come to the fore, and these lead naturally to questions of responsibility. Then too: shall we distinguish between doings that have effects on living creatures and doings that do not? Kicking a dog is surely different to kicking a ball.

The subject is complex. In order to clarify what I mean by *do*ing in an ethical/moral sense, I shall have to take positions on all of these questions rather more rapidly than philosophers would like.

STARTING WITH the last proposition: Only if an action has an effect on a living creature, including the doer, can it be judged good or bad. If one inanimate object affects another inanimate object—if a lifeless meteor crashes into a barren moon, say—then "good" and "bad" do not arise. Disrespectful things done to corpses have bad effects only upon the doers and witnesses, not the corpses.

If an action is involuntary or accidental (i.e., is not intended by the actor), then it has much-reduced or no ethical import, as Aquinas argued and as modern law inscribes—except that if an unintended action does affect living creatures negatively, then we are obliged to seek ways to bring such actions under intentional control and/or to reduce their consequences or chances of happening again.[29]

---

29 *Some might argue that involuntary or accidental actions that have positive effects ought to be brought under intentional control too, and so made more likely to happen* >

Many of the things we do habitually can have ethical import. This is because the first instance of choosing-to-do-X implies a degree of will on the part of the doer and a degree of control remaining thereafter, even if it is not complete. The same applies to actions taken on "orders from above," as when we are part of a bureaucracy or firm. Standard procedures, rules, and orders never fully justify the actions that they command; nor are they fully responsible for them. There is always a remainder—often a critical remainder—which requires that we be individually aware of the larger purposes and consequences of our actions. This awareness calls upon us to decide each time whether *or not* to follow a standard procedure, whether or not to apply a rule or carry out an order.

If an internal change-of-state occurs that has no external effects, like a not-acted-upon "change of heart," then it is not a doing at all. This is not to say that changes of heart are unreal or unimportant; just that they have not, as of yet, *done* anything to or for anyone or anything else.

In sum: To "do" something with ethical import is to move, act, behave, speak, gesture, or communicate in a way that affects the quality of life, thought, or actions of a person, sentient being, or living creature, not excluding oneself. On this definition, a belief held but not *acted on,* a thought had *but not communicated,* a dream dreamed *but not told,* an intention felt *but not realized,* a plan conceived *but not executed,* an understanding reached *but not applied...* is not a doing until and unless it has an impact on a life. Until then, it is not subject to ethical judgment.

Not all religions (or philosophies) would agree. The idea that unexpressed thoughts are neither good nor bad is more Judaic than Christian or Muslim. Say the latter two: God knows what you're thinking; he is affected by it, and it therefore matters what you think or dream even if you *never* act upon that thought or communicate that dream to someone else. (Besides, even if God did not know, *you* would.)

Judaism tends to take a more pragmatic position. As does post-Enlightenment common law. To wit: while it's *better* to think good thoughts than bad ones because they will probably lead to better actions, the privacy of the imagination is absolute. Besides, any attempt to censure or constrain "bad thoughts" will only increase their charm, not to mention

---

‹ again. I agree. But note that imposing conscious control sometimes decreases the chances of that good thing's happening again. In those cases, matters are best left "naturally occuring," unintended. Other things being equal, a good action is better allowed to happen than commanded to. God does not have to be manhandled into existence. Nor does our recognition of "God's face" depend on our having willfully painted it, as it were, then and there, ourselves. God can be produced from life-as-lived the way music is produced from windchimes: prepared for, yes, but not played. Good buildings are like wind chimes.

damage open discourse. Contra the Pauline (and Lutheran) tradition in Christianity, conduct is what counts. No harm is done, then, and no good either, even to the thinker/dreamer, until his or her life is affected or someone else's is. In this the theology of theopraxy concurs.[30] God increases life at the involuntary expense of none.

Thus, again: God is the good we *do,* not the good we once did, see done, or imagine doing, unless the good we once did (e.g., create a charity organization) continues to do good (distribute aid to the needy), the good we see done inspires us to do more, or the good we imagine doing results in our taking action. It may be in our imaginations that God is conceived in various ways, and in mere words that God is discussed, but it is as our doings-unto-others—and sometimes unto just ourselves—that God is materialized, enacted, and performed into being. It follows that unless and until something good is being done because of them, none of *these* words about faith and philosophy, nor your reading them, nor any rote ritual practice—be it prayer, ablution, visiting Mecca, reading the Bible, or meditating for hours on end—makes much difference to bringing God into being.[31]

FOR ALL this, we cannot erase the fact that actions are based on beliefs and vice versa. We cannot (and I do not) argue that changing beliefs will

---

30 *This is not to condone inflicting pain upon oneself in private. One is oneself a living creature. Nevertheless, I am inclined to the liberal-libertarian view that sovereignty over oneself is complete...until it affects others. Ethics, in my view, as in Martin Buber's, is inherently relational: it arises between people, and between people and living creatures. An ethical relationship to oneself makes sense only if one thinks of one's future self as another person, as the philosopher Derek Parfitt argues we should do. On this definition studying is a form of doing, some but not all reading is, and some but not all dreaming is. The test is whether or not the activity turns out to affect the quality of the doer's life, and/or someone else's.*

31 *Here is a young Ralph Waldo Emerson, not yet the complete deist, in near agreement: "He who does good, in the moment that he does good, has some idea of God." Or "We form just conceptions of [God] by doing God's will." I say 'near agreement' because the theology of theopraxy maintains that only the doing (of good) is God fully, not the idea of God, which partakes of God's existence, as it were, only if and as it increases the frequency and quality of good-doing. Emerson was here following Immanuel Kant—who was himself following Aristotle—in distinguishing pure or theoretical Reason from practical Reason, arguing that any God we can know and experience (as opposed to think of, or argue about) belongs to practical Reason, and is made real by our following of moral principles with our free and actual behavior. The truth of this, alas, did not prevent Kant or, later, Emerson from privileging principles over deeds and intentions over results. See Gustaaf Van Comphout (1999) pp. 50-51, 67-68.*

not result in actions that are better or worse.[32] Complicating the picture for those who would emphasize belief (or faith) over behavior (or "works") is the fact that not all beliefs are known by their believers to *be* beliefs. Many strongly-held beliefs fly below the radar of consciousness. Indeed, one has often to be exposed to strange and contrary beliefs in order to realize that one holds certain beliefs at all. For example, one might have to meet a happily married and perfectly healthy couple who long ago decided not to have children in order to realize that *having children* really is a choice, a choice that depends upon what one believes about the charms and benefits of family life, about the merits of population growth, about the duty we have, or don't have, to provide grandchildren to our parents, to carry on the family name, and so on.

Add to this that much of what happens to us we bring upon ourselves, this as people and nature respond to how we have "happened" to them. We are not in *complete* control, of course. Nor is everything that happens to us what we deserve or would prefer. But in the long run, cumulatively, and within the parameters of our particular time, culture, and accident of birth, we do indeed "reap what we sow."[33] I mention it because in this sowing and reaping process beliefs play a large role, and false or dispiriting beliefs play an even larger one, whether or not we know that we hold them.

For example, believe (it true) that people of group X are basically untrustworthy, and sooner or later some individuals in that group will be happy to justify that belief for you, if only in response to the way you behave toward them.

Lie because you believe that protecting feelings is more important than telling the truth and you will be lied to in order "to protect your feelings."

Believe that capitalists are thieves or that managers are fools, and in spite of your best efforts—even your own skill—you will likely be a lowly worker all your life, chafing at the unfairness of the System and idolizing "honest labor." (Or you might become a leftist professor.)

One more example, more generalizable than you might think at first: Many older people, on beginning to lose their hearing, believe that stan-

---

32 *Indeed, what is this book but an attempt to develop improved beliefs about God, among which is the improved belief that God is not real until we act on behalf of all life, not excluding our own?*

33 *"What goes around comes around." "How you make your bed is how you sleep." The Hindu doctrine of karma long ago magnified the wisdom of these sayings into a cosmological principle.*

dards of clarity of speech are declining. Shouting, and forcing others to shout, missing a great deal of what is being said (and denying it), enjoying the extra attention and not being dissatisfied, in fact, with the quietness they live in and the fact that they can now indulge their long-time preference for speaking *at* other people rather than listening to them, the quality of their lives slowly deteriorates. Friends melt away. Family members withdraw. Information stops coming in. Conversations dry up rather than flow, turning into simple proclamations and instructions. Boredom ensues, and loneliness, together with the withering belief that "no one has anything interesting to say any more," which is now true in their experience...and all this because they would rather not admit they are older now, and should be wearing hearing aids.

In sum, we often hold onto beliefs long after they have lost the capacity to engender happiness, other people's or our own. We also hold onto them long after they have been discredited by facts we accept as facts. Why? For several reasons:

Because we think that acquiring new beliefs would be too difficult intellectually.

Because we think it would show others that we were wrong all along and we are loathe to go around apologizing or explaining.

Because a new belief would cause havoc among other beliefs that we hold and that are still workable.

Because we judge it socially ill-advised to break rank with a community whose members hold those beliefs (or *apparently* do, for they too might be holding them for membership or profit-seeking reasons).[34]

But just as often it is because we do not realize that our behavior is based on beliefs *at all,* much less false or dispiriting ones. And rarely do we notice how many of the beliefs we hold engender the very actions, on *our* part, that keep them necessary.

IF CERTAIN beliefs bring about the very realities that then justify them, we are fortunate that some beliefs are "enspiriting" and life-promoting. Perhaps the most important of these is belief in the inherent dignity and equal worth of all human beings. In the Declaration of Independence, to

---

34 *This takes us into the larger territory of beliefs that we hold strategically rather than with personal commitment. They are things we sort of believe because they're plausible; because others do, because they are useful, and not too hard to sacrifice if necessary. We present them to each other, and move them about rather like chess pieces in an attempt to gain control of the board, and at the same time defend the King. And what is the King in this chess analogy? The one belief without which we would be as nothing, defeated.*

choose one prominent example, Thomas Jefferson called this belief "self-evidently" true (rather than commanded). This was brave, given how few people, then as now, acted as though it were true at all.

But that, of course, was exactly the point.

Jefferson was trying to make true by commitment what was not true in fact or by default. Commit yourself to thinking of others as worthy, he knew, and they will endeavor to deserve your high opinion. Trust them and they will labor to prove your trust justified. Be kind and you will likely receive kindness; tell the truth and you will more likely hear the truth. This evocation process is hardly mechanical, of course, hardly sure to work every time. One must expect disappointments. But there is no other method for increasing the general good in the long run than the steadfast application of the belief in other people's capacities as well as your own, belief in their inherent worth as well as your own, belief in the genuineness of their desire to do good as well as your own. "Before ever we have discovered whether a man has worth in him or not," wrote Felix Adler, "the moral law enjoins us to ascribe it to him, to treat him as though he had it, to see in him the light of the possibilities which he has never made good and which he never wholly will make good." [35]

By the same token—by the same process of evocation—no authority is sweeter than the authority people freely give to you because they judge that you judge well, because you bring out the best in them, because they cannot bear that you would *not* have it. This is truly moral authority. Many people have it to some degree. Properly understood, God has it fully.[36]

---

[35] *This requires humility about our own moral perfection. "The moral law is wholly misunderstood," Adler goes on, "if it be founded on the actual worth or value of men, for none of us has great worth or value." Felix Adler (1905) p. 41.*

[36] *More about how we might understand God's authority in* EXPLANATIONS 15.

8 : Theological hyperbole

IN THE most vivid imagery they can muster, Judaism, Christianity, and Islam alike portray God as infallible in wisdom and absolute in power. Given how little objective evidence there is that God is either—much less both—we might go straight to the obvious question: *why the hyperbole?*

One purpose, surely, is to impress children, this on the analogy of God being like (or quite unlike!) their natural fathers: wise and powerful, but infinitely more so. Later on in life God might be seen as a king, but again, as an ideal king, indeed, as the King of Kings. All this Freud pointed out.

But when, in maturity, faith seeks evidence, theological hyperbole serves a different purpose, and one less easy to criticize.

WHAT HAPPENS when we want to believe that God is infallibly wise and absolutely powerful?

This: We proceed to marshal the evidence. We apply our most hopeful explanations to God's every move. We direct our attention to seeing signs of God's wisdom and power everywhere. We seek not falsification but verification. We come to interpret all events as willed by God no matter how dispiriting or disastrous they are; or if not willed, then at least permitted by God as part of a greater and ultimately good plan.

Beliefs like this have many consequences. For one, they lend a certain circularity to reasoning about ethics, and for another, they support fatalism and passivity. Score two for atheists. But there is another consequence that both believers and unbelievers tend to overlook, and which is to the good; namely, that paying attention to anything—in and of itself—magnifies its object. Examine any little thing long enough and carefully enough—a fly's wing, a simple decision, the wording of a Biblical passage—and it will become immense, a world unto itself. Likewise, attention to God's wisdom and power magnifies its object, *which needs magnification precisely because it is the youngest and weakest force in the universe,* namely, the force of the good.[37]

---

[37] *I mean no blasphemy, but the parents of mildly autistic children engage in similar behavior. Disbelieving the diagnosis of autism, they desperately seek signs of normal development and encourage their child in every way. Such parents are also apt to imagine that their child is preternaturally gifted in some way (which many autistic children in fact are). In denying reality, one might say, parents create a new and better reality; namely, a child, loved by devoted parents, becoming the best adult he or she can possibly become. The child is not God, but what is happening here is.*

As though in acknowledgment, wisdom through the ages has countenanced considerable hyperbole about God. In his *Guide for the Perplexed,* for example, the 12th-century religious philosopher, Moses Maimonides, argued that God in his infinite wisdom gave different levels of understanding of himself to different kinds of people, according to their intellectual abilities. The young and ignorant *need* the hyperbole, he said; the old and learned do not, or at least not hyperbole of the same kind. Important religious texts like the Bible should therefore be read at several levels, from the literal level (at the bottom) through the symbolic and allegorical (in the middle), to the mystical (at the top).

Maimonides would not agree, however, to our explanation for his otherwise-accurate observation—the explanation, that is, that says that most people know, at some level, that in daily life God's power is so weak and his wisdom so hard to come by that they need all the amplification they can get. Maimonides would not agree that interpretations of Scripture by people like himself have the same magnification effects upon the actions of God in the minds of intellectuals as colorful stories, plays, rites, and sayings do that illustrate God's power and wisdom to the hoi polloi. For Maimonides as for devout conventional believers, it would be laughable if not dangerous to think of God as "weak" and in need of our sustenance. And as for God's wisdom, the good rabbi would find it ridiculous to assert that God had anything to learn from us.

Let us call ourselves more informed on this score. Should we now join the atheists in mocking religious faith? Can we now disregard God?

No, and no again. Although we might disregard God for several reasons, the one reason we ought *not* to disregard God is because we believe that God is actually weak and so can't punish us, reward us, move mountains, part oceans, and so forth. On the contrary. On the metaphor of God's being a young and tender being, God's weakness ought to call out to us. All the more should it call out to us because God is truly and not just metaphorically *good.* That is why (to speak metaphorically again) we need to pay attention to God's slightest inclination, to God's every yearning.

In short, "God," the word, denotes not the oldest and strongest but the youngest and weakest force in the universe; namely, the force of the good, which is a force exerted exclusively by us.

Two thousand years ago, a small group of Jews began celebrating the birth of a certain child in Bethlehem a hundred years earlier—a child who was already one with God, who was, they soon said, God come to earth. Of course, Jews of the time imagined *every* newborn child to be blessed by God and potentially a/the saviour, just as they do today. Ignore this for now. The intuition—the implicit message—was as easily overlooked then as it is today: First, that God is incapable of doing harm. Second, that God is ours to cherish, not fear.

LET US admit that theological hyperbole has helped enlarge God's influence. We ought to be happy. But we cannot be entirely. Today perhaps more than ever, theological hyperbole must be questioned. And this for two reasons:

First is the license such hyperbole has long given to brutality. I mean the wars, crusades, pogroms, inquisitions, scapegoatings, repressions, invasions, genocides, and bombings that have been carried out in God's or Allah's name and/or because the Bible or Qur'an seems to legitimize them. So involuntary has been the suffering and so enormous the cost to innocent life, that only a hyperbolically fierce, partisan, and, let us note, male God could possibly be thought to support them, let alone *will* them. There is no room in the coming world for wars fought for God or against "infidels" unless they are "wars" against ignorance, disease, and poverty.

The second reason theological hyperbole must be questioned, even hyperbole as well-intentioned and lovely as that which echoes from prayerbooks and hymnals, is because over the last few centuries, certainly, it has provoked as much atheism as faith.[38] No thinking person can believe in God's simultaneous omniscience, omnipotence, *and* omni-benevolence. As many have observed, at least *one* of these attributes (if not all three) has to be less-than-absolute if the suffering of the innocent is to be explained. Doctrinal demand for complete trust in God, even when "His ways" contravene our deepest moral intuitions, breeds faith that is simply submission or atheism that is simply arrogance, leaving thoughtful believers everywhere to wonder whether, or what, they *actually* believe.

---

38 *After Auschwitz, Hiroshima, Cambodia, Sarajevo, Rwanda, Darfur...we can no longer associate mass death with punishment for sin against God, a God who cares, a God who, if he exists "as advertised," deserves worship and praise. Alain Finkielkraut (1997, p. 79, 80) puts a finer point on it: "(B)y weighing (God) down with words of praise, by envisioning him as frightful, imposing, powerful, and as our instructor, we do less offense to the Eternal One than we do the victims of his care. There is not just an analogy between defaming our neighbor and adoring divine perfection: glorifying God is that superior form of defamation that gives useless suffering the seal of necessity." "If God does not exist, then everything is permissible," wrote Dostoevsky through Ivan Karamazov. But, Finkielkraut counters on behalf of all skeptics: "...if our century has robbed (God) of the attributes of being, if we hesitate to say 'God wished, God chose, God ordered'...it is precisely so that all is not justifiable, and so that suffering remains foreign to the principle of reason."*

There are other ways to keep God ineffable, of course, and thus out of range of our salvos of complaint: locating "him" in Logos or Being, in "unspeakability" or majesty, for example. How many are the ways of avoiding God's at-handness!

Theological problems like the "problem of evil" just mentioned (and to which we will turn our attention in ARGUMENTS 7 through 16) cannot be resolved by applying more hyperbole yet, as when theists faced by the contradictions so relished by atheists declare: "God is beyond human understanding!" and then feel vindicated, as though the very difficulty or absurdity of their faith was proof of its worthiness. We must imagine instead, I suggest, that God does not want us to sacrifice our trust in logic, law, observation, or rationality; that God does not want us to give up hope for earthly justice. We must imagine God benevolent. Permitting more personification, we must imagine God wanting more from us, surprising us, being open to the future with us, *and* being worthy of our unqualified devotion. By dropping the "requirement" that God also be the all-powerful, all-knowing, and unknowable Creator of the universe, the theology of theopraxy offers contact with a God that—or a God *who*—does not have contradiction at the base of "his" existence. By removing from our image of God—or rather, by refraining from attributing to God—everything that terrifies, everything that explains the indifference of stones and the evil in men's hearts, we are offered contact with a God beyond rebuke. *This* God—this hand-cupped flame, this whisper that will not be silenced, this gentle lifting force, this "child" of humaneness, this sacred activity—is second to none.

Set metaphors aside. Here is God as God simply and truly is: all goodness in deed, all the good we do. A modest God compared to the Bible's? Yes. A minimalist God? Yes. A remnant? In a way. But the true God at last, and wonderful enough.

9 : The weakest force

THE PREVIOUS chapter used several familiar metaphors for God. Except for "force," they were human, personal, Biblical. Here I should like to offer a more scientific metaphor, or rather, analogy, one that helps us visualize how the "youngest and weakest force in the universe, the force of the good" can be effectively omnipresent, but limited.

• Consider gravity. Gravity is the most universal and reliable physical force we have discovered. It permeates every pore of the universe. It forms gravitational fields, it causes agglomerations of mass, it bends trajectories.[39] But for all its pervasiveness and lawfulness, gravity is limited in several ways.

For one, gravity never repulses. It is limited to *attracting* (bringing masses closer together), which is only one of two possible directions. There is no such thing as anti-gravity, as far as we know.

For another, gravity exerts itself only along the line connecting the centers of mass of any two objects and *not* in any one of an indefinite number of other spatial directions, or in rotation.

Another: the *strength* of the force of gravity between any two masses is finite, and it changes at a rate that depends rigidly on the changing distance between them.

And one more: as physical forces go, gravity is rather weak, at least here on earth. Although gravity can't be turned off or screened, it is easy to work around by deploying the mechanisms of engineering structures, flotation, ballistics, and flight.

• Now let's make the analogy. In everyday life, the force of gravity attracts things downward, toward the center of the earth. This makes the experience of seeing things fall quite common. Then too, no fear is more primitive than the fear of falling, and no feeling more familiar than the tug on our bodies and limbs we call weight. Flying, walking, jumping, crawling, dancing, or swimming, all living creatures seek to avoid sinking down. Why? Because being down for very long means sickness and death. *Up* in general means *good,* and *high* is usually better than *low.* Who wants to have a heavy heart? Our language is soaked through with examples of this natural assignation of meaning through physical metaphor.[40]

---

39 *Cf.* EXPLANATIONS 4.

40 *There are very few exceptions. See George Lakoff (1980).*

It is in this frame of mind that we can think of "the force of the good," the force that God exerts, as an *attractive* force *upward*. God exerts a lifting/lofting force, drawing us upward. Like earthly gravity, this upward force is rarely strong. It is a force as gentle as it is persistent, as easy to frustrate and deflect as a helium party balloon. And it applies itself everywhere someone is making a choice and acting upon it.

• Because the force of the good is weak, it is not God (according to the theology of theopraxy) who causes tornados, floods, conflagrations, or earthquakes. God wields no mighty hammer. But it is God who steadily defeats our weariness, who helps us pick up the pieces and build again more firmly or flexibly. It is also God who, as it were, suggests weather forecasting, seismic testing, insurance, and having a National Guard.

Because the force of the good is weak, it is not God who causes or permits gross injustices for reasons we can never understand. After an injustice has been done, however, it is the gentle force of the good that makes us want to go on living *justly* nonetheless. God does not cause sickness, but helps us heal. God does not lose our sheep, but helps us find them. God does not guide bullets, but dissuades us from shooting. God entreats us to prefer forgiveness to revenge and forgetting to painful memory. "He leadeth us beside still waters." He walks in the garden after the heat of day. God is a gentle, one-way force, making "come-back kids" of us all: slapped-down balloons.[41]

THERE IS a wonderful story—a joke, actually—which speaks to the point.

A man of great faith moved into a house in a neighborhood prone to flooding from a nearby river. One day the river flooded its banks and began to fill the streets. Neighbors urged him to leave, but he declaimed:

---

41 *Some will be reminded here of Dietrich Bonhoeffer's* Letters & Papers from Prison: *"God is weak and powerless in the world and that is precisely the way, the only way in which he is with us to help us." But closer reading shows that Bonhoeffer holds to a faith in a transcendent biblical God, just one who at will forsakes us for our own good, and one who, in "his" wisdom, refuses to act supernaturally on demand. Even atheism "stands before God" and is not without God's approval: "God would have us know that we must live our lives as those who manage their lives without God.... Before God and with God we live without God." (Both passages quoted by John Shelby Spong [2001] p. ix.) Similar conclusions are often reached by holocaust survivors. They might say: "If there is a God, he evidently wants us to live without him. That is, he wants us to be good because simply, defiantly, and without underwriting, we choose to be." The theology of theopraxy is the only theology this side of existentialism that reconstructs God, as it were, from this last statement, which is to say, very nearly from scratch.*

"Have no fear, the good Lord will take care of me." The floodwaters rose. Police arrived in a boat and urged him to come aboard, but he refused, declaiming again that God would take care of him. The floodwaters rose ever higher until at last he was on the roof. A National Guard helicopter arrived. Hovering over his house, it dropped a ladder, and a crewman shouted for him to take this last opportunity. Again the man refused, putting his faith in God.

Eventually the waters swept him away to his death. Upon arrival at the pearly gates, the man petitioned to see God. Petition granted and head bowed, he tremblingly asked: "Heavenly Father, I was faithful to you and loved life. I put myself in your hands. Why did you do nothing and let me die?" And God replied: "Do nothing, my son? What are you talking about? I sent you caring neighbors; I sent you a boat; I even sent you a helicopter!"

10 : Persons and deeds

WHEN GOD is good doing, God manifests "himself" not as a spirit hovering over individual human beings, nor as a spirit dwelling within them, but as the substance and character of certain human *acts*. Neither you nor I as a whole, as persons or creatures, *are* God, however, even when you or I are doing good. Why? Because, for one, we are not wholly the good we do. We are also the bad we do and everything else we do too, from digesting food to sorting socks to fantasizing revenge. We are neither co-terminous with God nor part of God. To a first approximation one might say that God is part of us—the part that does good. Strictly speaking, however, God is not that either. God is good freely being done by us, as we do it, and as it flows from what we did. God is the deed, not the doer. God is the flame, not the match; the gesture, not the arm.

When you witness someone doing something of significant and surprising goodness then, don't say to yourself: "that person is divine," or even "that person is good." Say to yourself: "There's God in action," and consider it practice. For after a while even the smallest decency will provide the same evidence, the same feeling. And you will see God everywhere: in and as every genuine smile, every ungrudging service, every smallest charity, every well designed thing, every minute of peace. Then and there, you will see God being spun in evanescent threads all around, and that moment will become as a Sabbath day.

WHAT DO we mean, anyway, when we say (as we do all the time) that this or that person *is good?* We could be saying one of two things.

We could be saying that they are especially effective, accurate, or efficient in some activity. They are good baseball players, say, or good cooks, good artists, drivers, marksmen, or teachers. This is "good" in the sense of being skilled at some practice, ethical or not, which has conventional criteria for excellence. Thus, one could be a good hitman for the Mafia, a good terrorist, and so on.

We could also (or alternatively) be saying that the person is good morally, good ethically. This would evidence itself in many kinds of practice too, but not all. One could never be a good hitman, for example, or a good thief. The skill component remains, however, because saying that someone is a "good *person*" is saying that they are *skilled at doing good,* i.e., at preserving, promoting, and honoring all forms of life in everything they do, whatever they do. They are, in a way, doubly good.

An easy and commonsensical distinction, this. But note that our judgment in both cases depends continually on the *evidence* of deeds. A good concert pianist might be forgiven one or two off performances before she is no longer a "good concert pianist"—but no more than one or two. A good baseball batter is as good as his current batting average. Similarly, to say of a person that they *are* good (ethically, morally) can only mean that he or she has an above-average "batting average" at doing good, that his or her decisions and actions are supportive of life significantly more often than most people's are or would have been in the same circumstances.

Note too that in both versions of "good" it is actually the deeds that are meritorious, whether they are home runs, flawless musical performances, or acts of compassion. *It is the deeds whose light, as it were, shines or reflects well upon their doers.* The same is true of all virtues: in the end it's their performance that proves their possession. So even when we feel most comfortable praising *people* as good, we see upon closer inspection that it is what they did that we are praising and not what they are. Good-doing is episodic. In the theology of theopraxy, so is God.

Do you recall this creditable piece of Christian moral advice: "Love the sinner, hate the sin?" It would seem to disagree with our analysis, but it does not. Here is its wisdom: We are to love freely-chosen good deeds, i.e. God; we are to hate freely-chosen bad ones, i.e. sin (or the devil). We are to love *people,* however, as steadily, patiently, and unreservedly as we can, because people—those long-lived engines of action—are capable of good deeds and bad deeds both, and when loved steadily, patiently, and unreservedly are more likely to perform good ones.

11 : On being wanted

AT SOME time or another, most children will want to hear the story of their births: how it happened, where the family was living, and so on. Above and beyond the colorful details, what they want to hear is *that they were wanted,* that their birth was cause for celebration. A child who hears from his or her parents that their conception was accidental, or that they were "a mistake" has quickly to be reassured that the family was overjoyed to learn that he or she was on the way. Parents might say: "you were a surprise gift from God!"

To feel that our personal existence was intended, to know that we were welcomed from the beginning in and for our uniqueness, to be assured that we are on the planet legitimately in the eyes of all already there, and that we were, at least once, of inestimable value to our parents...these are some of the deepest desires we harbor, even into adulthood. I mention them not just to encourage their satisfaction, but to note that Western religion takes it upon itself to extend these desires and their satisfaction beyond the familial arenas in which they arose. It seeks to extend them indefinitely, casting God as the parent and the whole human race—humanity—as the child. It is important to us to feel that God (or The Universe) *wanted* us to be here as individuals, as nations, as a species.

One can see this logic at work in the first chapter of Genesis. There, at the end of each day of creation, God judges his work "good, very good." But only after creating Adam and Eve does he rest satisfied. We are a culmination. God made the earth and populated it with other living things so that we would have a home. But humans wrote Genesis, of course. On this knowledge, we can ask: does the Genesis story not represent the child in all of us pronouncing the parent good—good, for *wanting* the world and us to exist, good for conferring upon us a special legitimacy and authority over the rest of nature?

We see this logic again in the legendic imagery of Christmas, the nativity of Jesus. The Christ-child is welcomed by all, including representatives of the animal kingdom, of other nations (the three wise men to whom the birth was foretold), and of the cosmos itself, the star over Bethlehem.[42]

---

42 *Becoming convinced of Jesus's unconditional love for you, individually, can alleviate some of the pain of having been born unwanted or accidentally, or becoming an orphan. Clearly Jesus's unconditional love—i.e., God's love—works as a stand-in for the uncar-* ›

At the other end of the faith spectrum, we can see the same pattern in the scientist's cosmological "anthropic principle," which reports with barely concealed delight that many of the physical constants of the universe—like the ratio of the strength of the nuclear weak force to the strength of gravity, $10^{28}:1$—"just happen" to be *precisely* the ones that permit star formation and life on earth. It would seem that The Universe too wanted us to exist from the beginning! Deism supported!

And with few exceptions, cool-headed philosophers agree: existence is self-evidently better than non-existence, life better than death. But we can ask: What is this "better than" if not a de-sentimentalized affirmation of life and of self, with reality-as-a-whole cast as the good Father/Mother/cradle of humankind?

"Congratulations!" says the atheist. "You have seen through the myth to the truth. The anthropic principle especially proves nothing about God or man. Had the fundamental constants of the universe been different, the universe would have been different. End of story. That *we* are here to marvel at it all was simply the luck of the draw. Other creatures in other universes, with different constants, would thank *their* lucky stars; and universes without creatures at all would just be...universes without creatures. And as for existence being better than non-existence, well, all one can conclude from *that* is that the judge is probably not a potential suicide."

THE THEOLOGY of theopraxy asks us to pass up the idea that the cosmos is intrinsically good just because it exists, as well as the more reasonable idea that it is good because without it neither we nor any other sentient creature would be here to do good. It asks us to pass up these ideas in favor of a more challenging and ultimately truer one, namely that *goodness is something new in the world, and so is God.* Because responsibility for good's continuance lies with individual human beings, it follows that God's continuance does too.

Atheists mistakenly imagine that disproving the existence of a Creator-God "gets rid of" God. It does not. Discrediting the idea that the universe is intrinsically good does not get rid of God either. Nor does presenting evidence of widespread evil, and neither does pointing out that belief in God as Father rather conveniently helps our species feel at

---

‹ ing or missing parents' love. But more than that, Jesus' own plannedness by God but unplannedness by humans makes him the perfect receiver of your identity/legitimacy anxieties. If all children were welcomed and given love no matter the circumstances of their birth, such stories would not be necessary. God would be at work without our mentioning "him."

home—wanted and legitimate—in what is really a vast and indifferent universe. This is because the God that atheists "get rid of" was a straw God to begin with. Strong words, I know. But according to the theology of theopraxy, the God left standing after the atheists have had their way is finer by far than the God they dismiss.

12 : The real divinity of Jesus

FOR MODERN Christians the question of whether Jesus was wholly human, wholly divine, or somehow both without being "half-" either, remains equivocally answered. For some, Jesus was God himself come to earth: "Word become flesh." For others, Jesus was God's only begotten son, distinct in himself and yet joined with God (the Father) through the Holy Spirit. For Christians of liberal stripe, Jesus was "just" a man to whom God gave extraordinary insight, eloquence, and courage, a man whose short life God filled with such brilliance and pathos that his teachings, which were also God's, would not soon be forgotten.[43]

Jews and Muslims have little trouble with the last formulation. It makes Jesus a prophet who deserves great admiration, but leaves God, and only God, the proper object of *worship*.

The view of the theology of theopraxy on this score is complex. With Hegel, it sees Jesus not only as an remarkable prophet in the Hebrew tradition, but as a pivotal figure in the evolution of the idea of God. For the figure of Jesus Christ begins a fundamental shift away from the idea of Man—of humankind—being solely "born of" God the Creator, to God also being "born of" humankind, and thus being creat*ed*.

How so?

FIRST WE might note that in Genesis, Adam, the first human, is not portrayed as God's child or God's son but as God's creation. Adam is not the product of insemination, gestation, and birth. Nor does he experience boyhood. He is *manufactured* from inert matter, from dust. God *made* Adam; God *fashioned* him and breathed life into him. Eve is made roughly the same way, albeit from the substance of Adam. Moreover, Adam and Eve are thoroughly and recognizably human. Like us, they had no divine powers. Before the Fall, they were like innocent children; after the Fall, like care-worn adults. Like us, they made mistakes; like us, they worked, they had children, they died. In short, Adam and Eve were made *by* God and in his image, but they were not made *of* God, from his

---

43 *This was certainly the view of Thomas Jefferson and of many Enlightenment-influenced Christians of the 19th century, as well as of Unitarian Universalists today. But its roots lie earlier, in Ebionitism, named after the Ebionites, a small, ascetic Jewish-Christian sect circa 100 A.D. who believed that Jesus was an extraordinary and inspired prophet, but entirely human. See S. Gannon Murphy (2001) and Stephen Prothero (2003).*

substance. And indeed, throughout the Hebrew Bible, people are people, and God is God. The difference between human beings and God could not be greater—nor communication between them more frustrating.

Now let us look at the figure of Jesus. Jesus was not made by God and set upon the earth completed. He was—as it was once written and is now believed by conservative Christians—*born of* God through a human mother by the agency of the Holy Spirit; and he grew up a boy in Galilee.[44]

To Jews, and later to Muslims, this was heresy. This was the Greek idea of human demi-godhood illegitimately and unnecessarily imported into Judaism.[45] For Christians, however, Jesus came to represent—to prove—that God and humankind *could* fuse and that the conflict of kind between them could be resolved. Jesus was God's only begotten Son. More than a prophet, he was Christ-Messiah. More than that, he was God incarnated *as* a human being.[46]

Jesus himself gave grounds for the claim not just by the miracles he performed or the acuteness of his moral insights, which no thoughtful Jew or Muslim would gainsay, but by how he referred to himself, which was usually as the "Son of Man" but more than once the "Son of God."[47]

---

44 *In the synoptic gospels Jesus is born Jesus (Yeshua) of Nazareth and becomes Christ (Messiah) upon his death, resurrection, or exaltation (accounts vary). In the later-written gospels (like I and II John, and the letters of Paul) Jesus's divinity is projected back, as it were, to his birth. There Jesus was born Christ. And this is the image that became Church doctrine.*

45 *The Qur'an is emphatic on this score. In the third-to-last and most important of the suras called "The Unity Revealed at Mecca," we read (my emphasis): "In the name of Allah, the Beneficent, the Merciful, say: He is Allah, the One! Allah, the eternally Besought of All. He begetteth not nor was begotten. And there is none comparable unto Him."*

Canonical Christian belief by contrast might best be summed up by this credo from the United Methodist Church website: Jesus "is the eternal Word made flesh, the only begotten Son of the Father, born of the Virgin Mary by the power of the Holy Spirit. As ministering Servant he lived, suffered and died on the cross. He was buried, rose from the dead and ascended into heaven to be with the Father, from whence he shall return."

46 *Whether Jesus was wholly God or God in (a) man (the so-called "Aryan Heresy" named after Bishop Arius), was the source of great dispute for hundreds of years, ultimately forcing European Christianity to split into two factions, once centered in Rome, the other in Constantinople.*

47 *But see for example John 17:1–4. Of course, we shall never know what Jesus really said—of himself or anything else. (Ditto Socrates.) The synoptic gospels were written forty or so years after Jesus' legendary death, resurrection, and exaltation, and John much later than that. From the point of view of the theology of theopraxy, it doesn't matter whether Jesus himself actually uttered the words we are told he uttered. The word of God is any-* >

Certainly, others referred to him as the Son of God many times, and he never denied its appropriateness.[48] The pathos of his death and the wonder of his resurrection seemed to close the case for those who heard the gospel: Jesus *was* the Son of God, made of the same substance. More than that: he was God (in the form of) *the Son,* who, along with God (in the form of) the Father was made of the substance of God (in the form of) the Holy Spirit.[49] One need not be a Christian to understand how this belief could spark a new era of faith, retrograde in one sense but progressive in another. For established, now, was the possibility of God-in-human-form issuing from God-in-ethereal-form—not just from *a* god, *à la Grécque,* but from *the* God, the one and only God of the Torah.[50] Here

---

‹ one's to try to tell. *As Jesus (apparently) said: "It is by their fruits that we should judge them" (Matthew 7:19-20). The Bible is the work of many well-intentioned hands, and it is full of contradictions and metaphors. It is for that reason, paradoxically, that it is to be trusted. There is more wisdom in the Talmud by far than in the Torah, even though—or rather, precisely because—the Talmud held the Torah to be the unerring word of God (which it is not) for thousands of pages.*

48 *At the crucial moment of meeting Caiaphas, Jesus deflects the question (Matthew 26:62–64, Luke 22:66–70) and goes back to his usual self-appellation, namely, "Son of Man." But as reported in Matthew 16:13–20 and in comparable places in the other gospels, Jesus clearly allows the imputation.*

The term "sons of God," sometimes translated as "divine beings," appears first in Genesis 6:1-4, which tells of a time, long ago, when divine beings impregnated the loveliest of human women, and gave birth to a generation of superior humans. One sees an echo here, or a remnant, of the ancient Greek and Phoenician myth of the Titans, born of earth and sky, and tales of a time when the great ancients—"Nephilim" in the Bible, meaning "giant men"—strode the earth.

The phrase "sons of God" appears again in Job 1:6 and 38:7 in obvious reference to Genesis 6:1–4, as well as the concept of rare divine beings, perhaps angels, who are able physically to approach God. A "son of God" also appears in Daniel 3:25, where it depicts what we would today think of as an angel.

Now, the Bible that Jesus knew, from Genesis to the later prophets, told that there were many angels, many "sons of God." Jesus could therefore not have thought of himself as the first, last, or only son of God. Indeed, when Jesus defends himself against skeptical Jews (John 10:34) he refers to Psalms 82:6, where God chides his divine sons, in the plural. Jesus may have thought of himself as being in their exalted company, but the disciples thought him singular, exceptional, in the company of none but God. To them he was not a son of God but the only son of God, christos, savior-messiah. And Jesus, if we are to believe the gospel writers, let it so stand. It was John who most strongly insisted upon Jesus' exclusive divinity, and John's view was to become Christian orthodoxy.

49 *See Matthew 28:19 for the New Testament's first suggestion of God's tri-unity. The Epistles of James and Peter, which pre-date Matthew, make no reference to it. Trinitarianism as we know it was to become Christian doctrine only four hundred years later, based on the writings of Irenaeus, and Tertullian.*

was the Lord God of the universe, a distant and terrifying figure for so long, choosing to be "born of Man" through a woman, choosing to make himself real and vulnerable, as though to see what it is like to be human, but in fact to demonstrate his teachings and thus bring us back to him.

God, born of Man. A misinterpretation, perhaps, of God *borne in* Man, but there it was! There was the proposition upon which the fate of Jesus actually turned, the one underlying the more obvious blasphemy of an angry young man with hair and teeth claiming to be descended from God in a literal way, which could have been dismissed as delusion. In the view of the theology of theopraxy, Jesus's deeper proposition was not that he was the "Son of Man" *or* the "Son of God," but that he was somehow both; that he represented, by example, the possibility of the equivalence between *God the Son of Man* and *Man the Son of God,* where "Man," capitalized, means humankind, male and female, worthy of honor, and "God" means the source and judge of all goodness, beauty, and truth. Moreover, as Jesus said more than once, it was not just himself but *all* men and women—all "sons of Man"—who could be Sons of God.[51]

---

50 *The gods of ancient Egypt, Greece, and Rome behaved a great deal like humans. They fought, they married, they loved, and several were "literally" half-human, i.e., offspring of man (or more usually woman) and god. Among them, Osiris (Egyptian), Persephone and Dionysus (Greek) and Attis (Phrygian and Roman) were unjustly murdered and later resurrected.*

51 *From the Sermon on the Mount: "Blessed are the peacemakers, for they shall be called the sons of God" (Matthew 5:9). The disciple Paul elaborates this implication: "For all who are led by the Spirit of God are the sons of God...(If) you have received the spirit of sonship...it is the Spirit himself bearing witness with our spirit that we are the children of God. (Romans 8:14-16). Again: "(I)t is God which worketh in you both to will and to do of his good pleasure...that ye may be blameless and harmless, the sons of God (Philippians 2:13-15 [King James Version]). The apostle John wrote, as an older man: "See what love the Father has given us, that we should be called the children of God," (I John, 3:1), and later in the same passage "whoever does not do right is not of God, nor he that does not love his brother" (I John 3:10, my emphasis).*

"If I am not doing the works of my Father," said Jesus to a group of skeptical Jews in Jerusalem, "then do not believe me; but if I do them, even though you do not believe (that I am a son of God), believe the works, that you may know and understand that the Father is in me and that I am in the Father" (John 10:37-38, my parenthetical words). Note the reversiblility of identity using the irrational metaphor of mutual inclusion (irrational because A cannot logically be in B and at the same time B be in A). Note too that the "works" to which Jesus refers in this context are probably his by-then-well-known miracles. "Works" take on another meaning in Paul's emphasis on faith over works as the road to redemption. In his letter to the Galatians especially, "works" denote "works of law," where "law" refers to rites and rituals performed without the proper spirit. No wonder Paul privileged faith over works: he did not mean by "works" what it means in the Epistle of James ›

We can see, further, that if "son of..." in Biblical metaphor means "created by" or better, "emergent from," then the story of Jesus prefigures what the theology of theopraxy today proposes: that *humanity* (meaning humane-ness, decency) and *divinity* (meaning God) bring each other into being. "I am in the Father, and the Father is in me," said Jesus. Note the reciprocality; note the sense of *borne in* or *borne by* rather than born *of.*

Where Christianity draws the line at Jesus as Christ, the theology of theopraxy asserts that in myriad acts of mercy and joy, love and courage the world over, a vast number of men and women before Jesus and since him have been signal in the process of humanity-divinity co-creation: good people creating God, God creating good people. A vanishingly tiny number of these individuals have had their lives recorded for posterity. We do not know them even though everything good in our lives depends on what they did. Their memory died with those they served and taught, loved and perished for. None *were* God. No one *is* God. All, however, bore God into the world by their actions, and wove God into the fabric of our present-day reality.

The "Kingdom of God is among us" because of them.

‹ *and almost everywhere else, namely (remarkably good) deeds of all kinds.*

Note finally that Jesus would have known of the three references to "sons of God" in the Hebrew Bible mentioned in Note 48.

In all, we see a trend to watering down, if you will, the powerful phrase "son of God" from (1) a handful of angelic beings or minor gods present at the Creation, to (2) Jesus, who appears concretely as a man but is God, to (3) any good man or woman who accepts Jesus' message and divinity...and then a reversal with post-Nicean Christianity, back to (2). See Geza Vermes (2000).

13 : The Kingdom of God (and a prayer)

THE KINGDOM of God has established itself already. It is in our midst, as Jesus said. But it is not whole, and may never be. It has the shape of an archipelago, with islands that rise up and sink down continuously, sometimes connecting together to form a larger mass, sometimes breaking up into hundreds of smaller pieces or disappearing entirely. The king that rules this archipelago has no permanent palace or throne, but as many temporary ones as there are people who are doing good, knowing they are free to do otherwise.

May you live on one of those islands of peace, happiness, and good will. May it surround you and be in your heart. May it grow larger and join with others; may it grow over in complexity and variety, order and lifefulness, until the time of your children and beyond.

14 : On nature's beauty and ordinary goodness

TODAY AGAIN, the sun sets over the ocean. Tonight the sky will be dusted with stars. The crickets will sing and the tiger will turn its head. Beautiful! But natural beauty is, after all, just beauty. There is no goodness in it, or evil. It has been said that the ancient Greeks worshipped the goodness of beauty while the Hebrews worshipped the beauty of goodness. But the truth is that only in human works can beauty and goodness be united, so that we may see one in the other.[52]

It's late afternoon on a Sunday. I sit in my front yard on a terrace of stone, which is cupped from the street by a weathered cedar fence covered in ivy. It is fall. The air is fine. Three large oak trees twist up into the sky. Their bark is black and their myriad leaves stand silhouetted against the blue while the sun turns the trees across the street a brilliant gold. A neighbor rakes his path, *scraaaap, scraaaap*. A single-engine plane drones across the sky. A car passes; a dog barks and another answers far away. A snatch of rock-and-roll escapes from a teenager's car as he slams the door. A mother calls her child to dinner. A leaf falls on my lap.

All this is beautiful too. But beautiful in a different way, and, I want to say, better way than the stars. In the form of a painting or a piece of music, a building or a garden, beauty made by humans is more than just beauty. It is the crown of thousands of years of civilization, of law, of peace, and of a certain wisdom in design both with and against nature. This house in which I write was built, these stones were laid, and these trees were planted more than fifty years ago when the neighborhood was developed. Together with the hundreds of homeowners who have lived here, this neighborhood was laid out and constructed and planted and maintained by people who were neither angels nor creative geniuses, but who contained in their professionalism and general decency enough human goodness to make this place and this moment beautiful and good. It did not have to be so. The good they did lives on.

---

52 *John Keats ends his well-known* Ode on a Grecian Urn *like this: "When old age shall this generation waste/Thou shalt remain, in midst of other woe/Than ours, a friend to man, to whom thou say'st,/'Beauty is truth, truth beauty,—that is all/Ye know on earth, and all ye need to know.'" "Thou" refers, of course, to the urn, a human work of art; but Thou also refers to God, for whom Keats speaks.*

And so, while I am deeply interested in the beauty and complexity of nature as such, and while I cannot help but recognize myself reflected in, prefigured in, and related to all forms of life, I am not touched by nature's beauty the way I am touched by the smallest act of genuine human altruism, not as impressed by Mount Everest as I am by our agreement to drive on the right, or the left. Because, for all its grandeur, Nature's beauty is actually the picture and result of fifteen billion years of randomness-leavened, micro-scaled automatism. The Milky Way, waves on the beach, the most delicate honeycombs, the Grand Canyon reflected in an eagle's eye...all these things are just cooling gas, "computer art," a gigantic screensaver.

Human art, on the other hand (and it need not be "great"), glows with a light that is no longer a simple reflection of the sun and the moon. It glows with improbable skill, with love, and with longing, as does every life-promoting act and every healing gesture. Human goodness proceeds with the kind of persistence, generosity, and "uphillness" of which the furious stars know little. All the stronger do their deeds glow when the people who act in this way—let us call them "artists of good"—imagine they are doing what anyone else would do.

15 : God's authority versus God's power

It has been said that *authority* is given while *power* is taken.[53] Let us look into this distinction.

Power is the ability to project the credible threat of violence and/or the promise of protection from it. Power can be had in greater or lesser amount therefore, depending on its wielder's strength or indestructibility relative to those around. Those who have power have no need of permission to use it—no need, at least, to receive permission from those whose power theirs exceeds.

Authority is a gentler force. It is held by those who have permission to wield power but very rarely do so or need to. This permission is granted to them on approval, as it were, by those who will be protected or by those who have greater power yet. Although authority is backed by power, it is only legitimate when it is backed by laws agreed to by all, which apply to all, and which publicly establish the criteria and procedures by which authority is granted and peacefully taken away.

Power must periodically be demonstrated. Authority must periodically be earned. Power is something one submits to; authority is something one obeys out of respect.

Now, according to Bible and Qur'an, God has power over both nature and humankind: God could smash them to pieces at will. God's authority derives from that power alone. According to the theology of theopraxy, however, God has authority but no power—and then only the authority that humans vest in God. God has no taken or self-given power at all, and God is nowhere to be found in nature except in and as the life-promoting doings of human beings.[54] When "God" is understood as goodness-in-action personified, it becomes natural to *want* a world that we can say God rules completely, and to grant God every permission to make it so through us.

It is not we, then, who might be "elect of God," as the Calvinists have it, but God who might be "elect of us." God is elected by us each time we

---

53 *I have not found the provenance of this saying. Close, but not quite, is this definition by Jacques Maritain (1951): "Authority and power are two different things: power is the force by means of which you can oblige others to obey you. Authority is the right to direct and command, to be listened to or obeyed by others. Authority requests power. Power without authority is tyranny."*

54 *But see Note 10 of this chapter.*

elect to do the good and do it. In this mirror held up to the standard view, the Israelites of five thousand years ago were not the chosen people; they were the choos*ing* people. They chose *one* God, Yahweh, to be the Lord (of all) God(s). With no small urging from Moses, they elected Yahweh, and accepted His commandments, and in so doing became the Jewish— the Yahwist—people.[55]

---

55 *In the liturgy of Yom Kippur one reads: "For we are Your people, and You are our God. We have chosen You, and You have chosen us." In the light of the theology of theopraxy, the logical (not to say moral) equivalence of the two choosings becomes plain, although in the body of the text I emphasize only the counter-traditional side.*

16 : The truth of theopraxy

SINCE THERE are as many understandings of God as there are major religions, and as many shades of those understandings as there are sects, we might ask: does it make sense to look for the one true God in the small set of theological postulates that all religions have in common? Some would say yes: the truest view of God lies in the *intersection* of all ideas of God. Others would argue, however, that the truest understanding of God would be the one that coincides with the *union* of ideas of God, that is, all of them, taken together, logical conflicts notwithstanding.[56]

One must also consider the possibility that for any given time and place there are ideas, metaphors, images, arguments, and practices that best address (or most please) God because they maximize the production of beauty over ugliness, truth over delusion, kindness over cruelty, life over lifelessness—in short, goodness over badness—then and there. It might be the case that Christianity's *Father, Son, and Holy Spirit,* that Judaism's *Adonai Elohenu, Melech Ha'Olam* (Lord our God, King of the Universe), and Islam's *Allah Al-rahman, Al-rahim* (Allah the Beneficent, the Merciful), different as they are, are still the best and most realizable ideas of God for today's Christians, Jews, and Muslims respectively.

Intersection

Union

But it might just as easily be the case that these "versions" of God have lost their ability to nurture the best in each of these groups, or to be nurtured in turn by what each has become. To judge by the religiously-based conflict in the Middle East, India, Pakistan, and Indonesia, not to mention American Christian-evangelical empire-building, international Muslim-fundamentalist terrorism, and European "secular" national chauvinism, there is room for improvement.

The theology of theopraxy holds that what lies at the intersection of all religions and moral philosophies is the mandate to preserve, honor, and promote all forms and instances of life. One might call this mandate God's will, which we come to know "in our hearts" through, with, and

---

56 *For a popular example of the "intersection" approach, read just about anything by Ken Wilber or visit www.beliefnet.com/story/141/story_14148.html. Unitarian Universalism, as its name suggests, employs the mathematical union strategy.*

behind all manner of imagery. Or one might call it moral intuition. But we need to see (proposes the theology of theopraxy) that God's objective and actual existence depends upon that will's execution by us, in this world. God's will, on this view, is God's will to *exist*. And it comes not from on high, but from human life flowering as a cosmic phenomenon.

Big words, these. Perhaps too big. Let us focus the discussion upon a small but emblematic point. If the effectiveness of prayer depended upon the literalness with which one believed in a traditional God, then *that* idea of God, although problematic in one sense (theoretical), would be unproblematic in another (instrumental or practical). If traditional religious beliefs work best to do good, then their proponents are justified in calling other religious beliefs not *wrong*, perhaps, but not as *true* of God.[57]

Indeed, if it could be shown that the good that results from believing in a Biblical Creator-God is greater than that which results from belief in any other God, or no God at all, then the Biblical God is a *good* version of God—perhaps the best—which, *because* it works and *as* it works, is God (according to the theology of theopraxy). By its own criteria, the *theology* of theopraxy would recuse itself as a perspective worth offering there. It would become, at best, an intellectual curiosity presenting some small enticement to atheists, or just one more Path for already spiritually-inclined people to experiment with. But if, on the other hand, the theology of theopraxy proves equally effective or more effective at engendering goodness in this day—if it leads to more freedom, more beauty, and greater life-length and life-quality for more creatures—then our theology will have satisfied its own highest criteria. It would be theopraxy itself—which, it claims, all religions and moral philosophies have unwittingly been aiming at.

---

57 *Norman Podhoretz (1999): "Jews are good by virtue of the commandments they follow, not the theological niceties they accept. I heard an anecdote illustrating the force of this ethos from an Israeli friend who had become an atheist in his teens and whose father was Orthodox. One day, while having an intense argument about the existence of God, my friend's father looked at his watch and said to his son: 'Well, God may or may not exist, but it's time for the evening prayers.'" The view is far from exclusively Jewish. See for example Eric O. Springsted (2002),*

17 : The rightness of Genesis 1 and 2

"In the Beginning...God created the Heaven and the Earth..." The next thirty-one verses of Genesis 1 go on to describe the creation of the world in six days. In what sense can it be said that this best-known of all creation stories is correct? How can it be believed, not just beloved?

Certainly, it is not an accurate description, even in literary summary, of the way the world actually came into being.

But it is also not "half-right," the way religion-friendly scientists like to concede, saying something like: "Given that the universe was actually created *ex nihilo* in a primeval Big Bang some fifteen billion years ago, followed by galactic formation, planetary formation, biological evolution, and so forth on up to us, the story of the six days of Creation is *roughly* true. Order arises from chaos, the heavens precede the earth, the inanimate precedes the animate, the animals precede humans... all true and in order. It's just that each 'day' lasted about 3 billion years!" At this point the scientist chuckles: "Not bad. Not bad at all, considering that Genesis was written some three thousand years ago!"

The truth is, however, that the Creation stories of Genesis 1 and Genesis 2 (they are a little different) are as helpful, and in a way as right, as any account of our origins given by modern science, Big Bang, evolution, and all. One just has to see that the subject matter of each account is different.

The great scholar Maimonides proposed that Genesis reads like a children's story because God, whose word is the Torah, knew that the general populace could not understand anything more complicated. It was up to scholars and sages to probe the Torah's depths, to turn over every word and phrase to find the truth encoded there. We can agree. The story of creation as told in the first chapters of Genesis are true, perhaps not in exactly the way Maimonides would accept, but certainly in the spirit he encouraged.

For one realizes that the opening verses of Genesis do not so much describe the world as *in*scribe one, bring it into being. The kind of being that Genesis brings the world into is not simple physical Being *(Sein)*, but phenomenological being, *human* be-ing (what Heidegger called *Dasein*). *Dasein* appears as the cosmos, but as a cosmos always-already humanly understood, humanly categorized, humanly experienced, and humanly valued in its entirety—including by scientists. The cosmos as modern science would have us pretend to understand it, i.e., "on its own terms," is a pitiless place, foreign beyond foreignness, neither beautiful nor sublime, neither large nor small, neither old nor young. It is without future or past or up or down. It is neither our home nor *not* our home. It is not even interesting. (Or rather, it *is* interesting, but only because we "find" it so.) As even our most objective scientific language betrays, the universe cannot be understood "in its own terms" since understanding involves blood-pumping, click-counting, instrument-squinting, theory-making, hope-having, beauty-judging *us*. There is no view from everywhere, just as there is no view from nowhere. The simplest act of *counting*—1, 2, 3,...— depends on ignoring differences among the things being counted, and is thus selective, motivated.

Consider Carl Sagan's famous invocation of "billions and billions" (of stars, light-years, miles). Was it not notable for the emotion it conveyed? Cosmologists are still a-titter with their project.

No, galaxies by the billion careening through the icy 'dark matter' of space without privileged center, edge, or direction do not a world make, a world that feels like home. Genesis does. The first chapters of Genesis are human world-creation written down.[58] Who else but humans (and perhaps some animals) would partition the cosmos into "the Heavens and the Earth," and the earth into dry land and sea? There's nothing incorrect about that. Does the sky not still cover your town with a blue dome? Does the sun not "come up" in the "east" and "go down" in the "west"? Do the stars not "come out" at night? Does a weed not blossom by your door. Do your flowers not "need" water? Do you not care for your dog, and regret having to kill for food? Is your beloved wife or husband not a "help-meet"? Is your living not earned by the sweat of your brow? Or someone else's?

Consider Genesis's inscription by description of a seventh day of Creation, which is when God rested and appraised what he had done. This sitting-back in reflection and appreciation, emulated by the great Western religions with their Sabbath rituals and now adopted worldwide, speaks volumes about the difference between *Sein* (Being *per se*) and *Dasein* (being-here humanly). The universe that science reveals to us spins and burns endlessly, tirelessly. It contains nothing that "works," nothing that "rests." There are no weeks in it, and no weekends; no minutes and no hours. The world that Genesis both describes and inscribes, on the other hand, is *our* world, not The Universe, and as real. And that makes the first chapters of Genesis true in an unexpected way. [59]

---

58 *I should say "Western European and Islamic world-creation written down," since there are many world creation stories globally (see for example Hamilton, 1988). All, however, have the same anthropocentrism as the Biblical account, if not more.*

59 *See also* ARGUMENTS 20, *Note 96.*

18 : Responsibility to and for

"THE POTTER is greater than the pot." Descartes thought the truth of this proposition self-evident; as did Aristotle; as do people of common sense today. It follows that God (as traditionally conceived), who is the Potter of us all and who, moreover, made the very clay he shapes, is greater in every conceivable way than his creation.[60]

When the theology of theopraxy proposes that "God is in our hands," then, does it not make human beings the potter and God the pot? What a hideous reversal! Has our theology replaced God with *ourselves*? What hubris. For if God (God forbid) should turn out to be our creation, or we believe this to be the case, then how could God (be thought to) command us to do anything? Where would obedience go? Who would stop us inventing a new God every day according to our fancy? And what happens to God's incomparable grandeur if he's "just us"?

From the perspective of conventional religious belief, theist or deist, these are real concerns. I brought them up in Chapter 1 of this Book and will return to them several times. Here let me suggest that things are not as bad as they look: the theology of theopraxy is not as dangerous as traditional believers might think it is. Or as heretical. In the matter of results, quite to the contrary. It suggests that traditional religions can and should be embraced in those forms that make the best of us. After all, when you believe that God is the good we do, it matters not very much what master narrative *exactly* brings you to bringing God into being: ones that deny this formulation are fine too. As though in reciprocal agreement, most renderings of the Biblical/Qur'anic God have God preferring good non-believers to bad believers. Did Jesus not say: by their fruits shall you know who is and who is not "of God"(Matthew 7:19ff.)?

THERE ARE three further ways to allay the worries people might have about the theology of theopraxy's mutualizing of the creation of God and humankind—three ways, that is, to explain its apparent and perhaps alarming confusion of Potter with pot.

The first comes from understanding evolution.

In biological evolution, certainly, the later, descendant species *can* be "greater" than the earlier, descended-from species. The child can be greater than the parent; the pot greater than the potter. The three components of

---

60 *The potter-pot metaphor is Biblical, originating in Jeremiah 18:6.*

the biological evolutionary process—namely, reproduction-with-inheritance, random variation, and natural (or sexual) selection—repeated over and over in an increasingly complex environment, virtually guarantee that the "latest model" of a species will be greater than its earlier counterparts—"greater" meaning smarter, stronger, larger (probably), more efficient, more complexly organized, and inclusive of the earlier model's qualities. Evolution's way of *causing* things is not like simple mechanical imposition, i.e., like a fist to the chin or a hand upon clay, like a wrench to a nut or even a paintbrush to a canvas. In evolution, new phenomena, new entities, and even new laws emerge from myriad simpler ones interacting. They flower, as from seed. Wrinkles get wrinkles until a new shape appears, a new capability, a new and stable state-of-affairs that in turn constrains its constituents to being what they are.[61] Unlike craftsmanship, which involves imposition, evolution with emergence describes a path not of *descent* in complexity, organization, and capability—potter over pot—but of *ascent:* from the inanimate to the animate, from the animate to the more animate yet, and from the "more animate yet" to the animal that can care for all animacy, for all life, to wit: the enlightened human being. In a world of growing complexity and increasing diversity, things can and do get better, more various and more particular, more particular and more coordinated. In short, in an evolving universe the Apocalypse is not assured.

By itself, the long-term uphill direction of evolution on earth (and perhaps elsewhere too) does not logically *entail* the emergence of God, although some have argued precisely this.[62] I cite evolution only to coun-

---

61 *For an eloquent treatment of "emergentism" rather than reductionism as the new paradigm in physics, see Robert Laughlin (2004). For a broader view, see Harold J. Morowitz (2004). Among physicists for whom diversity and its increase are somehow the universe's intention or business, see Freeman Dyson (2004 [1989]). Not all Judeo-Christian theology is inherently anti-evolution. See, for example, John F. Haught (2001), who portrays God as actively involved in the directions that evolution takes.*

62 *For example, the Oxford philosopher Samuel Alexander (1950, [1920]) and the Jesuit paleontologist-turned-theologian Pierre Teilhard de Chardin. The driving idea is that God did not intend the Universe; the Universe intends God. Our theology avers: no, only humans do.*

Here is Harold J. Morowitz (op. cit., p. 195) all but agreeing: "Note that God's transcendence was not meaningful before the emergence of humans and human culture. Violation of the natural law is only meaningful to individuals capable of knowing natural law. Divine transcendence arose from immanence and emergence and coevolved with Homo Sapiens. Transcendence is an emergent property of God's immanence and rules of emergence. We Homo sapiens are the mode of action of divine transcendence."

ter the idea that causes are always "greater" than their effects.[63] But evolution and emergence as descriptions of how the world works do leave open the *possibility* that God need not have started things, or have designed them, in order to be here and deserve our ultimate respect. God can be greater than we are even though we are God's "effectors" and God is ours in the moral sphere. Already, everything seriously said and thought about the divine over the short history of philosophical theology has grown to more than any one of us can hold in one brainful. God is at the very, very least "greater" in this way than any theologian.[64]

THE SECOND way to counter worries about our theology's "heresy" is to appreciate, perhaps more fully, the power of *ideas*.

Most will agree that ideas deserve respect. Not *all* ideas deserve respect, of course, just those that convey truths about the world, or that give our lives meaning, or that promote virtuous behavior. (It goes without saying that the best ideas do all three.) Take "democracy," "freedom," "honor," "destiny," the "virtues" or "art," for example. These are ideas that people "made up." Yet we find it entirely rational, indeed supremely admirable, for people to devote themselves to realizing them in everyday life. Moreover, when we devote ourselves to realizing ideas in everyday life, and do so generation after generation, these same ideas begin to "make us up," you and me. They become part of our constitution, not just our Constitution, and we find ourselves dreaming of their perfection as ideals. This is cultural evolution at work.[65]

We might respect traditional ideas of God, then, out of admiration for their age, beauty, and importance. But we need not stop there. Respect given, we can continue to *improve* our ideas of God, which means improving their effectiveness in producing good, which whole process, according to the theology of theopraxy, is the same as God improving us. We are talking about full assent to God as God really is without full assent to God as pictured by this or that religion. God, after all, is no one

---

63 *There are other counter-examples: in complex systems, the tiniest of causes—a crack, a slip, a minuscule error—can multiply into huge effects, even mechanically. Think of avalanches.*

64 *Some readers might be reminded here of St. Anselm's famous definition of God as "something greater than which nothing can be conceived." Since existing-in-fact is "greater than" existing-only-in-theory, Anselm argued, God must actually exist. This argument became known as Anselm's Proof of the existence of God.*

65 *...and alas, sometimes de-evolution at work, as when a generation of children is taught to hate certain foreigners. How can war not ensue?*

person's idea or personal friend. Nor is God any one era's privilege or any one religion's privilege to see. Realizing God is a panhuman quest, each generation handing off to the next a set of descriptions and prescriptions that needs rational justification and more: a theology that narrativizes God, that fantasizes God, and that, in so doing, amplifies the capacity we all have to recognize the good when we see it and long to do it ourselves.

Saying that God is an idea, then, is no great heresy if you have sufficient respect for ideas to start with. Still less is it a heresy if you think that God is more than a good *idea* of God, which is to say, if you think (as Anselm did with a different idea of God in mind) that God-realized is greater.

A THIRD way to worry less about the possibly bad effects of believing that humans create God (even if we believe also that God in turn creates our humanity), is to look more carefully at the creative act itself. Why? Because the creative act is often where the divine is located, not just in universal first Creation but in everyday creation too, especially artistic creation. It is here, some would say, that the Holy Spirit enters us—in-spirits us, inspires us—and emerges as new beauty, new goodness, or truth.[66] Of course, when art was mostly religious in theme it was easier to say of an artist—or for artists to say of themselves—that their inspiration came from God or the gods. But an element of this claim remains in all uses of the term "inspired," aided and abetted by the fact that human creativity remains neurologically and psychologically something of a mystery.

Rather than theorize what creativity really *is,* however, I want look into creativity's social/ethical dimension.[67]

Take the concept of *responsibility*.

People are responsible for what they create. In what is perhaps the canonical case, parents create (or initiate the creation of) their children.

---

66 *Indeed, there is much to be said for thinking of God as* creativity *itself, as I did in* DECLARATIONS, *and as the Harvard theologian Gordon D. Kaufman does in Kaufman (1993 and 2004). As in process theology, what Kaufman has in mind is universal, cosmic creativity, which includes, but is not limited to human creativity. The idea of theopraxy focuses on human creativity. Closer to our thinking on this score is John Wall (2005).*

67 *One theory gaining plausibility is that creativity is merely evolution speeded up and/or seen from the outside. Think of moments of creativity as pearls on a string. If we were to look inside each pearl we would see evolutionary processes at work at smaller scales and much speeded up because they are rendered at neurological and even molecular scales. Certainly, this seems true of the human mind. See Gerald Edelman (1987), Daniel Dennett (1978), William H. Calvin (1996), and Michael Benedikt (2007).*

Certainly, they are responsible for their children's very existence, and can fairly be asked "why did you have children?" They are also morally responsible for their children's health, education, and behavior, at least until the children are adults. Engineers, architects, and designers are responsible for what they create too. Professionally they have to stand behind their work, and can be sued for negligence. It is on this model that we can hold God (as traditionally conceived) causally and therefore morally responsible for the world he created.[68]

But creators are also responsible *to* what they create. In the case of progeny this is clear: we are responsible not just *for* our children, but *to* them. Our children have claims on us, and we must do right by them. Many artists feel the same way: they are responsible not just for their works but to them. What they create has certain rights: the right to be completed in a certain way, to be part of a trajectory of *oeuvre* that has its own logic, to become part of the larger, humanity-wide project called Art, and to be protected from wanton destruction even by the artist him- or herself. Art collectors, for their part, are protective of the art they own, and not just for the work's financial value (insurance can cover that), but for the preciousness of their unique "being."

Scientists often feel this way about their research projects, as do entrepreneurs who create companies, architects who design buildings, people who cultivate gardens...all truly creative people. And perhaps God, as traditionally conceived, feels this way about his creation too.

Now, the theology of theopraxy proposes that we are responsible for God. No hubris is intended by this view. Indeed, humility is the appropriate attitude precisely because our responsibility *for* God is matched by an equal—let us even say, greater—responsibility *to* God. Traditional religions insist on the responsibility-to component exclusively, this on the model of our being the eternal, dutiful child to the eternal all-wise, all-knowing parent who brought us into being. The theology of theopraxy does not want to eliminate this feeling but to add to it the feeling

---

68 *Here the discussion usually veers off into the problem of evil and how or whether God can be blamed for the mess we make of things. When the analogy is made to parents and children, it can be claimed that humankind is no child to God anymore, but grown up, and given freedom, and therefore culpable in the way no child can be.*

69 *We realize that the statement "God is in our hands" has two slightly different meanings: (1) that God's existence depends on our actions, and (2) that we are responsible for looking after God, caring for "him," once "he" is here (as perhaps instated by other people's actions).*

that grown-up children properly feel toward their own children, namely, responsibility-for.[69]

What creates can also have been created. What has been created can also create. Responsibility is similarly twinned: there is responsibility-to *and* responsibility-for. Why would our relationship to God involve less than both?

19 : Knowledge and faith

MANY WOULD agree that religious faith arrived at in maturity is better than faith inculcated at childhood and maintained by habit.[70] Similarly, faith chosen knowing the difference between faith and knowledge is stronger than faith accepted unreflectively, i.e., "on faith." Let us think about this for a moment.

Those of scientific bent (positivists, to be exact) maintain that faith is inferior to knowledge. One has faith when one does not *know*. Faith is permissible, but only as a transitional state, as when we "take on faith" that something is true—for example that "the logarithm base 2 of 2 is 1"—on the assurance of understanding *why* it is true later. At best, say positivists, faith is an amalgam of partial knowledge and trust. At worst, it is conviction "achieved" by turning a blind eye to the weight of evidence against the matter believed.[71]

Defenders of faith, on the other hand, see it as a better and firmer state of mind than mere knowledge. For one, they say, knowledge is open to revision by experience, while faith is not, or is less so. Where knowledge is slippery and fickle, faith is sticky and loyal. Where knowledge is "knowing only in (or with) one's mind," faith is "knowing in (or with) one's *heart*." Faith is what warriors must have. And not just warriors. When you or I launch upon any course of action on the basis of a promise, what are we doing but "acting on faith," since no promise is sure to be fulfilled? Indeed, faith is what everyone acts on all the time, even positivists, and it is optional only in theory. This is because complete and certain knowledge is never granted to us: not knowledge of what another person did,

---

70 *One might think here of the writer C. S. Lewis turning from atheism to Christianity at age thirty-five. One might also think of the great Rabbi Akiva (c. 100 A.D), who lived the first half of his life as a shepherd. Or indeed of the Biblical Abraham, who was 75 years old before God's oneness occurred to him.*

71 *I found this passage in the* Encyclopedia Britannica Online, *under "Aspects of Christian Philosophy," instructive: "As unforced belief, faith is 'an act of the intellect assenting to the truth at the command of the will' (Summa theologicae, II/II, Q. 4, art. 5); and it is because it is a free and responsible act that faith is one of the virtues. It follows that one cannot have knowledge and faith at the same time in relation to the same proposition; faith can only arise in the absence of knowledge. Faith also differs from mere opinion, which is inherently changeable. Opinions are not matters of absolute commitment but allow in principle for the possibility of doubt and change. Faith, as the wholehearted acceptance of revealed truth, excludes doubt. "*

or is thinking now, or will do in the future; not knowledge of the tens of thousand of facts in history, law, medicine, or science that we simply accept as true as we go about our lives; and certainly not knowledge of what God (as ordinarily understood) has in mind.

Moreover, say defenders of faith, what one has faith in often *matters* more than what one has knowledge of. After all, what is known (or thought to be known) with certainty is, in a sense, dead, ready for the archives. Toward what is known with x degree of certainty the proper attitude is x degree of acceptance of its being the way things are, and $(1 - x)$ degree of questioning or doubt. It is belief, it is faith—and the hope for, and vision of, a better future—that closes the $(1 - x)$ gap, that enables us to go forward still in doubt, and that invests the *given* world with interest and emotion.[72]

And then there is the fact that the future, being at least partially undetermined, makes the course of events open to our creative intervention. Because we act on what we *take* to be true and *hope* to be(come) true, not just on what we *know* to be true (already), it is often faith, not knowledge, that triggers the activities that make the world what it will be. Consider: whatever we can *make* true by our own actions we can predict will *be* true. The gambler who puts his hand on the roulette wheel is hardly gambling: *making* it true that the wheel stops at 22 Red turns his "predictions" into self-fulfilling prophecies. Of course, putting your hand on the wheel of a scientific experiment in order to get the result you want is not a good way to do science (and it's an illegal way to gamble). But the environment in which most people live is neither a laboratory nor a casino. People are immersed in life itself, the real thing, with a great deal of what will happen (legally) determinable by the decisions they will make, which are based in turn upon what they *want* to happen as well as what they know might (or might not) happen apart from them.

So while we cannot move the stars or adjust the value of the gravitational constant, what happens in the realm of ideas, culture, law, social relations, or art very much depends on what we make happen. There we are free to try to bring about what we want to bring about: games, laws, songs, dances, stories, buildings, movies, theorems, human relationships... love, honesty, possibilities. These things are no less real than the stars,

---

72 *Theologian Alvin Plantinga is well known for arguing that belief in the existence of God (along traditional Judeo-Christian lines) is basic, which for him is to say, does not and should not require "sufficient evidence." Argues Plantinga: there can never be sufficient evidence for any belief, let alone for beliefs as important and consequential as belief in God.*

and all begin with nothing more than someone's conviction—someone's faith—that they can be helped into being by their own free actions.

That is why actions based on faith in God help bring about the kind of God one has faith in. God cannot abandon you of "his" own accord. Only you can abandon God. Why? Because God is nothing without you (cf. 2 Chronicles 15:2 and James 4:8). God has prophets, just as Bible and Qur'an tell us. But prophets are possible because God is the ultimate self-fulfilling prophecy.[73]

BECAUSE GOD is the ultimate self-fulfilling prophecy it matters a great deal what sort of God you believe in. If you avenge proudly, then your God will be vengeful. If you prize mercy, your God will be merciful. If you admire freedom from desire, your God will be free of desire. And all these conditionals operate in reverse: God's presumed character shapes ours, at least in ambition and in what we regard as self-evidently praise-worthy: *imitatio dei.* The God of the Bible is expressed in the actions of those who believe in God as described in the Bible (albeit differently from book to book). The God of the Qur'an is expressed in the actions of those who believe in God as described in the Qur'an. From the perspective of the theology of theopraxy, all versions of God become *factual* to the degree that believers in them make them *ac*tual.

Now, atheists who understand this and follow time-tested secular moral teachings (like the Golden Rule) are well-positioned intellectually. *Their* actions, they can say, are guided by reason and by results. They believe in peace, compassion, prosperity, fairness, and so on, because these ideals have proven themselves essential to the long-run promotion of human life and curtailment of human suffering. No *God,* they declare, is necessary to underwrite such ideals. Indeed, not only is God unnecessary, but faith in God too often stands in the way of realizing them. Moreover, God just *cannot* be the omniscient, omnipotent, and omnibenevolent creator and sustainer of the universe that traditional believers say he is, and at the same time be so patently indifferent to the suffering of innocents, so blithely tolerant of injustice and calamity. More than perplexing morally, the supreme, all-swallowing (and, let us note again, distinctly male) God of Bible and Qur'an is impossible, logically. How could belief in this God *not* issue in misguided behaviors?

---

73 *It was precisely the unfalsifiability of self-fulfilling prophecies that drove philosopher Karl Popper to distraction about the truth-claims of theism, communism, and psycho-analysis, his three favorite targets. But again, and as he conceded: theism is not a science but a meaning-giving, ethics-yielding system of thought and practice. It can only be wrong ethically. Ditto communism and psychoanalysis.*

THE ATHEIST makes a strong point.[74] I shall not go into the standard ripostes from believers, except to note that there are at least a few believers who grasp God's impossibility more profoundly than do most atheists. The difference is: they want this impossibility embraced. They understand that God's absence from vast swaths of life is real, not apparent, but go on to argue that it is precisely God's absence that calls forth the resolve to *make* God actual, to make God present in and through what *we* say and do. God's existence on-high, they accept, is problematic; but it is problematic, they offer, by (God's own) design. It has yearning built into it. God takes the shape of a guest we long to see, who promises to come, but who hardly ever arrives, which makes us long for his or her presence all the more. To love God with all one's might, then, and at the same time to admit God's unreliability—to admit, even, "his" fundamental metaphoricity—is to enter into ceaseless striving to *make* the world the kind of world in which God, as traditionally conceived, could convincingly be said to have arrived triumphant.

This is not so odd a view. We can find traces of it in Bonhoeffer, in Lévinas, in the Lurianic Kabbalah, in Maimonides, and in a much earlier Jewish prophet: With his life ebbing away on the cross, Jesus cried out, "My God, my God, why hast Thou forsaken me?" The sky darkened, and injustice took wing. How can our hearts remain unstirred? But the truth is that Jesus's cry—his utterance *in extremis* of the first lines of Psalm 22— has been the cry of the ages. *Forsaking* is what God of the Bible seems to do best; and that is intolerable. God must be. God must be through us, in us, and as us doing God's will (which is to do good) or God will not *be* at all.[75]

WHEN WE keep a promise, we make something true that was in our hands to make true. There is, in general, a kind of truth that comes from realizing the object of one's faith or one's imagination in one's actions— "realizing" in the sense of "making real," and also in the sense of "suddenly understanding." In the case of theopraxy, it means putting evidence of God into the world for all objectively to see. And what is that evidence? It is goodness itself, which, as it happens, is the very substance of God before one's eyes. This self-fulfilling, truth-*making* process is not a failure

---

74 *Probably no one made it more resoundingly that Robert Ingersoll in the early 20th century.*

75 *"(F)orgive them," Jesus then whispered, "for they know not what they do." (Luke 23:34) I like to think that Luke misreports, that Jesus had looked down and was addressing these words not to God but to the appalled onlookers at his feet.*

to be scientific, but an essential part of living in existential freedom. Scientific proof of the existence of God will never be found as long as the God sought after is imagined to be the almighty, all-knowing Creator who is by definition ineffable. Scientific proof of the existence of God is easy, though, if you imagine God to be he who—or that which—is brought into being with every good deed. One need only look around.

The theology of theopraxy shares with all other religious and secular moral philosophies the insistence that living-in-freedom be done ethically. But with its peculiar warrant for that insistence, it becomes more than a set of arguments for being ethical, and more than an epistemology—a theory of knowing—interested in the kind of truth that promise-keeping and artistic creativity have; which is to say, the kind of truth one might call "religious truth" in the sense of its being "binding" *(ligare)* upon reality and not merely passive with respect to it. It becomes a positive theology in its own right, compressible, if imperfectly, into maxims like "God is the good we do" and "God is in our hands," which try to modify extant understandings of God on the one hand, and make ordinary good-doing holy on the other. "God is the good we do" can be understood as an attempt to bracket every traditional attribute of the Biblical God but his omnibenevolence, understanding our freedom to be a gift from God, yes, but also a gift *to* God, because it is prerequisite to God's very existence. The maxim "God is in our hands," for its part, tries to make God as present as *we* are, and you and me responsible both to and for that fact.

Understand this and theodicy as an enterprise vanishes. Theological hyperbole all but disappears. Reason reigns with intuition rather than over it. We find ourselves with a set of insights—call them beliefs if you will, or simply ideas—with which we can invest traditional religious practices and their underlying theologies with new meaning, and so embrace them—perhaps again, perhaps for the first time—much as they are.

Do we always know what the best thing to do would be? No. But traditional believers are hardly better off. They do not know God's will in every situation either. Nor is there any guarantee that there *is* a single best, or even one satisfactory, course of action. Different people's ideas of the good can compete, and, none being bad alone, crash into each other in practice. Because of this, "theopractitioners" and traditional believers alike must decide at every moment whether to act now or reflect further, whether to think it through themselves or seek advice, whether to act alone or act together. The commitment of both is to doing the best they can. According to the theology of theopraxy, though: as and when we *do* do the good, and even as we genuinely try, God is there, God resplendent, God in full. One need not ask for more.

20 : Miracles

MIRACLES—OR RATHER, proclaiming the reality of miracles—is often the last line of defense for traditional theism. This is because miracles, over and above intellectual arguments, prove that God exists not as an abstraction or long gone creator-designer, but as an all-knowing, all-powerful agent who at critical moments can show himself by dramatic intervention in the course of events.

What sort of event qualifies as a miracle?

For a theist, the event in question must have no natural or logical explanation. The sea must part. The sun must stop in the sky. The lame must walk or the dead rise up. The event must also have distinctly moral consequences, or a lesson to teach, for otherwise black holes, gravity, turtle navigation, and all the other marvels of nature would equally be miracles. This is why miracles—true miracles—happen only at critical moments in the course of human lives and history. It is also why miracles save only the God-favored *(ipso facto)* and why they are summonable only by saints and sons of God.

Deists don't think that any of the miracles reported in the Bible (or since Biblical times) were really miracles. For deists, miracles are either as-yet-unexplained natural phenomena or they are illusions, even fabrications. Miracles might be marvelous, and everything marvelous might be a miracle (as in "the miracle of birth"), but, for deists, such events are simply the evidence of the grandeur of God's initial design and not of the application of God's will against nature as precipitated by human petition or a sudden change of heart by God.[76]

For its part, the theology of theopraxy sides with theists. It admits the phenomenon of miracles. It agrees nonetheless with deists that miracles are either as-yet-unexplained natural events, or they are fabri-

---

76 *Here is a nice description of the deist view of miracles, from a declaration of faith by the Unitarian Universalist minister Forrest Church in October 2002: "First...we believe in miracles. Not in the stopping of the sun. Not in the parting of the Red Sea. But in the miracle of the sun shining upon this earth and the miracle of the oceans teeming with life. The miracle of a newborn child. The miracle of consciousness. The miracle of hope. The miracle of fluttering leaves, felt tears, and open hearts." Fundamentalist and orthodox believers find their miracles in Scripture. Skeptics and materialists discount the very idea of miracles. Unitarian Universalists follow Ralph Waldo Emerson and say "All life is a miracle," from "the blowing clover to the falling rain." (www.allsoulsnyc.org/publications/sermons/fcsermons/one-light-many-windows.html)*

cations. How can our theology have it both ways? Because of the value it assigns to "fabrications." The miraculousness of a miracle lies not in the event's unexpectedness or uncanniness, since coincidence and nature provides these quite frequently. It lies, rather, in the event's conversion from freakishness-in-the-course-of-nature to appositeness-in-the-course-of-human-events by an act, precisely, of moral fabrication. Miracles lie in how uncontrollable events are taken, not how they are *given*. They are extraordinary acts of interpretation—human acts—brilliantly conceived to sweep paralyzing incomprehension into salvific activity.

Consider just a few of the miracles recounted in Exodus—miracles on the basis of which the Hebrews chose Yahweh.

Story: Moses commanded the Red Sea to part so that his people could cross over it on foot. When they were all across, Moses commanded the sea to close up again, drowning the pursuing army of Pharaoh.

Probable scientific truth: The Red Sea happened to be partially dried up when Moses and the Israelites crossed it. It was dry every ten years or so. Moses, as a member of the Egyptian court and a friend to the scribes, could have known about this cycle and timed the exodus accordingly. Or perhaps he was in a position to hear news from travelers. The Egyptian army probably chased after the Israelites, not hours, but weeks or months later, by which time the Red Sea was uncrossable again. Or perhaps it was not the Red Sea at all, but the Reed Sea, the marshy Sea of Reeds, which was crossable on foot, but not by heavy horses and chariots.

Theology of theopraxy: Look what the Israelites took the crossing to *mean*. "We were slaves of Pharaoh in Egypt," cries the Passover Hagaddah, "and the Eternal our God brought us out from there with strong hand and an outstretched arm!" *Now* it's a miracle.

Consider the "miracle" of the ten plagues God visited upon the Egyptians. Each can be given a natural explanation, including the tenth, the saving of the first-born sons of Israelite families while those of the Egyptians died. (If the Israelites kept largely to themselves, certain contagious diseases among the Egyptians would naturally have stopped at their community gates and family doorways). In an act of great political savvy, Moses gave cosmic meaning to each plague. Each was a reason to let his people go. Each was further evidence that the Hebrew God was punishing the Pharaoh for his "stiff-neckedness." Wherein lies the miracle? In the success with which Moses interpreted an unusual series of natural calamities as inherently moral events—as a display of divine power on behalf of an enslaved and suffering people. *This* was the work of God, not the plagues.

For the two generations that the Hebrews wandered in the desert, Moses had many occasions to despair. He despaired not only of his people, but of himself and his presumptuousness at leading them into starvation, homelessness, and a status among tribes barely higher than it was before. Did he wait for bad weather before going up Mount Sinai, just as he waited for the Red Sea to dry? It's possible that Mount Sinai was volcanically active. Did he bring a group of witnesses to a rock-spring that a scout had reported to him (and whom he had told to go back and block up), then remove a stone before them with his staff and make it flow again? How other than by cleverness, and, yes, subterfuge, could Moses give this people hope, establish law and order, and offer feelings of chosenness and high status among nations? How else could he transform these landless, wandering ex-slaves and children of slaves with only old stories to hang onto, into a confident army so that the land that was promised to Abraham could actually be gotten? He had to persuade the Hebrews they had the best God, the God of both deliverance and promise—the first, deliverance (from Egypt and slavery), freely given, but the second, promise, to be fulfilled on condition of observance of his Law.

What a bold idea!

SINCE ABRAHAMIC and Mosaic times many miracles have been reported. They occur throughout the rest of the Bible.[77] Jesus was responsible for many. Of the 10,000 saints in the Roman Catholic register, most were responsible for or witnessed miracles.[78] This is not just a feature of Catholicism. American Protestants today believe that witnessing a miracle is not only possible in the average believer's lifetime, but probable. A survey by the Pew Research Center for the People & the Press shows that the percentage of Americans who "completely agree" that "even today miracles are performed by the power of God" increased 14 points

---

77 *Mohammed, in the Qur'an, never claimed that he could perform miracles. In later legend and Hadis, however, miracle-working was ascribed to him.*

In post-Biblical Judaism, reported miracles are rare and play an ambiguous role, legends of the Baal Shem Tov notwithstanding. Witness this Chasidic story (S. Y. Zevin, 2000): "There was a man whose wife had died leaving him an infant, and he had no money with which to hire a wet-nurse. A miracle was worked for him, and he developed breasts like those of a woman so that he was able to nourish his baby. Hearing this Rabbi Yosef exclaimed: 'How great is this man, that such a miracle should be wrought for him!' Said Rabbi Abayae: 'On the contrary—how blameworthy is this man, that the natural order of creation should be disturbed for him!'"

78 *There have been several hundred canonizations since 1983, which is when Pope John Paul II, in a sweeping review of the process, made responsibility for at least one miracle after their deaths (!) one of the criteria for sainthood.*

between 1987 and 1997, to 61 percent.[79] Are we witnessing an increase in supernatural events? This is hardly likely, even in reaction to the advance of science.

Are we witnessing an increase in the frequency of divine intercession in human lives? It all depends on what one means by "divine intercession." In the view of the theology of theopraxy, the answer might be: yes. Miracles begin in natural, if unusual, events that generate extraordinary feelings of gratitude in us. To the extent that these feelings are used to heal, inspire, and guide us in more moral directions, they are correctly attributed to God. They are "miracles."

---

79 *Mark O'Keefe (1998) p. 1.*

21 : The creed of "deed over creed"

Think not that I have come to abolish the law and the prophets;
I have come...to fulfill them.

—Matthew 5:17

FROM MORMONISM to Christian Science, from Scientology to the Unification Church, from Jehovah's Witnesses to dozens of New Age spiritual practices, America has been the breeding ground of new religions for two centuries and more, and host to as many from other cultures and countries.

This book is not an attempt to found yet another religion. Theopraxy, "the practice of God," is not a religion. It is ordinary good-doing sanctified. Its theology does little more than offer a perspective on religion and ethics based on a unique understanding of who or what God is. This understanding, it is hoped, might allow people troubled by religion's supernatural claims, inconsistency, and frequent intolerance of other religions, to practice the faith familiar to them in a new and more enlightened way, in a more life-reverent, critical, and creative frame of mind. It is based on the notion that as we mature as individuals, and as we evolve as a people, so God grows with us—God the idea, to be sure, but more importantly God as realized in everyday life, in "deeds not creeds." Whenever the project is more goodness, more beauty, more life, and more truth in the world, God's project and ours are the same.

BESIDES, THERE is no safe way to devise a new religion out of whole cloth or by collaging together the parts of many. This can only lead to bestiaries, to cults. Healthy religions grow like trees, reaching up by developing new branches and leaves from the same trunk, reaching down by extending the trunk's root system, searching for nutrition.

In reaching up, a religion finds new air and new light from the science and philosophy of the day; it finds new energy and insight to provide another round of interpretations of the old stories. In reaching down— unafraid, for example, to treat the Bible as history *and* myth—a religion acknowledges the soil it shares with other religions, older and younger, each of which fructifies that soil in a different way.

That is why, as times change, it becomes ever more the duty of every thoughtful religiously-inclined person to seek plausible re-readings of the hallowed texts and rituals of his or her home religion so that new meanings can be seen, so that new morals can be drawn, and so that new and Godly actions can be taken. Fundamentalism in any religion is a mistake in large part because it is a refusal of the essential character of life, which is not stasis or simplicity but burgeoning complexity, growth "upward" in currency *and* "downward" in depth simultaneously.

The theology of theopraxy, of course, has as yet no history to call its own and only one distinctly theological claim: that God is the good we do. It is not a branch of any established religion and so offers no distinctive liturgy, no peculiar rituals on the occasions of birth, confirmation, or coming-of-age, no unique ceremonies for marriage, burial, or mourning. The theology of theopraxy, one might say, is a meta-religion, one that makes goodness-produced the only criterion by which to judge any theology's truth, or religion's or philosophy's value. Its aim is help us to produce God *from inside* whatever creed, philosophy, or "language game" we are born into or choose.[80]

ONE CAN arrive at a similar conclusion from a different direction.

Zoroastrianism is a religious tradition that emerged in Persia nearly 3000 years ago. Today, Zoroastrians number only around 135,000, almost half of them living in Bombay. Its modern tenets are simple. "Zoroastrianism lays stress on...morality. Do justice, fairness, honesty and righteousness. When you are standing, lift up the poor. God has given you wealth in excess, use it to help the downtrodden." Zoroastrians do not proselytize; they do not convert others. "In this time, this is the best policy. We believe you must follow the religion of your birth and seek salvation from your own religion."[81]

This emphasis on good action is not the only thing our theology shares with Zoroastrianism. It also sees the wisdom of the recommendation to "...follow the religion of your birth and seek salvation from your own religion."

---

80 *In this it is similar to the Sea of Faith movement founded by Don Cupitt. See* www.sofn.org.uk.

81 *Firzone Kotwai, a contemporary* dastur, *or high priest, of Zoroastrianism, quoted by Gustav Niebuhr (2000, p. A15). Zoroastrianism was not so liberal or "modern" in the 3rd and 4th century BCE, when it influenced the Judaism of the day, and later Christianity, with such powerful notions as a Last Judgment preceded by a general resurrection, an afterlife in which the wicked would be punished and the good rewarded, the writing of our life-stories in a heavenly Book, and angels that had names and different functions. See Lloyd Geering (2002 p. 28).*

THE THEOLOGY of theopraxy aims to cultivate an attitude toward life and religion, and most especially one's *own* religion, which is based on an understanding of how God is brought into being by *praxis*, by doing: how good-doing, more than good, *is* holy.[82] It respects almost all traditional language about God's Creatorship, God's omniscience, omnipotence, and all-round magnificence, but brackets it as a picture—or perhaps two. One picture, suffused with longing, is that of a good and merciful God at peace in his kingdom; the other is that of the human heart stretching to make a home for itself and for all earth's creatures in a pitiless universe. They refer to the same reality.

One becomes a theopracticing Jew, a theopracticing Christian, a theopracticing Muslim, Zoroastrian, or Mormon. To the outside observer, a theopracticing Jew's ritual behaviors (at weddings, say, or on the Sabbath) or a theopracticing Christian's ritual behavior (at baptisms, say, or on Christmas Eve) would be indistinguishable from his or her more orthodox neighbor's. It is privately that these individuals are different, feeling on the one hand more detached, but on the other more dedicated. Prayerbook language becomes more obviously metaphorical to them, and at the same time more forceful and moving. How so? Because the obligation to discern and *do* God's will is more strongly felt at the outset, just as it ought to be if we are all God "has" because our good actions are all God *is*. This fusion of metaphoricity and literalness yields a rush of understanding of one's utter freedom from God's punishment together with a new-found respect for all the good and holy people who have lived and are now living. *No sooner does one realize that good-doing is radically voluntary than it becomes powerfully obligatory.* A paradox? Not if you've had the feeling. Then you know that there is freedom to be found only *in* doing good and from doing good.

Ideally, other than in extended conversation, one could not tell a "theopracticing" Christian from a traditional Christian of the same level of religious observance, or a theopracticing Jew from a traditional Jew, and so forth, as I have said. All three would preserve, honor, and pro-

---

82 *The conviction that goodness and holiness are of the same "substance" states, perhaps most succinctly, one of the major differences between the theology of theopraxy and those theologies wherein holiness is seen as qualitatively different (and superior) to "mere" goodness, issuing only from God, and at God's discretion. Taken to the limit, the theology of theopraxy sees all good-doing as God and thus sacralizes even "secular goodness," while Bible-based and Qur'an-based theologies sacralize only the supernatural occurrences that inspire or command good-doing. When the holy is held higher than the good, however, many not-good doings, like waging holy war, might be "commanded." In the theology of theopraxy, "holy war" is an oxymoron. Cf. ARGUMENTS 16.*

mote all forms and instances of life on earth as best they could, and do so with courage and creativity. It remains to be seen however, whether the cognitive and emotional layer that the theology of theopraxy adds to traditional belief will yield better behavior in non-ideal circumstances as well as greater happiness in the everyday.

At the very least, theopraxy has this beginning advantage: that God as described by its theology can exist exactly as described without logical contradiction, and without exhausted and ultimately dangerous superlatives.

The same cannot said for the others.

BOOK THREE

Arguments

1 : Prolegomena

OVER THE next twenty-three chapters the theology of theopraxy is presented as a set of arguments (and agreements) with other religious thinkers about problems that lie on the far side of disputes about whether God exists. God exists. The question is how.

Some of these problems are old and thorny, like "the problem of evil." Others are hardly newer, like the perils of zealotry, the proper relation of faith to works, the value of a single human life as compared to the lives of many, the sanctity of non-human life, or the right way to live when the definitions of "neighbor" and "love" are increasingly ambiguous. Yet other problems are quite new, like the ethical dilemmas posed by modern medical, genetic, and reproductive technologies.

There can be no solutions to such problems, I argue, or at least, no solutions coming from religious reflection, without reconceiving what "God" means in such a way that everything good about God is retained, everything impossible about God is eliminated, and yet most if not all traditional religious language about God—and most if not all practices in God's name—can continue to inspire, protect, and make sense of life for millions of people.

This God-reconceiving project is being carried on by others too, as we shall see. The theology of theopraxy hopes only to make a contribution.

2 : Martin Buber and the "image of God"

IN DEGREE if not in kind, several abilities distinguish human beings from other animals. Among them are speech, laughter, cruelty, voluntary fasting, and the practices of art, science, and trade. To this somewhat arbitrary list we can add one more item and it is definitive in kind: an understanding of God.

Where does this understanding come from?

Genesis 1:27 and 9:6 tell us that "God created Man in His own image," a phrase that is as ambiguous as it is lovely. Human beings, it suggests, resemble God. They partake of God's nature and have done so since the outset. The reason we can understand what "God" means, then, is because the capacity to do so is written into our constitution. Our very breath, our spirit, is "his."

One can also assert, equivalently, that "the image of God was made in Man," i.e., in humankind. If you allow "was made in" to mean "evolved in," this rephrasing of Genesis's claim represents a more scientific view.[1] In that same vein, the theology of theopraxy says that God was not present in the Beginning. Certainly, an understanding of God developed not on the first but on the sixth day of Creation, which is to say, over tens if not hundreds of thousands of years of human biological and cultural evolution. Had the image of God not evolved in us (we can now say in hindsight), humans would likely still practice cannibalism, human sacrifice, and slavery, and men would universally still regard women as chattel. If the image of God does not continue to evolve in us (we can say in foresight), and if it does not do so in concert with science and reason, we will

---

1 *That faith is natural to humans, that religious belief and behavior is written into our DNA and/or the social contract, that our brains are pre-wired to understand "God"...are versions of the single proposition behind a slew of recent books from neuroscientists and evolutionary theorists, among them Dean Hamer, Pascal Boyer, Joseph Giovannoli, Andrew Newberg, Eugene D'Aquili, David Sloan Wilson, Matthew Alper, Carol Rausch Albright, Laurence McKinney, John McGraw, and Michael Shermer. Their conclusions are quite compatible with the notion of theopraxy. In religious philosophy, the claim that God is natural goes back to Cicero, through John Calvin's claim that every human is endowed with* sensus divinitatis *(a "sense of divinity") to Alvin Plantinga's assertion that belief in God is "properly basic" (like our belief in up and down) and thus in no need of special defense.*

certainly not achieve peace between nations, nor reach global ecological sustainability, nor reduce the suffering of innocents, nor bring the benefits of education and technology to all. The question is this: how should the "image of God"—our understanding of God—continue to evolve in order to ensure these results? The matter is in our hands, starting with yours and mine.

As the reader well knows, this book argues that the image of God as the universal first Creator must be modified. So must the image of God as Nature, God as Nature-and-More, and God as Process, which are the images of God offered by pantheism, panentheism, and process theology respectively. But you need not agree with me on this score in order to accept, or at least entertain, the argument that follows, which combines the views of the theology of theopraxy with those of the 20th-century religious philosopher Martin Buber.

No mental image of God can arise in a creature that is not aware of itself as a living being—an "I"—making choices whose consequences affect others. This is why God on almost any description of "him" cannot be thought *of* by infants, animals, or plants, and certainly not by stones and the stars. God as a *reality*, not just a potentiality, arises from an *I* doing good (says the theology of theopraxy), which in turn stimulates beneficence in others. What does it mean to say that God arises from "an 'I'" doing *good?* Borrowing a Christian metaphor, it means, among other things, that we are not so much the objects of God's love as the instruments of God's love, the successful exercise of which means preserving, honoring, and promoting all forms and instances of life. It also means what Martin Buber had in mind when he extolled what he called the *I-Thou* relationship.[2]

For Buber, not bare existence but existence-in-*relationship* is the primary reality of human life (and perhaps all life). The compound word *"I-Thou"* describes a particular mode or *kind* of relationship; namely, the kind that exists between two people where at least one of them, calling himself or herself *"I,"* addresses the other in the second person reverentially enough to mean *"Thou"* rather than merely "you" (even though they might say "you"). The understanding is that the other is also an experiencing *"I,"* not merely a thing, or an *"It,"* or a "hey you!" The *I-Thou* relationship is the only relationship between people (or between a person and any sentient being) that is reliably ethical, if for no other reason than that treating others as one would want to be treated oneself, and doing

<hr/>

2 *Martin Buber (1970). See also* ARGUMENTS 19.

so authentically, entails *experiencing* others as one experiences oneself, which is to say, as the center of a world and an end in oneself, as a nexus of sensation and feelings, as a thinker of thoughts and a possessor of interests, aims, rights, and free will...rather than as a means, or object, or instrument of some other person or "system's" will.

The *I-It* relation, by contrast, may or may not be ethical. For in the *I-It* relation, the *-It* half of the pair is addressed with a view to how it can be used to further some *I*'s happiness or its own happiness (yes, one can treat oneself as an *It*). *It*-s always have their uses. *Thou*-s and *I*-s never do.

Moreover, the *I* that forms part of an *I-It* relation is qualitatively different to the *I* that arises from an *I-Thou* relation.[3] As in physics, the nature of the bond modifies the atoms conjoined.

Buber suggests that whenever we enter into an *I-Thou* relation with another person (or sentient creature)[4] we *ipso facto* enter into an *I-Thou* relation with God. Why? Because God is the One *-Thou* behind all specific *-Thou*-s. He is the *-Thou* of *-Thou*-s, as it were, the very cause and source of *-Thou*-ness. Every time a creature is addressed fully as *Thou* by an *I*, a window, as it were, opens onto God, allowing us a glimpse of his reality.[5]

FOR BUBER, God is the *-Thou* of all *-Thou*-s, experienced through but not *as* the person or creature with whom one is in an *I-Thou* relation. God "himself" remains fixed as it were, eternal. In our theology, God is neither centralized nor eternal. For us, God does not exist apart from what men and women do. God comes to life in certain moments, like a flame that lights up here and there, or, multiplied, like the light of campfires on a vast

---

3 *The first is an ego, the second a person. Buber, op. cit., p. 111-12.*

4 *Earlier (EXPLANATIONS, Note 10) I admitted that God might be present in the actions of higher animals, but thought it wiser to restrict myself to making statements about humans. Nevertheless, it should not be necessary to play down animals' mental capacities in order to make ours look God-given. Many animals seem capable of being the -Thou half of an I-Thou relation with us. Buber is comfortable with this. And perhaps some animals are capable of being the I- part of an I-Thou relation too, with humans in the -Thou position. Interesting question: Can animals enter into I-Thou relations with each other? I think, probably not. But really, who knows? There's no profit in saying that God does not even glimmer in chimps or dogs or elephants. Indeed, God might already shine more brightly in the lives of some extra-terrestrial species, a species that would regard humans as "intelligent but rather limited" animals...rather as we regard dolphins.*

5 *For Hegel, writes Robert Williams (1997, p. 365.), "Genuine reciprocity in mutual recognition (which is quite different from the practical tit-for-tat 'I-It' reciprocity characteristic of economic relations)...results in Geist or Spirit." (My emphasis.)*

and twinkling plain: different, each one, but made of the same substance.

Buber's is a powerful and beautiful formulation of a core religious experience, one centered, like ours is, on an ethical and existential approach to life rather than an esthetic or cognitive-scientific one. But the theology of theopraxy wants to add something and take something away too.

If God is to be seen through certain relationships to other people, as Buber suggests, then what it wants to *add* is the requirement that the other person, or really both, be doing good, or be trying to do good, even if ineffectively or on mistaken assumptions. I cannot enter into an *I-Thou* relation with someone who is knowingly destroying life and expect to experience God through them. But I can try to *produce* God by the engagement.[6] To turn someone from evil by addressing the fullness of their being with the fullness of one's own is difficult, of course, not to say hazardous. But it is theopraxy.

What it wants to take away is more metaphysical: the habit of thought, typical of monotheism so far, that demands that goodness have a source elsewhere, in a singular Creator-God burning like the sun rather than here in tiny local fires, and in these only. For Buber, the *I-* glimpses God through the *-Thou*. Our theology sees God as every *I-Thou* relationship (in which there is good) as it passes through both rewarding encounters and vexing ones.[7] And it sees God in other places as well, ignited, as it were, by different materials. If I might explain further:

IMAGINE AN elderly woman, her family far away, who lives alone and is in failing health. It is surely a very good thing to befriend her, to help her with home repairs, shopping, conversation, cooking, medical visits and the like. Now imagine five cases in which neighbors volunteer to do these

---

6 *For more of the notion of "producing" God see* ARGUMENTS *18 through 20. Since the vast majority of animals must be thought of as innocent of the intention to do evil and unable freely to choose good, entering an* I-Thou *relationship with them must be done unilaterally by the human* I-, *without expectation of symmetry. All the purer is the relationship for it, say some, and the closer to God. Not so, say others, since love of another who could but does* not *return the love—or who relates to one in* I-It *mode but could relate in* I-Thou—*is more difficult (and thus praiseworthy) than love given to another who cannot love as much, or as personally, or at all, by their very nature. See also Note 4 above.*

7 *Later, in* ARGUMENTS *19, I will wonder further whether Buber is indirectly instrumentalizing the other (the -Thou), and turning him or her, and even oneself into an* -It, *by suggesting that the* I-Thou *relationships are a means of reaching/seeing/experiencing God. It would seem that either we should enter into* I-Thou *relationships with no such ambition or knowledge, or we must accept that having multiple, coexisting motivations is a part of human nature.*

things, and do them, but for different reasons:

The first person does them to win recognition at Wednesday night church meetings.

The second person does them with a view to receiving God's blessing at some time in the future.

The third person does them for God without expecting reward.

The fourth person does them on call of duty, because of the woman's circumstances, without expecting reward.

The fifth person experiences the unique subjectivity of the woman, shares their own with her, and now cannot *but* be involved in her life—which fact they accept and embrace. Help and companionship are offered more erratically, perhaps, but also more humanly, less "religiously."

Many a religious person would sanction the second and third person. Kant would privilege the fourth, but Buber would deem the fifth closest to God.

How would the theology of theopraxy rank-order these motivations? First, let's take a step back.

I-Thou relationships are good, says traditional religion. One need not go all the way to proclaiming "God is Love" (and only love) in order to see that people cultivating *I-Thou* relationships fulfill God's desire that we love our neighbors as ourselves.

I-Thou relationships are more than good, says Buber. Through the compassionate interaction of two human beings in the fullness of their being, God himself is experienced.

I-Thou relationships are good, says the theology of theopraxy. Indeed, they *are* God if and as they preserve, honor, and promote life. But not only *I-Thou* relationships are God. The person who helps the old woman for *any* of the five reasons given above (and as many others), does the same good if they carry out the same actions (helping, shopping, talking...) with more or less the same grace and tact. They also light the flame that is God. Underlying motivations, in and of themselves, matter not one whit. Or rather, they matter only as they affect the quality of the doing. They are as kindling to the fire.[8]

---

8 *Motivations matter, of course. The question is: matter to what, if not to deeds? On the largely Protestant view, good things done for bad reasons are only apparently good. Indeed, God would rather we did bad things with good intentions than good things with bad intentions. From this it is but a short step to inferring that God cares more about your motivations—for what's "in your heart"—than for actions; i.e., what you actually do. Christians of the Eastern Orthodox Church, by contrast, hold that goodness of motive and deed are equally essential. Rabbinical Judaism leans further to the right: in God's ›*

If ONE *must* judge and rank motivations nonetheless, then here is the right question to ask: Under which of the five (or other) motivations is the *most* good done with the *least* harm in the *long* run for *both* parties and all those affected by their relationship? It might turn out that the most good is done under the most selfish of the five motivations, i.e., improved social standing in some morality-conscious community like a church, or, more selfish yet in our scenario, for consideration in the old woman's will. It might also be the case that the fourth or fifth motivation I list is best. Or yet some other, such as a salary for being a social worker.

At this point Buber and most theologians would object to the "whatever-works" *pragmatism* of the very way I put the question. Pragmatism (they would say) is no gold-standard of morality. Moreover, it begs the question to have some outward assessment of the quantity and quality of the good done by an action either trump or rank-order the *reasons* people typically have for doing that action. Who is to say we shouldn't judge

---

< *eyes good motives are nice, but good deeds are essential. The right feelings and motivations follow from right actions as much as lead to them.*

These are important differences among faiths. Our commentary:

No one applauds hypocrisy. No one applauds people who feel, believe or say one thing, and then do *another or do nothing. The problem with insisting that motivations and behaviors match each other perfectly, however, is that our motivations are notoriously varied and simultaneous without any of them (necessarily) being* bad*. Which one of our several motivations shall we deem* right *enough to eclipse the others? We tend to tell others (or worse, tell ourselves) that we undertook action x for only the* best *or most socially-approved reasons for doing x, this from among the many less noble reasons we actually had for doing x. This too is hypocrisy, as common among politicians as family members, among clerics as atheists. And what do we do with the undeclared motivations? We keep them to ourselves.*

Then too: what if I cannot bring myself to feel like doing what *ought to be done fullheartedly? ("I could* do x, *but I don't really want to. Since doing it halfheartedly would be hypocritical, and hypocrisy is a sin, it's better I don't do x.") Think of the good that remains not done because people judge (or report) themselves insufficiently pure-of-heart to act. Between these things and things not done out of inertia (and what is moral inertia if not multiple motives neutralizing each other, or thought unacceptable to express?), would these goods not constitute around 90% of what most needs doing? As William Miller (2003) asks rhetorically, what do the virtues of, say, courage and civility consist in but overcoming with actual behavior the perfectly natural feelings we have of fear and dislike, which don't go away?*

Complexity abounds. Here is a simple conclusion: While everyone would agree that best of all is authentically wanting to do something good and actually doing it, when it comes to deciding which is the lesser failure—(1) wanting to do something good but not doing it, or (2) doing something good but not wanting to, or doing it hypocritically—subscribers to the theology of theopraxy would choose (2). If "truth to oneself" must confront "truth to goodness," then truth to goodness wins.

motivations and intentions *only*, using actions, if necessary, to retrodict what those motivations were? Perhaps purity-of-heart is the proper object of our attention.[9]

The objection is well taken. The theology of theopraxy can only reply that its central tenet—namely, that God is the good we *do*, and not the good we only dream of, intend, plan, report, feel, or remember—does indeed represent Piercian/Jamesian pragmatism taken to a logical conclusion. God is as God does. Or put in more conciliatory language: God (in us) *is* as God (through us) *does*.[10] Noble intentions, private piety, felt sincerity, inner selflessness, hoped-for rewards, and imagined grandeurs and perfections on behalf of God and/or "his" prophets, matter only to the extent that they have effects on our *doings*. Religious myths and stories have only this purpose: to encourage the doing of good, which is God.[11]

In many places the Bible would seem to concur: "You will know them (true prophets) by their fruits," said Jesus (Matthew 7:19–20, recalling Proverbs 11:30: "The fruit of the righteous is a tree of life"). "Every one who hears these words and *does* them will be like a wise man..." says Jesus a little later (Matthew 7:24, my italics).[12] The Epistle of James fairly crackles with the pragmatism of deed over creed.

OTHER CRITICS would discourage the very study of how different motivations yield (morally) different results—ironically, on pragmatic grounds. The very process of the research, they might say, would compromise the phenomenon it sets out to study. Case in point: *I-Thou* relationships would be ruined—their spell broken—if participants in them

---

9 *Besides, they could say, even if we accept the pragmatism, because people have less control over outcomes, which are external to them, than they have over intentions, which are internal to them, it might well be more pragmatic to focus on intentions and motivations! A good rebuff? Maybe not. It is not at all clear that controlling one's desires and intentions is easier than controlling one's actions, which are that much more closely linked to external outcomes anyway. Again, this is a more Judaic than Protestant view.*

10 *"It is God who is at work in you, enabling you both to will and to work for his good pleasure." Paul in Philippians 2:13*

11 *Cf. Santayana's view, outlined in* REFLECTIONS 6, *and Dewey's in* REFLECTIONS 7.

12 *For all that they urge good-heartedness and sincerity over evil-heartedness and hypocrisy, both the Hebrew Bible and the New Testament are replete with admonitions about the insufficiency of good intentions by themselves. In the New Testament, the Book of James, as I have remarked, is the most insistent on the superiority of "works" (meaning good deeds, not miracles or religious rituals as Paul means by "works"), and even works alone, over faith alone. One wonders whether William James, as a very young man, took note.*

were made aware of their various and possibly less-noble motivations, or allowed themselves to be the subjects—the *"-It-s"*—of some scientific study. Sometimes outcomes should be put out of mind, neither sought for nor awaited, if good outcomes are wanted; just as, sometimes, one must profess baser motives than one has in order to carry out acts of genuine altruism.

Again, proponents of the theology of theopraxy would agree. Back to our case in point: The relational state of *I-Thou* is as fragile as it is precious. And it's no good destroying anything precious until and unless (1) there is something better to take its place, and (2) an easy and voluntary transition between them can be made. In order, then, to realize the benefits of the theology of theopraxy—such as they are—without jeopardizing the good that people are already doing being involved in *I-Thou* relationships, these same people would have to have the mental flexibility to fuse two images into one: an image of all-the-good-now-being-done-anywhere-on-earth-for-any-reason, and an image or "feeling-memory" of *their* experience of *I-Thou*-ness repeated over the face of the globe... these two images fused into one "three-dimensional" image of God, God "holographic," God whole in every part.[13]

We pick up Buber's thought again in ARGUMENTS 19.

---

13 *I John 3:10 puts it most simply (my emphasis):* "(W)hosoever does not do *right is not of God, nor he that does not love his brother."*

3 : Russell and Shaw: no atheists

BERTRAND RUSSELL, famous through most of the 20th century for the eloquence of his atheism, wrote the following in his autobiography:[14]

> *Often I feel that religion, like the sun, has extinguished the stars of less brilliancy but not less beauty, which shine upon us out of the darkness of a godless universe. The splendor of human life, I feel sure, is greater to those who are not dazzled by the divine radiance; and human comradeship seems to grow more intimate and more tender from the sense that we are all exiles on an inhospitable shore.*

Russell's complaint, like that of all atheists, is against an older idea of God: the God that Nietzsche proclaimed dead and that some consider not dead enough yet.

But this does not mean that every (or any) atheist is Godless, or that the universe is Godless if atheists, by their own measure, are right. In the view of the theology of theopraxy, the universe cannot be Godless when it contains a Bertrand Russell. Russell was not one of atheism's best exponents, but one of its best refutations. The truth of this is what the theology of theopraxy tries to show. Russell might have been the world's best-known 20th-century atheist, but his faith in humanity was all but religious. So was his passion to enlighten, to lead, to work for world peace and to diminish suffering until his 97th and final year. And all this from a logician and philosopher who knew everything there was to know about the attractions of an abstract rendering of the cosmos. If Russell, who was a friend and colleague of Alfred North Whitehead (they co-wrote *Principia Mathematica*), had any sympathy for his friend's "process theology," it was because he saw his own every act, too, as part of the God process.

As Russell's contemporary, George Bernard Shaw, put it in 1909: "To me the sole hope for human salvation lies in teaching man to regard himself as an experiment in the realization of God."[15]

---

14 *Bertrand Russell (1967). Actually, Russell called himself an agnostic. It was everyone else who called him an atheist, and hence his fame as such.*

15 *Quoted by Gregg Easterbrook (1999, p. 3). This statement comes from later in Shaw's life, when he had renounced his loud and youthful atheism in favor of a vitalistic mysticism close to Henri Bergson's. "Conceive of the force behind the universe," he said in a speech in 1907, "as a bodiless, impotent force, having no executive power of its own, wanting instruments, something to carry out its will in the world, making all manner of ›*

"An experiment in the realization of God." If we take Shaw at his word, and Russell at his, then in place of theism—belief in a person-like Creator-God—or deism—belief in an original or underlying Intelligence—and in place too of pantheism and panentheism, we have theopraxy: God as the very practice of realizing God. This is the only God we need as well as the only God who has been God all along. And neither Russell nor Shaw were atheists.[16]

‹ experiments, creating reptiles, birds, animals, trying one thing after another, rising higher and higher in the scale of organism, and finally producing man, now and then inspiring that man, putting his will into him, getting him to carry out his purpose." (From "The New Theology"). In EXPLANATIONS 9, I likened God to the force of gravity, or rather, anti-gravity in the sense that the direction in which God urges us is upward. The analogy served to imagine the "force of the good" as weak, persistent, non-centralized, but (breaking the analogy) new, and felt only by humans and perhaps higher animals. Shaw's view is closer to Bergson's, more forceful and cosmic: God is a/the coherent moral-life-force at the very base of all Nature, gathering itself, driving us and all life forms relentlessly forward. Evolution is also God experimenting—and not always successfully—to find the greater good, like a Great Scientist in His Laboratory. In this marriage of teleology to evolution, both Bergson and Shaw as well as Teilhard de Chardin were strongly influenced by Hegel. For a modern expression of this line of thought, see Gordon D. Kaufman (2004).

16 Erik Wielenberg (2005) picks up on Russell's argument, and on Marian Evans' (George Eliot's) too (see ARGUMENTS 19). We can hold to moral values without belief in any religion's God, argues Wielenberg, and so avoid religion's unfortunate consequences. Hope, charity, courage, compassion, and so forth can be "believed in" on purely naturalistic grounds. They are intrinsically good for life. From our point of view, of course, the very presence of these virtues (with or without reference to God) is proof of the existence of God—not specifically of the Biblical God of course, nor of any more modern version of God...except the theology of theopraxy's.

4 : Abraham's obedience

THE TRADITIONAL theist says: there is good in the world because there is God. I think we can equally say: there is God in the world because there is good.

The difference between these views manifests itself in an older theological conundrum: Is honoring your father and mother good because God commands you to "honor thy father and mother"? Or does God command you to honor your father and mother because doing so is good? Is rape bad because God forbids it, or does God forbid rape because it is bad?

If we *know* that certain behaviors are good and others bad, just as God does, then why do we need God to tell us so? Which is to say, if God only underlines or points out what is already written into the code of life, as it were, then God's chiming in is nice, but not necessary. If, on the other hand, behaviors are neither good nor bad *until and unless* God declares them so, then how are we to deal with conflicting reports as to what God deems acceptable? Nowhere in the Bible or Qur'an, for example, is slavery forbidden. On what grounds did we abolish it? Galatians 3:28, which reads "There is neither Jew nor Greek, slave nor free, male nor female, for you are all one in Christ Jesus," was the slimmest of beginnings.[17] It took nineteen hundred years to pay heed to.

ONE CAN put a sharper point on all this. If God says "do x!" and we *know* x is bad, should we do it? Shall we really *put to death* anyone who curses their father or mother, as Exodus 21:17 recommends? Some would doubt whether they heard God aright. Others would subjugate their own judgment and *do* x on the grounds that if God wants it done then, "by God," x is good.

The classic Biblical example of this dilemma, of course, is Abraham's willingness to sacrifice his son Isaac (Genesis 22:3–18). Abraham does *not* kill his son, we read, because "an angel of the Lord" stays his hand at the

---

17 *The Hebrew Bible is fairly accepting of the institution of slavery...except that Exodus is the story of its non-acceptance, that is, of the God-aided escape of a whole people from slavery in Egypt. In the New Testament, most passages about slavery are simply admonishments to slave-holders to treat their slaves well. Indeed, the modern Passover Hagaddah notwithstanding, one could argue that the exodus from Egypt was not from slavery as such, but from harsh treatment. We also need to remember that slave-taking in war was and remains an improvement on genocide. God works in stages.*

very last moment and provides him with a substitute (a ram caught in a thicket). One wonders what to make of all this. Was the angel an interfering angel, disobeying God? Did God change his mind? Was God merely testing Abraham's faith, planning all along to stop the sacrifice just in time? This last is the Bible's own explanation. Abraham had trusted all along that a sacrificial animal would be provided at the right moment—and tells Isaac exactly this on the way (Genesis 22:7-8). He was right.

From the theology of theopraxy's point of view, however, another answer offers itself, and it is closer to the first and second options (i.e., the interfering angel, God changing "his" mind): The voice that stayed Abraham's hand was Abraham's own God-evolving, God-creating, and God-created conscience.[18] God's sparing of Isaac represents a step forward in the moral evolution of humankind and of God. After Abraham, God was merciful because Abraham was merciful. After Abraham, God took pity on actual individuals because Abraham did. Because Abraham took it upon himself to correct an unnecessary and brutal ritual (the sacrifice of first-born sons was not uncommon at the time), God could un-make and re-make religious customs. Henceforth, consecration of the first-born would do (Exodus 13:2).[19] It was after God had become these things that Moses could compose the Ten Commandments on Mount Sinai and at the same time feel them being dictated to him from the heart of mysterious fire.

For subscribers to the theology of theopraxy, reaching a better understanding of what "good" means represents far more than an academic exercise. Understanding what purposes "God" serves when God defers

---

18 *And perhaps the angel that spoke to Abraham after he had saved Isaac—the angel who blessed Abraham and promised to make his descendants "as numerous as the stars of heaven and the sands on the seashore"—was Sarah herself, her cheeks streaked with tears of joy as she welcomed the two home.*

Angels often appear as humans. What are we to make of this? The three who appeared to Abraham in Genesis 18, appeared to him as men, *and they are treated to Abraham's extraordinary hospitality as men (and rather curt ones at that). Only after the three had experienced Abraham's hospitality does one of them predict Sarah's giving birth to Isaac in the near future. We might say: only then did they rise to being messengers of God, for Abraham's goodness to the strangers was theopraxy: God was kindled there. With what love Abraham must have later turned to Sarah, who was still laughing…*

Franz Rosenzweig (1970, p. 15) remarks upon the same passage thus: "Abraham is the religious man par excellence *for he sees God in the human situation." We can go further: Abraham is the religious man* par excellence *because he brings God to life in the human situation.*

19 *Much later, ritual animal sacrifice would come to be eliminated too, just as, in the distant future, the eating of real animal flesh (by humans) will likely disappear completely.*

to the good is more than a search for an adequate defense of faith. It is theopraxy, the very practice of God. Indeed, the chicken-and-egg-like quality of the question "Which comes first, goodness or God?" is the hallmark of all evolutionary processes. If God strengthens as human behavior improves and vice versa, then the squabble between theists and humanists as to whether God or humankind has ultimate authority in defining the good simply reflects the workings of a cycle, first one and then the other pressing (cultural) evolution forward in lifefulness, first one then the other calling itself progressive and the other conservative. The truth is that any (idea of) God that does not reliably produce more good in this world is not a good (idea of) God. In the view of the theology of theopraxy, we may drop the qualifier "idea of:" God must pass our tests of goodness, just as we must pass God's. In the fullness of time the God that fails dies off, just as populations and nations die off who for too long ignore God's call to honor, preserve, and promote all forms and instances of life.

THAT SAID, and at least provisionally believed, we are led to ask: what are our prospects? Speaking as an American, I should like to try to answer.

For centuries we have, at best, promoted *human* flourishing at the expense of any and all other forms of life. At worst we have promoted only our own flourishing as individuals, as communities, and as nations, against all others. The rise of environmentalism in the late 20th century together with the notion of animal rights, the growing recognition of the economic interdependence of nations, the proliferation of intelligence-assistive technologies, and a resurgence of interest in what religion—call it true religion or enlightened religion—can offer, give us reason for hope.

5 : Personification and "the death of God"

IF GOD is simply the good we do, then God as we have been referring to God in this book—which is to say, with all the usual personal pronouns and ascriptions of will and agency—is clearly the-good-we-do metaphorized, *personified*. Why not drop the personification, leaving God a (particular) process or activity only, i.e., *good-doing*? Would this not be more precise, more honest? Is personifying God (or Nature, or fire engines) not for children, a throwback to primitive thought?

Not necessarily. Many modern theologians continue to "resort" to personification knowing full well that God is not a person. And so do we, for three reasons:

The first is so that we can construct useful sentences about the-good-we-do cast as both a source of inspiration and an object of admiration, like a person who calls upon us to *act* and to whom we can feel *responsible*—rather than as an inanimate, non-agentic, a-moral, and alienatingly vast abstraction like God-or-Nature (Spinoza), Absolute Spirit (Hegel), Process (Whitehead), Being (Heidegger), or Invisible Ground of Being (Tillich), which just is, everywhere, implacably, without *particular* instantiation or call.

The second is so that we can critically and yet respectfully carry on the tradition of trying to understand what "God" means by asking "who" God is and what God "wants" using the rich arsenal of poetics, metaphorics, feelings, and facts that apply to human beings in relationship to each other and to other living creatures—which, not coincidentally, is where the bulk of good-doing is played out.

And the third is so that we can find ways to accept and adapt—rather than discard or replace—the practices, rituals, and commitments that constitute long-evolved religions, which, although they preserve old and even wrong understandings of God—and perhaps in part because they do—are beautiful and moving in the way no deistic, humanistic, New Age, or purely civic equivalents can be. Continuity is essential to God's evolution and ours.

FURTHER TO this third reason: When Nietzsche proclaimed God of the Bible "dead" in the modern age, the image he used was not of an old God's graceful death and transfiguration, but rather of deicide: a god/

king/father exposed, deposed, decapitated.[20] Accept this metaphor, however, and you might well accept what typically follows, which is a new and more ambitious God's ascendence to the throne, a God with a man's name or an -ism's, or an -ocracy's...a God all too eager to fill the vacuum left by the disappearance of the old one.[21]

Such fears of succession may well motivate many religion-shy Americans to fill the void with intentionally-diffuse New Age "spiritualities"— quasi-religions based largely on Buddhism as interpreted by once-Christian or once-Jewish writers, and as mixed with mysticism, psychotherapy, Kabbalah, yoga, popular cosmology, nutrition lore, and ecology. The price paid by followers of syncretic New Age spiritualities, however, can be steep. I mean: dependence on a class of gurus and spiritual guides that might be no more admirable than the evangels of the religions they are fleeing from, loss of connection to family members, and a hole in the heart where God was.

No, the core narratives and rituals of old religions cannot be discarded without leaving holes in the heart—Pascal's "God-shaped vacuums"—and they cannot be erased by atheistic regimes without dire social consequences. This Nietzsche knew. Rather, a transformation must take place, one that leaves God's authority intact even as God's image steadily changes from all-knowing, all-powerful, all-good, justice-and-mercy-dealing Creator-God who is separate from his own creation and whose ways and reasons are unfathomable to humankind, to an immanent and contingent God, chosen *by* us to represent and inspire the best we can do, and who depends on us, on *our* individual commitment to caring for all forms of life, for "his" success. Understood deeply enough, I believe, all religious metaphors, allegories, and metaphysical claims point us ultimately in this direction.

It is out of the conviction that the God who is the good we do has been *God* all along—the one and only—that I can say with confidence that God is not dead. It is also why I can continue to capitalize the word "God" in these pages and hold, where appropriate, to the older appellations of "he," "his," and "him."

---

20 *"Whither is God?" he cried. "I will tell you. We have killed him—you and I. All of us are his murderers. What...are these churches now if they are not tombs and sepulchers of God?" (Friedrich Nietzsche, 1974, Section 125). Freud was to enlarge the metaphor of deicide in* Civilization and Its Discontents *and* The Future of an Illusion. *For 20th-century radical theologians like Thomas J. J. Altizer, God-of-the-Bible's death is/was prerequisite to Man's freedom.*

21 *Nietzsche, for his part, thought* science *was the usurper-God, and argued instead for a new spirituality based on acceptance of the body and our natural will to power—a sort of Dionysian humanism.*

6 : Stephen Weinberg's atheism

IN EXPLANATIONS I was critical of cosmologists and physicists who feel qualified to make pronouncements about God by virtue of their advanced scientific understanding of cosmic beginnings.[22] I regretted that many modern theologians (not to mention science journalists) ceded them the special authority to do so.

As a case in point, consider the following passage from an article about the physicist and Nobel Laureate Stephen Weinberg:[23]

> *Dr. Weinberg professes belief in his own kind of conviction, the idea that the scientific effort to uncover a complete theory of the universe is one of the things that can in itself add dignity and meaning to human existence.*
>
> *As for conventional religion, though, his views are uncompromising: it is not only silly but damaging to human civilization. "The whole history of the last thousands of years has been a history of religious persecutions and wars, pogroms, jihads, crusades," he said. "I find it all very regrettable, to say the least."*
>
> *Actually, Dr. Weinberg does occasionally entertain the possibility that there might be a God. While sitting in his study, with its striking view of Lake Austin, he imagined himself in the role of the Biblical Abraham, whose faith God tested by commanding that he sacrifice his own son.*
>
> *"Even if there is a God," Dr. Weinberg said, "how do you know that his moral judgments are the correct ones? Seems to me Abraham should have said, 'God, that's just not right.'"*

Of course, "God, that's just not right" is effectively what Abraham *did* say, as I suggested earlier (ARGUMENTS 4). Like most scientist-philosophers, Weinberg's aims his atheism at notions of the deity that modern theologians have long since transcended, while complaining that theologians (and the like) do not fully appreciate the subtleties and grandeur of modern science.[24]

---

22 *As intelligent human beings reflecting upon the* whole *of life, they are, of course, as qualified as anyone else—and certainly as qualified as I am—to express theological beliefs.*

23 *James Glanz (2000). See also Stephen Weinberg (1999).*

24 *Weinberg's unwillingness to penetrate the surface of religious literature and Biblical hermeneutics is far from rare among scientists and philosophers of science, for whom the Enlightenment story is the true(r) romance. Here, for example, is philosopher-of-science* ›

Weinberg is right about science. Scientists are seekers of truth the way few others are, and this is ever to their credit. Science's pleasures in the classroom, its adventures in the laboratory, its promises in the boardroom, all happen at the boundary of knowledge, and its mathematics makes us feel as though a great code is being cracked. Science holds out the promise of understanding the world completely, and true, it has little need to hypothesize God.

We can go one better on behalf of science, however: I see no reason why science cannot trace, in outline and in principle if not in every detail, how nature goes from physicality to morality, how—on earth at least— nature took a path from processes subatomic and molecular through processes biological to human life, and thence human freedom, ethicality, and God. This would not be explaining God away, as science (up to now) is wont to do; it would be explaining God here. It would be reasoning *toward* God rather than *back* to God, which is the path deists have long taken. Although Hegel showed this "forward" way, and Teilhard de Chardin tried to make it epochal and Christian, the long path of spirit's emergence from dust has yet to be scientifically traced.[25] The evolution of God from *"his"* beginnings in the life of sentient creatures is a story that remains to be told scientifically *and* reverently. This dual attitude is available only in the theology of theopraxy. One certainly cannot get

---

< *Richard H. Schlagel (2002, p. 109) in the middle of three hundred pages of revelling in the inconsistencies of the Bible (as though he had discovered them himself, as though the rabbis were not perfectly aware of them all): "It is unfortunate (except for some beautiful literature and inspirational writing) that the Holy Bible was not called the Wholly Babel, which would have spared us a lot of superstitious nonsense." How scientists love to admit that the Bible is "beautiful and inspiring;" that it has "great stories." Big of them. But sources of beauty and warning and inspiration (not to mention law) as monumental as the Bible are not to be condescended to, even if the science in them is found wanting. No great work of fiction is just fiction, much less the thousand-page poem called the Bible which has been redacted and pored over by hundreds of interpreters for nigh on three thousand years. Recording Middle Eastern history accurately from roughly 5000 BCE to 100 CE is the least of what the Bible does. For better—and yes, often for worse—the Bible has made law, and thus history, from at least 2000 BCE onward. The Bible is a first-rate subject for science, not a second-rate textbook of science.*

25 *Some readers would insist that philosophers like Alfred North Whitehead, Samuel Alexander and Charles Hartshorne have done precisely this. I would argue they have not, since the God they end up with was not, first, the gods of ancient world, then the God of the Bible, the Way of Heaven, and the Tao, then the man-God Jesus, then Spinoza's God-or-Nature, and then...well, that's what we're struggling with now. The evolution of God, understood scientifically, would yield the "clades" of God as they actually unfolded historically. Hegel might have seen into the story at the broadest scale, but he was not a paleo-ontologist.*

to it by holding that physics, pursued far back enough in time to small enough scales and dense enough energy concentrations, will reveal God's face or "plans."[26] There was nothing there, then, and certainly nothing intelligent.

Now, Weinberg also refers to the harms that have been committed in the name of God by organized religion. Many others, of course, have made the same observation, exhibit number one being, perhaps, the thousand-year reign of poverty, illiteracy, war, and disease in Europe called the Dark Ages, which was launched and fueled by the process of Christianization.[27] This was hardly the legacy Jesus had in mind. One might, in defense of the faithful of that time, point to the Fallenness of humans, shrug, and insist we do better. But the problem for conventional faith is bigger than that. From the Flood to the present day, God of the Bible (and Qur'an) would seem to have endorsed if not ordered a great deal of killing and dying, to have presided, seemingly unconcerned, over countless natural disasters and random calamities, and to have induced extremes of fatalism and hubris in response.

This is why solving the so-called "problem of evil"—i.e., answering the question as to why an everywhere-present, all-powerful, all-knowing Creator-God who was also wholly good would permit all the suffering of the innocent, all the outright evil and senseless accident in this world—has for thousands of years remained the strongest single impetus toward atheism on the one hand, and toward reaching a better understanding of God on the other. This is the problem to which we now turn.

---

26 *To his credit, Weinberg does not believe this either. He is no deist. It would, however, describe Stephen Hawking, who wrote this at the end of his best-selling book* A Brief History of Time: *"Even if there is only one possible unified theory, it is just a set of rules and equations. What is it that breathes fire into the equations and makes a universe for them to describe?...(I)f we do discover a complete theory....then we would know the mind of God." By way of antidote, one might read Nobel Prize-winner Robert B. Laughlin's 2005 "emergentist" tract,* A Different Universe: Reinventing Physics from the Bottom Down.

27 *The Muslim conquest of Spain, North Africa, and the Middle East all the way to India over roughly the same time period might not have been prettier in terms of bloodshed, but the Muslim conquerors were, at least, known for their tolerance for the religions and scientific learning of those they conquered.*

7 : The problem of evil

FIRST WE should note that "the problem of evil" is rather poorly named. It ought to be called "the problem of the existence of evil" or better "the problem, for monotheists, of the existence of evil," since unlike the "problem of duckweed" or the "problem of government corruption," solving the problem of evil would not eliminate evil—at least not directly. It would just explain why there is evil at all in a universe completely governed by an all-knowing and entirely good God.

If there were more than one God, then, of course, the problem of evil would not arise. For we could say that some gods bear ill-will toward humans or that there are conflicts among the gods that spill over into human affairs. When no *one* god must account for everything, the existence of evil needs no more explanation than any conflict we see between different essential natures, as between, say, a dog's and a cat's.

If there is *one* God and Creator of the universe, however, one God who is infinitely powerful, all-knowing, completely good, and self-consistent, then we have a *logical* problem with the existence of evil. For if God's control is total, if God's wisdom is complete, and God's goodness is constant and unassailable, then why would—or rather, how *could*—God cause (or allow) children to be raped, airplanes of vacationers to explode in mid-air, volcanoes to smother cities, terrorists to believe they will go to heaven, executives to run off with pension funds, etc., etc., not to mention innumerable famines and genocides?

This is "the problem of evil."

Among traditional (mono)theists, several explanations—several "solutions"—to the problem of evil have been offered. These solutions can be summarized and grouped into three types. Each attempts to preserve God's absolute creatorship, goodness, power, knowledge, and wisdom. Why? Because explanations that do *not* keep all of God's traditional attributes intact are not considered explanations of—are not considered "solutions to"—the problem of evil at all. Here are the three:[28]

1 **Totality Explanations.** We (humans) cannot and will not ever understand God's plan or methods. Thus, what may *seem* to us like evil really

---

28 *This tripartite division is certainly not the only way to parse the problem of evil. For a detailed overview of recent thinking about the problem of evil by logicians and philosophers, see Michael Tooley (2004). What follows is a far rougher treatment.*

is not, in the larger picture. Perhaps God is saving us from worse evil yet. Perhaps he is teaching us a lesson we need to learn. Or maybe God is testing our faith (to see whom he will reward). In all these cases it is *human* understanding of love, justice, and goodness that falls short. Ditto our understanding of the nature of God and our interpretation of events. Blind to the Big Picture, ignorant of God's plans and methods, we cannot judge. The world he made is good. Indeed, it is the best it can be and still be a world governed by laws.[29] God's ways are surpassingly wise because he is good and considers *all* eventualities.

2 **Freedom Explanations.** God, who has absolute freedom, created human beings in his image, which is to say, as having freedom also. This freedom includes the freedom to do harm unintentionally or intentionally, which is to say, innocently or culpably. (Some argue only the latter is evil.) Either way, say Freedom Explanations, because God is wholly good and humans might or might not be, the fact that evil exists proves that God values our freedom more than any of his other gifts to humanity—in fact, more than he values our goodness. God prefers us to *choose* to do good rather than do good (or do anything) automatically, robotically, unable to conceive of doing anything else. So evil is simply a nasty side-effect of freedom, which we would be wrong to give up on that account.

3 **Finite Knowledge Explanations.** These solutions to the problem of evil combine elements of the first two. But they focus on another limitation that humans have and God does not have, namely, limitations in ordinary, factual, this-worldly knowledge. Thus: whereas God has complete knowledge of (not to mention power over) the world in every detail, we do not. The future remains opaque to us, as does history in detail, and as do the myriad facts about the world that surrounds us now. Under these circumstances, the best we can do with the best of intentions is not likely to be good enough to ensure that the right things happen. There will be mistakes. There will be unforeseen outcomes, accidents, coincidences, and so forth. Nor can we control the consequences of decisions we have already made, forcing unfolding events toward the good we wanted to see and had aimed for. To be good, and always and only good, *requires* perfect knowledge of con-

---

29 *If the world were not "governed by law," it would be without regularity or system, and neither we nor any animal could learn about or adapt to it. In essence, this is the answer to Job given by God.*

ditions initially and/or perfect control over events thereafter, as well as perfect education as to the nature of the good. Since God did not endow us with any of this knowledge (this he kept to himself), nor, apparently, with the ability to acquire it all, the whole panoply of harms and evils caused by ignorance, error, or stupidity remains possible, even likely.[30]

THE ABOVE three paragraphs represent a *very* brief treatment of how mainstream theologians in the Judeo-Christian tradition have tried to explain the existence of evil without taking anything away from (their picture of) God.[31] The question is: do any of these explanations succeed? The answer, I think, is no. Because although each type of explanation offers some comfort, each takes something away from God as traditional believers suppose God to be.

For example, Totality Explanations (which say we cannot know God's plans or ways) diminish the "omni" component of God's supposed omnibenevolence. For they admit that God, albeit for the best of reasons, does not have good-will toward *all* people and *all* creatures *all* the time. He has ill-will toward sinners, for example, at least for a while, until they

---

30 *To go on with this third answer: our freedom can be seen not as a gift that God gave us out of the goodness of "his" heart, but a gift God had to give us as a consequence of the limitations God also imposed on our knowledge and power. The reason we have the freedom to choose is because the process of imagining options, choosing among them, acting upon our choice, and assessing the outcomes—in short, the process of guessing, choosing, and learning from experience—is the only way to go forward rationally when knowledge and/or power are limited. A creature that knew everything from the start and/or that was able to control everything to suit its desire would have to decide nothing except what to desire in the first place. Once it had decided to want the good (and it would know infallibly what good was), no further choices would have to be made, and no further freedom would be needed. It follows that God, as traditionally conceived, does not have to be free. Only we do. For an expansion of this argument, see T. J. Mawson (2005, pp. 55–69) and a riposte from Wes Morriston (2005).*

31 *I omit Gnosticism, Manichaeism, and other mystical traditions that posit the existence of a "dark force" or evil god equal in power to Yahweh. My remarks assume genuine monotheism. For a more extensive treatment of (the problem of) the problem of evil, see J. L. Mackie, (1990) and Susan Neiman (2002).*

32 *It doesn't help to argue that God has good will toward those whom he punishes, like the "tough love" strict fathers rain down upon wayward children. For one, no father would kill his child, which God (as traditionally conceived) does or allows with regularity. For another, no punished child can be blamed for imagining his or her father genuinely angry, and genuinely if temporarily wishing harm upon them, which belief is probably better for the mental health of the child than the alternative. Consider: is pain caused by someone* ⟩

repent and/or repair what they have done.[32] Nor does God seem to mind the slaughter of millions of animals every day so that we can have lunch. God's being "all good, all the time," we realize, actually only guarantees that God is interested in some *greater* good, one we can't necessarily see, and for which some people and creatures just have to suffer.[33]

Totality Explanations also undermine rational faith in God's omnipotence, for they say that God is incapable of so arranging laws and/or events that no one has to suffer for the sake of the long term or for the sake of others. It says that even God cannot make an omelet without breaking some eggs (to borrow Lenin's phrase). God becomes the Supreme Utilitarian, arranging the most good for the most people that he can, i.e., according to his plan and within the laws that he Himself cannot or will not change (or reveal to us).[34]

Totality Explanations have one more undesirable result for theists. To admit that our comprehension of God is limited in a permanent way, indeed in principle, is to admit that we might not know much about God at all. This in turn opens the possibility that God might not be wholly good. Perhaps God *likes* a little sin, discord, and mayhem to "spice up his life"... in which case we have to wonder: just how much is "a little" to

---

< *who hates you (hopefully temporarily) not preferable to pain caused by someone who, as they punish you, assures you they love you without cease, that they're "doing it for your sake"? You might reply "Well, no. My dentist causes me pain and loves me (in a way)." But unlike a good dentist, God of the Bible rarely explains himself to sufferers; and, as though to add insult to injury, He has a way of rewarding (or allowing reward to accrue to) people who are clearly sinners. Traditional believers find they must take refuge in what they would dearly like to explicate, which is God's inexplicability. No wonder the doctrine of heaven and hell—compensatory reward and punishment after death—puts itself forward.*

33 *"Have to suffer," of course, implies an unwillingness to suffer, which raises the possibility that if one is always willing to suffer—so great and so constant is one's faith in the wisdom of God's plan—then one's suffering, now voluntary, transforms itself into profoundly meaningful self-sacrifice. Alas, even if one found this response healthy and life-affirming (which I personally do not), it does not cover the bulk of suffering in this world, which is the suffering of innocents who are not so devout (not to mention the suffering of billions of animals who, after leading miserable lives, daily become our food, who did not volunteer to do so, and who are incapable, anyway, of the requisite faith). Or shall we say that not believing in God's Plan and sacrificing oneself to it unquestioningly is crime enough to be the legitimate target of God's punishment? There are many religious fundamentalists who would say "Yes, this is so. If you suffer, if you die, it is God's (good) idea that you do." Atheists are quick to point out the fatalism and circularity of the whole argument.*

34 *Of course, if God cannot change the law then God is once again not omnipotent, and if God will not, in the cause of alleviating suffering, God is not omni-benevolent.*

God? To us it often seems like a lot. The point is that incomprehension of God, once accepted as inevitable, opens the door to the acceptance of everything that happens—from genocides to children dying of cancer to your beloved dog being run over—as part of God's plan, as well as acceptance of the possibility that God might endorse evil.[35] Indeed, God might have attributes of which theologians have yet to dream.

FREEDOM EXPLANATIONS raise different sorts of problems.

Let us agree from the outset: freedom is wonderful, even essential to human life. Let us also agree that we cannot be *totally* free, free to walk though walls for example, to change the past, or to converse with the dead. But it does not follow from this that being free—even being *very* free—requires us to be free to do serious wrong or harm.

What do I mean? Freedom entails the ability to make choices. A traditional believer can imagine that God sets those choices before us and hopes that we will choose well. Now think of a banquet buffet, with, say, fifty dishes to choose from. Is it necessary that some dishes—say four of them—be poisonous? Surely not. Let us take the four poisonous ones off the table. All forty-six of the remaining dishes could be good, all could

---

35 *There is a tradition, rooted in Judaism, of understanding God and humankind to be in partnership, working together—not alone—to repair or perfect the world* (tikkun olam). *In this tradition, God needs us as much as we need him. This is why God enters into covenants—contracts—with people at all. We are not God's slaves or puppets. The implied limitation of God's power in this scheme cannot be overlooked, however, which is why the "partnership hypothesis," though admirably pragmatic, cannot be thought to solve the problem of evil for Judaism or for theism generally. Saying that God in his infinite wisdom chose to work this way (i.e., to limit his power) amounts to a dodge, not a doctrine. (Can God take full power back at any time? If so, then God never gave up his power.) And it does not undo this concession: if God needs us to do his work—indeed if God needs anything—then God is neither omnipotent nor perfect in himself.*

Besides, let us look at the partnership from a purely human point of view. Would you voluntarily enter into a partnership with a person whose modus operandi *included unilaterally killing off members of your family and other innocents in order to get his way, and then saying (if he bothers to say anything at all) "trust me"? This would be a partnership with the Godfather, not God the Father, and certainly not God the Holy Spirit. Says our theology: if God is good, only and entirely, and doing good is up to us, only and entirely, it follows that God's very existence is up to us.*

36 *Leibniz famously solved this particular problem in theodicy by having God in*capable *of doing anything* logically *impossible, like make something at the same time be wholly black* and *wholly white or having 1 plus 1 be equal to 3. The laws of logic are in a sense above God, conditioning of Him. It is simply not possible to have a world without conflict, to have races without winners and losers. It follows that the world we live in is the best logically possible one.*

be healthy, tasty, good-looking, and so still allow a great deal of room for choice and preference on the part of the guests. If God had arranged the world so that all available options were pretty-good actions, would we not have been free enough?

The point is, if he could not so arrange the world, then he is not omnipotent.[36] And if he has not and will not, then he is not omni-benevolent.

Then too, if we are free to choose evil, then surely so is God (on the traditional view of God). If God cannot choose evil—what with being all-good—is "he" less free than we are?[37] It would seem so, on purely logical grounds. It would seem that in order to make sense of God's total goodness, freedom ought to be available fully only among good alternatives, for God as well as for us.[38]

---

37 *Jean Paul Sartre said that either God (as traditionally conceived) is free, or we are. Some have argued that God's "inability" to do evil may indicate nothing more than his utterly consistent choosing not to. Yet others propose that God may have deliberately limited his powers for our sake. In Christianity, the doctrine of kenosis describes God as having reduced himself to living in the world as Jesus out of compassion for humanity. In medieval Judaism one has the Kabbalistic doctrine of tzimtzum (see* REFLECTIONS 18): *God is imagined to have withdrawn himself from Creation, to have limited his powers soon after the first moment so as to leave room for human actions, for chance, and for material reality itself...this out of the desire to have something other than himself to love. Had God not done so, the universe to this day would be nothing but pure light—God's holy light, filling everything, immaterial, without real extension or duration—and neither sun nor moon nor any living creature would exist.*

Some might see the similarity between this doctrine and the cosmogonist Alan Guth's hypothesis of cosmic inflation. Here, however, we could entertain ourselves by speculating whether God as described by the Kabbalah might not also have voluntarily reduced himself to being the God proposed by the theology of theopraxy, i.e., simply the good we do. Has "he" not the power to do so?

38 *There is one more objection to traditional theodicy, credited to John Hick. Why did God choose freedom to be the supreme value for humans? Did God have to? If so, then God is not free, and this non-freedom has nothing to do with logical possibility, as Leibniz argues (cf. note 36). Surely God could have chosen any feature of life, any virtue, to be the most valuable one—language, dexterity, happiness, strength, fructitude—one that would not logically entail evil and might well require giving up quite a lot of freedom...and we would have agreed, indeed "concluded" with all sorts of emotion, that this was God's supreme gift to humanity.*

39 *There is a minority opinion among liberal theologians that God does not know the future. Possibilities exist for God as well as for us. God takes risks. God does not know what we are going to do; God does not know what "he" is going to do either, because it depends how things develop and, at least a bit, on our cooperation. These concessions go a long way toward neutralizing the problem of evil, of course, but they do not solve the problem of* >

FINITE KNOWLEDGE Explanations also fall short of defending traditional monotheism.

For one, they do not make evil a necessary feature of the world, just a probable one. Sooner or later, they say, human stupidity if nothing else will cause something bad to happen. Very well. But if we are unable to do the good reliably because of our perceptual-cognitive limitations, and if God wanted it that way, the question arises: Why doesn't God step in to save us from ourselves and from natural disasters?

Here's an analogy. Believing in the benefits of freedom, imagine that you want to offer your two-year-old nephew, soon to visit, maximum run of your house. You would probably remove all protruding sharp objects, fragile valuables, and poisons. You could not and would not remove all possible dangers. He could still fall down the stairs, run out into the street, or drown in the pond. Because such dangers are not eliminable, then, you would stay in attendance, hovering close enough by to swoop in and prevent calamity. On the Finite Knowledge view, God does not seem to want to offer us the same protection. He lets us hurt ourselves in the most irreversible ways. As fathers go, he seems about as caring of his brood as a fish.[39]

THE PROBLEM of evil has been a significant intellectual challenge for theists for more than three thousand years, and only slightly less a problem for deists, who must agree that the world is the way it is by divine design. It puts into words the average believer's nagging doubts; it represents the skeptic's best shot in his or her argument against faith in a Biblical God. Philosopher Susan Neiman (2002) argues that solving the problem of evil has been the consistent if unstated theme of *secular* moral philosophy since the seventeenth century, and she is probably right.

From strongly traditional believers, however, the response has been different: not rationality or argument, but comfort taken in one, two, or all three of the above explanations, together with renewed faith in God— faith beyond the sort that says "ignorance is our lot, so *trust*," which one might call rational faith, to faith that says "believe in God against all contrary evidence, logic, and argument," which can only be called irrational or blind faith.

‹ evil because no solution *would compromise any of the classical attributes of God, which "the open view of God" does, to wit "his" omnipotence, omniscience, omnipresence, or omnibenevolence; as well as, possibly, "his" eternity or creatorship. See Clark Pinnock (1994), John Sanders (1998), or Gregory Boyd (2000) and a critical reaction to the idea in Bruce Ware (2001). In Judaism, the idea that God genuinely needs humankind to fulfill his purposes is not that unusual or heretical. See for example Abraham Joshua Heschel (1997).*

The theology of theopraxy cannot solve the problem of evil in the terms set up by theism. No rational philosophy or religion can. Something about what most people mean by "God" has to give.

8 : The problem of good

Unlike other forms of theism, the theology of theopraxy proffers that God has only one of the attributes traditionally ascribed to God, namely, perfect goodness. In the theology of theopraxy, what is *not-good* is simply *not God*, no matter how entertaining or useful or real it might be. Crimes and cruelties, therefore, are never justified by the larger achievements in which they might eventuate, much less the esthetic qualities they might exhibit.[40]

The existence of evil is not a problem that the theology of theopraxy *has* to explain because it does not posit a God who knows all or who can do all in the first place. God, it argues, cannot break the laws of nature in order to divert certain trains of events from causing harm. Nor did God design or create the world as we find it, which is a world where rigidity, chaos, indifference, misinformation, mediocrity, and selfishness are common. In a world like ours, the miracle (if one wants miracles) *is that there is good at all.* Put another way: *God* is the miracle.

The problem for atheists, it follows, is not the problem of evil, which provides ready ammunition for an attack on traditional theism. The problem for atheists, rather, is *"the problem of good."* For if there is no God in any sense, including the theology of theopraxy's, then whose image or what thought-patterns inspired Moses, Solomon, Isaiah, Jesus, Francis of Assisi, Ghandi, Schweitzer, Wallenberg, and Mother Theresa,

---

40 *Crimes and cruelties are by definition impositions on unwilling others, and so cannot be justified. Pain and suffering, however, can sometimes be justified. Two examples: when lesser pain* must *be endured in order to prevent greater pain (think of dragging a child to the dentist), and when those who will feel the pain agree voluntarily, beforehand, to risk pain or to sacrifice themselves for the sake of the larger good envisaged, a good that they also voluntarily agree is larger, and good enough. Put another way: the end never justifies the means unless those to be used as a means agree that the end is worthwhile, and also to being a means for achieving it.*

Are these exceptions exploitable? Alas, yes. With regard to the first, one can falsely attest that a worse pain is inevitable unless the subject undergoes the presently proposed one. Religious fundamentalists turn the second to their advantage by advocating that everyone volunteer for everything that might happen to them, on the grounds that, since whatever happens to them is the will of God (and thus for the best), one should "beat God to it" as it were, and will *whatever appears inevitable. Of course, this makes a mockery of God's gifts to us of* intellect, *which would include the right to question seeming inevitability, and of* freedom, *which would include the right to refuse, without penalty, to volunteer for suffering.*

to name a famous few, to do what they did? Set these heroes aside: how does everyday kindness, decency, and honesty arise? Whence supererogatory—"above-and-beyond-the-call"—acts of philanthropy, altruism, and love? Whence honor in business and even war? These are not minor achievements, and situation-by-situation, calculated-from-scratch self-interest does not explain them completely. The question is: how could a world without God—i.e., without (according to the theology of theopraxy) goodness exemplified and embodied all around in small and large ways—bring about any of these things? This is "the problem of good."[41]

While it might or might not be a problem for atheists (we will look at their reply in a moment), the existence of goodness in a bad or indifferent world is not a problem for our theology. Or rather, it poses none of the *logical* dilemmas that the problem of evil does for theism. This is because the theology of theopraxy does not posit a single locus of dominion over all good or evil: God is present where good is being done and absent where good is not being done: God is good-being-done. Some long-lasting *idea* of God might be what carries some of us from one good deed to another, but only *in* the deed and *as* the deed does God literally come to life. God's job, as it were, is to redeem the world through us, and ours to redeem the world through "him," properly conceived.

If, then, there is no logical problem for us in the fact that there is goodness in the world, a mystery remains nonetheless. When God's power is our power and "his" wisdom is our wisdom, when God "sees with our eyes and hears with our ears" as Confucianism too pictures it (cf. DECLARATIONS 9), then the problem of good is better called the mystery or wonder of good. For truly, the radiance of the slightest genuine kindness is equal to the light of the stars. And it is harder to explain.

"STOP, STOP," cries the atheist. "Why do you speak of 'wonder' and 'mystery'? There is no *wonder* in the existence of good; nor is there anything remotely divine or mysterious in any part of the process. 'Good' is merely what we call those behaviors, rules, and tools that have proven beneficial to the ongoing life of human beings, starting with ourselves and *our* people, but becoming more inclusive as we do better in our own, longer-term, best interests."

---

41 *John Horgan (2002) poses the problem of good nicely: "This is by far the greatest gift that mystical experiences can bestow on us: to see—really see—all that is right with the world. Just as believers in a beneficent deity should be haunted by the problem of natural evil, so gnostics, atheists, pessimists, and nihilists should be haunted by the problem of friendship, love, beauty, truth, humor, compassion, fun. Never forget the problem of fun."*

And the atheist might go on: "Your theology should be content with *natural* explanations for morality, along the lines offered by sociobiology and evolutionary psychology.[42] To wit: goodness, morality, ethics, law, religion itself...are instantiated in behaviors that are useful for the proliferation of the human species, that survive the selection process, that increase progeny who will repeat these useful—i.e., 'good'—behaviors.[43] There's no wonder or mystery here. Does the theology of theopraxy itself not say God evolves?"

These are strong challenges. Here is our reply.

Our atheist is not wrong, just one-eyed. One can explain a thunderstorm in Texas as what happens when warm humid air from the Gulf of Mexico flows over a body of dry cold air coming from the north and condensed water droplets by the trillion fall to earth. There's nothing wrong with this description, ethically or scientifically. But it does not explain or begin to describe the experience of running through a summer storm with thunder all around and water seeping into your socks with every splashy step. Likewise, understanding the chemical composition of foodstuffs and their transformation by heat can help us be better cooks, as would knowing the history of world cuisines. But those same facts have another face when they become the taste of a sauce taken off a hot spoon. And it is actually this "face"—the experience—that is the culmination of the art of cooking.

Similarly, we can accept that our moral intuitions emerged from biological evolution and from tens if not hundreds of millennia of living together as human beings. Understanding the process will be rewarding. But evolutionary explanations of goodness yield facts that have the same two-sided character as the facts that describe weather and cooking: one side that is all "fitness indicators," "genetic predispositions," "kin selection," "social utility," and so forth, and another side which is how goodness *actually feels to someone who is doing it or witnessing it.* One gets this side from good novels and movies, and one gets it from living life oneself.

Such dual explanations are not the same as duelling explanations. Dual explanations support each other. Duelling ones do not. Evolutionary explanations of the roots of ethical behavior might well, if they are good in the scientific sense, help us do good in the moral sense.[44] But when

---

42 *For overviews, see Robert Wright (1995), Matt Ridley (1998), or Frans de Waal (1996).*

43 *See David Sloan Wilson (2002), Pascal Boyer (2002), and Loyal D. Rue (2005).*

44 *Steven Pinker (2002) makes this point, as do all who argue that finding evolutionary logical reasons for contemporary practices does not* ipso facto *condone them. In fact, by and large, they do the opposite. Going* counter *to our natural impulses is most often the moral* ›

naturalistic explanations come around to illuminate and enhance the experience of seeing, deciding, and enacting what is good, they have a much better chance. The experiential side of the coin is the side that counts as much; it's the side that people recognize and the one that educates.[45]

One has to realize, in sum, that *evolution-in-process* feels like *life as lived.* One has to realize that when the phone rings we are all suddenly existentialists, cast into a world we didn't make and as spontaneous as cats.

EVOLUTIONARY, BIOLOGICAL, and even humanistic explanations of "where morality comes from" challenge traditional belief in God. But they support the theology of theopraxy's entirely. When God is a production of human experience as real as color, music, or democracy and "closer than the vein in your neck,"[46] God's mystery and wonder do not depend on revelation in the Biblical sense: no voices from thin air, no angelic light, no ladders into the clouds are required. It is simply the wonder of being touched by ethical action firsthand, up close. Here is a child offering her blood for transfusion into her sick brother; here is a man risking his life to lead a dog off a busy road; there is a woman anonymously channelling her wealth to charity; there is a man steadily forbearing insults to himself and offering goodwill in return. On such occasions a familiar amalgam of emotions is elicited: awe, gratitude, joy, hope, pride in being

---

‹ direction. *There are, after all, evolutionarily "good" reasons why women have inferior social status to men (I shall not go into them here), just as there are evolutionarily "good" reasons why stepfathers are more likely to harm their stepchildren than fathers are their own children. There are reasons to take revenge that make perfect sociobiological sense. Etc. Being civilized, however, means not perpetuating these behaviors. Understanding the evolutionary origins and uses of these behaviors helps in not perpetuating them because it helps us devise practices and laws that avoid the circumstances that trigger them and/or that offer more tempting and less harmful alternatives: soccer, not war.*

45 *A great deal of science goes the other way, of course: starting in phenomenology—which means starting with extreme sensitivity to the structure, texture, and content of actual experience, probably one's own—and only then moving to generalizations and quantifications. It takes a phenomenologist* extraordinaire *to compare, in all seriousness, the experience of a person in an closed, upward-accelerating elevator to the experience of a person in a gravitational field, as Einstein did for his Theory of General Relativity (calling it the Principle of Equivalence). The physics laboratory is a virtual haven for phenomenologists. Would that there were an equivalent for moralists.*

46 *The phrase is Qur'anic (Sura 50:16). If traditional, Bible-based theism would let go of its objective, prior, 'out there' existence-claims on behalf of God in favor of phenomenological, existential, produced-by-life claims for the existence of God, it too would be unfazed by evolutionary and humanistic explanations.*

human. Just as the experience of being scalded is not nullified by knowing that it is "just" billions of fast-moving water molecules battering the nerve endings under our skin, so the wonder of goodness is not at all undone, and is perhaps intensified, by the knowledge that it emerged from billions of years of selfish, witless, life on earth becoming conscious—the light of stars becoming light of another sort. Think this, and the mystery and wonder of God can come from something as simple as the pleasure of realizing that one is alive, free, without pain, and at the same time of benefit to others who deserve the same experience.

And who deserves that experience? Every baby born.

THE TRUTH is that some measure of goodness is all around. Every iota of tact, every laugh among friends, every moment of patience and offering of help, is an instance of God. Every obedience to law, every washing of hands, feeding a pet, or letting someone sleep is God at work. This is what it means to know that God is immanent *and* in our hands. That we can walk peaceably and work respectfully among other people, that we tolerate their foibles and can expect the same from them, are miracles that do not appear miraculous because they are "normal." And they are normal because they are built upon millennia of learning and transmission of the Word of God (or Way of Heaven), which itself evolves over time. We need only contemplate with the existentialists our ever-present freedom to do almost *anything*—including lie, murder, steal, dishonor, and abandon—to see that good-doing is always up to us, that it is always a choice, and a choice of which we can later be proud even if we were not fully aware at the time that we were choosing.

Recall the hells-on-earth that dot human history. Bring to mind the ones that exist right now somewhere on the planet. Now look out of your window. Every bird not shot, every walker not carrying a gun, every car waiting patiently for a traffic light to change, every repairman writing up a job fairly, every person dying in a fresh hospital bed rather than on a battlefield or in a gutter, every street that is swept, every bush that is trimmed, every toddler studying a worm... is God evidenced and instanced.

Look upon these things and be glad. Rejoice at peace and decency. See that for the most part your "cup runneth over," and more: that by your actions *you* are one reason for that cup "running over" for others. Call it the wonder of doing. "The wonder of doing," Abraham Joshua Heschel thought, "is no less amazing than the marvel of being....and (it) may prompt us to discover 'the divinity of deeds.' (I)n doing sacred deeds we may begin to realize that there is more in our doing than ourselves, that in our doing there is something—nay, someone—divine. (It is) 'through the ecstasy of deeds' that we learn 'to be certain of the hereness of God.'"[47]

---

[47] *Maurice Friedman (1987, p. 265, 266.).*

9 : Evil from human nature

To traditional believers we have said: the problem of evil cannot be solved by applying ever stronger, ever blinder faith.[48] To atheists we have said: explain the "problem of good" if you can, not in remote and naturalistic terms only, like "kin selection" or "inclusive fitness," but in experiential and existential terms.

The theology of theopraxy, we have also said, does not need to solve the problem of evil because it does not believe in an all-powerful, all-knowing Creator-God in the first place, and it goes on to throw some light on the atheists' "problem of good." Nonetheless, can our theology offer something useful about the *practical* problem of evil, that is, about the presence of evil in everyday life?

On the definition of good offered in EXPLANATIONS 6, the theology of theopraxy sees evil—good's opposite—as the free and conscious doing of harm, where "harm(ful)" is what we call whatever action destroys, dishonors, or diminishes any form or instance of life whose thriving does not depend on harming equal or higher forms or instances of life.[49]

Extending this we can say: particular forms and instances of life that want *more* life for all forms and instances of life (with the proviso above) are apt to do right and good, while particular forms and instances of life that want *less* life for all forms and instances of life, or more life only for themselves or *their* form of life, are apt to do wrong or evil. What is *not* alive, however, or does not want (desire) anything, might be good or bad for life—we can decide which—but it cannot do (or be) evil.[50] The nearby supernova that someday will scatter our solar system through

---

48 *This is not to dismiss the extremely sophisticated efforts of theologians like Alvin Plantinga to rescue faith from skepticism by positing religious faith as* not in need of defense *on the grounds that it is no worse than, and probably better than, several other foundational, axiomatic beliefs—like the belief in reality, logic, or our own existence.*

49 *Cf.* EXPLANATIONS 6, and Footnote 26 there.

50 Not wanting *anything—expunging desire—is the larger part of the Buddhist solution to morality with the understanding, rarely stated, that the cessation of wanting is not to be caused by the surfeit of having. (Plato cut off this possibility by claiming that the desire for material goods and for power are intrinsically limitless, and ultimately destructive.) Like the older Hindu principle of* ahimsa, *the idea is this: that not-desiring leads us away from taking anything from anyone else using force. Acceptable, only, is receiving what others freely offer.*

infinite space like so much dust, will be bad—very bad—for life on earth. But it will not be evil.[51]

Is evil an entity or force? St. Augustine, Maimonides, Aquinas, and most liberal theologians since have disavowed the idea that evil is a "positive" force or entity usefully personified as Satan or the Prince of Darkness. Rather, evil is a privation, an absence, a lack, of goodness. They reject the Gnostic notion that Yahweh is a lesser god, as well as the Manichaean notion that agents of good and evil, cosmic in scale and equal in power, are locked in eternal battle with each other. Why? Probably *because it does no good* to believe it—less good, anyway, than believing in the far greater power and ultimate triumph of a God who is wholly good. But if we agree that "evil" means something more than the failure to do good (when it would be possible to do good) or prevent harm (when it would be possible to prevent harm), if it means "positively" visiting pain and anguish and death upon others, then we must admit to some slippage, some contamination by older notions of evil as a "positive" force. For it implies that evil is more than just nature's entropy at work in the form of error, randomness, breakage, aging, or natural death, and more than just a thwarting of good intentions by complications. Evil that deserves the name is wrong-doing intended, done, and condoned. It is someone's wishing harm upon another and then acting in ways that bring it about— ways that might include neglect or carelessness (i.e., forms of *not*-doing). It also speaks of evil's attractiveness—of the way that evil-doing can call to us in the name of justice, a little fun, or short-term gain in an uncertain world.

DEFINITIONS CAN get us only so far. What can be said about the practical problem of evil from the point of view of theopraxy? In the most preliminary of analyses, this: that evil occurs chiefly as the result of four features of human nature:

• The first is that people can be driven by the conditions of war, famine, addiction, sickness, poverty, imprisonment, or natural disaster to regress to a less-than-human state. Starved, threatened, or cornered, people will kill to save their own lives or the lives of their clan; humiliated, they will strike out to restore their dignity. They will steal, deceive, and destroy, or,

---

51 *It is the hallmark of modern philosophy, and commonplace today, to make the distinction between* natural *"evil" (like volcanoes, tsunamis, and other "acts of God") and* moral *evil, which is what we and perhaps a handful of other animals can do, and call only the latter evil.*

in despair, do away with themselves, which is hardly a better outcome.

It is obvious how to prevent evil in these cases, at least in theory: it is to do everything possible to prevent humanity-degrading conditions from developing in the first place, and, if the situation is already far gone, to do everything possible to reverse them.

Now, some might say: "Not *everyone* turns to evil under duress. *Good* people don't. People of strong faith don't. Only the morally weak blame their 'situations.'" True? Well, we can certainly find instances that illustrate the case. But, setting aside the evidence that tells us that chance and genetic factors make a significant contribution as to who will break and who will not, let us remember to check the intentions of those who push this only-the-weak-fail argument to the fore, because, aside from being logically circular, it can be used to persuade others to allow themselves to be tested to failure and then to blame themselves for having characterological flaws (weakness of faith, evolutionary unfitness), all to the persuader's advantage.

Even on the best of motivations, relying on extraordinary conscience, courage, or faith in God is not a good idea. Human beings are social animals, flexible and ambitious. This is why, in the act of writing laws or configuring institutions whose overall missions might unquestionably be good, it is still essential to avoid devising jobs, positions, titles, roles, or patterns of authority that by their very nature will put people in situations of despair or, more insidiously, that will put people in situations where *being good at their job* is at odds with, or even disconnected from, *doing good*.[52] The desire to be competent and be recognized as such, the desire to excel and to deserve praise, runs strong in human nature. Regardless of the activity at hand, there are few stronger threats to our personhood— from ourselves if not others—than feeling incompetent, ineffective, unable to attract attention or "hold up our end."[53] And this makes it easy, even natural, for us to put being *good at* something ahead of whether that something is *a good thing to do*. Indeed, many people would rather be good at doing bad than be bad at doing good. All the more is this true when our competence at doing X, rather than the goodness *of* X, has been so configured, institutionally, as to be source of our legitimacy or livelihood.

Lest you feel immune from this weakness, know that the nicest of us are capable of doing evil on this basis. The experiments of Stanley Milgram in

---

52 Cf. *EXPLANATIONS 5, 6, and especially 10.*

53 *Let's be honest: this is the downside of preaching that we should live to serve others. For if we're bad at it, why live?*

the 1960s and Philip Zimbardo in the 1970s have made that abundantly clear, not to mention the Nuremberg trials of the late 1940s or the Truth and Reconciliation Commission of the mid-1990s.[54]

God is the good we do. God is therefore interested—metaphorically, *selfishly* interested—in how good we are at doing good. Other religious philosophies are able to make this clear too, of course. But none place the distinction at the heart of a theology.

• The second feature of human nature that keeps us prone to evil is this: that only witnessing suffering firsthand evokes in us the undismissable, visceral responses of pity, empathy, or fear. Use remote means of warfare and the enemy becomes unreal. Hide abattoirs and we can all eat meat. Remove people of type C from our neighborhoods and their fate becomes academic. One of the drawbacks of continuing suburbanization, globalization, and technological advance has been the heightened production of just this sort of *social distance:* whole new classes of people whose lives do not intersect with ours in any direct way, whose faces, if they appear at all, appear on TV. Then too, the consequences of our actions—mediated as they are by scores of people, machines, market transactions, and bureaucratic protocols—fan away in all directions, becoming ever harder to discern, harder to assign. Under these conditions, moral accountability is diffuse. When everyone is rationally doing their part in some great System, no one person is responsible for the harm done...or the good done, for that matter.

It is ever to the credit of conventional theistic preaching, therefore, that it emphasizes our personal visibility and accountability to God. We are *each* to follow God's commandments, *each* to treat others as we would like to be treated, *each* to resist attempts to make others alien either by social definition or forced relocation.[55] The theology of theopraxy goes one step further. It holds that God is the good we do, not collectively as such (as in democratically making good law), but individually as we each *contribute* to that process. Whenever and wherever good is being done, solo *or* in contribution to a collective effort, then and there is God summoned up, "whole in every part." Every single encounter with others creates the potential for bringing God into being (or, if you prefer, for bringing God's goodness to life).

---

54 *See Stanley Milgram (1974), Philip Zimbardo, (2004, pp. 21–50),* www.prisonexp. org/slide-1.htm, *and* www.doj.gov.za/trc. *These people were just doing their jobs.*

55 *To my knowledge, no one has developed this theme better than Zygmunt Bauman (2000 [1989]).*

This view of God, I suggest, undoes tendencies to sacralize community *per se*, which many religions do, completely convinced, in the case of *their* communities, of its inherent morality. But in fact, taken too far, elevating "community" to religious status cultivates social distance from other groups, which sooner or later breeds enmity as well as bends individual conscience to community norms.

- A third fact about human nature, seldom remarked upon as a source of evil, is that people are prone to overcommitting to the ideal of *justice*. Consider: those who lie, steal, murder, or wreck others' lives in large and small ways invariably have a story to tell. And invariably it is a story of injustice, redress, and/or higher justice: They did it because their victim killed their brother; they did it because they were unfairly fired; they did it because they needed the money more than the insurance company did; they did it because their family was stolen from; they did it because their rights were ignored, because they didn't get what others got and didn't deserve (either). And so forth. The list is long because, in fact, *unfairness and injustice are endemic to life on earth*. Life's complexity is such that it cannot be lived with precise and inflexible rules of fairness-accounting. Without forgiveness or patience or hope, without doubt about the accuracy of hearsay, and without the capacity to absorb a modicum of unfair punishment and bad luck uncomplainingly, the grounds for evil-doing are laid again and again. Is nine-tenths of love not relaxed accountancy?

    Far from ignoring justice, repeated wrongdoers—"bad people"—are often *perfectionists of justice,* untutored that *goodness* is the higher ideal by far.[56] What greater priority can be given good-doing than identifying it with God "himself"?

- Finally, a fourth fact about human nature: We are only recently out of the tribal phase of human existence where (among other things) we imagine members of other religions or nations (i.e., "tribes") to be blood-

---

56 *By referring* ultimate *justice to God and* final *reward or punishment to the afterlife, Western religion aims at reducing the urge to level the scales of justice impulsively, or in ways that contravene goodness. This is a good thing. Or can be. Why, then, is the tendency to give justice priority over goodness so prevalent? Perhaps because* measuring *and* administering *justice is easier than measuring and "administering" goodness. Asymmetries of pain and benefit are plainer to see and simpler to correct than absolute volumes of love. The scales of justice measure* comparative *not absolute mass, after all. Moreover, justice more often than not is simply power authorized or revenge legitimized, and both power- and revenge-seeking are older instincts by far than offering generalized love or practicing goodness for life's sake.*

related to each other and therefore intimately knowledgeable of each other's doings. Deeper than that, we imagine them united under the skin, each individual being simply a mirror, a manifestation, of the archetypal Person-of-That-Tribe: an Arab, a Jew, a Pole, a Catholic, an American. It follows that to encounter *one* actual person of that descent or origin is to encounter *all* people of that descent or origin collectively, archetypally. It is upon this atavistic logic that the guilt of one Greek, say, becomes the guilt of all Greeks, and punishing *any* Greek becomes only marginally second-best to punishing the actual Greek that committed the offense. One might cite the shadow that fell upon all American Muslims after September 11, 2001. But history is replete with internments, discriminations, and pains inflicted upon the innocent through the ideas of national character and collective guilt. (And let us be wary, too, of the latter's seductive twin: collective merit.)

Now, to deny that there is any such thing as national character seems foolhardy. It would be to deny the role of culture, language, local history, and family ties in making the people of a given time and region similar to each other (for better *and* for worse) as well as more likely, however slightly, to know each other. Nor can one deny that a first meeting between strangers compellingly involves each party making suppositions about the other's character based on their apparent nationality (or social class). The sin—the crime—begins when matters stop there and no greater depth is sought or admitted to exist. When the daily encounter between flesh-and-blood people devolves to—or rises no higher than—a game-like encounter between two stereotyped national characters, the potential for evil is hugely multiplied. An attitude barely appropriate to soldiers-at-war is being allowed to invade daily discourse. This is how brutality comes to lurk just below the surface of smiles.

All this is well understood, and I shall not elaborate further. The question is: does the theology of theopraxy help us commit to seeing beyond national and cultural stereotypes to the more complex truth of the individual? I suggest that it does, by locating God in acts by individuals, acts in behalf of all life. God can be on no *nation's* side ever, by definition: nations don't act; people do. It is you and I who can choose to be "on God's side" or not, moment by moment. It is you and I who, to the best of our abilities, can help draft laws and construct situations wherein the good is both rewarded and easier to do than the bad—or if not easier, still well short of requiring heroism. Learning to treat no person as a national (or ethnic or cultural or racial) *type* for longer than one second—which is about as much time as human nature can be granted in this case—is a small but important step.

In summary, these four features of human nature have to be faced by all concerned with decreasing the evil in this world:

- our tendency to regress in maturity and morality when under physiological duress or when attempting to satisfy inherently conflicted situational requirements,
- our insensitivity to remote suffering,
- our tendency to prioritize justice over goodness, and
- our tendency to relate to people as types.

OTHERS HAVE written more eloquently about these things. But I know of no place where these four features of human nature are collected for inspection, nor, of course, a place where a response is offered from the point of view of a theology like ours. Secular humanists, certainly, would agree that although all four might be a part of human *nature*—and indeed might once have served a life-preserving purpose—each, then as now, is brought forth and then exacerbated or moderated by human *culture*. And this means that each can be addressed by institutional design and by education: education not only about the facts of history and nature, but about the varieties and consequences of our beliefs.

One important set of beliefs has to do with the nature of God. Attempts such as ours to reconceive what "God" means are attempts precisely, on the one hand, to undo the logical flaws and unethical outcomes of too enthusiastic a belief in a supernatural, justice-dealing, side-choosing Creator-God, and, on the other, to weaken the demoralizing effects of denying that holiness can be produced, and not just deludedly felt, by human beings in contact with God by (almost) any definition. Atheistic humanism, I submit, is handicapped by its disregard of *sensus divinitatis*—our sense of the divine. This is as much a feature of human nature as any I have listed, with the difference that it is entrainable to producing and sustaining goodness in copious amounts.

For subscribers to the theology of theopraxy, you know what *that* means: it means producing and sustaining God.

10 : Enthusiasm / extremism

CONVERSE TO the problem of evil, as I have noted, is the "problem of good": the problem of how and why there is as much *good* in the world as there is, given the indifference of nature and the brutishness that still characterizes human beings. It is here that the theology of theopraxy shines because it sees goodness not at Creation and thence in decline, but as the youngest and weakest feature of the universe, still in ascent.

Now, it is common to hear it said by Christians and Muslims that God is the source of all good and humankind the source of all evil. Judaism agrees more or less, but it allow human beings to originate—truly originate—good as well as evil. We have within us, the rabbis said, urges to both good and evil. We can be sources of light, not just reflections of it; agents of change, not just puppets.

Only in the theology of theopraxy, however, is God identified with goodness itself as and when good characterizes the deeds of people free to do otherwise. Evil originates in humans, to be sure, and not in God, in whom it cannot occur by definition. As Augustine said: "All that is good is God." And so, just as goodness-experienced teaches us who or what God is, God-contemplated helps us see what *good* is. Put another way: holding on to God-in-concept helps us bridge between occasions of seeing God in action (or enacting God ourselves). But human nature is such that the intuitive feel for God we get from experiencing goodness firsthand is often superior to the intellectual understanding of God we get by reading or theological speculation alone.

It follows (from God being the good we do) that if classical religious faith reliably yields goodness and prevents evil, then none of its fictions, contradictions, odd rituals or imponderables are nonsensical. It follows, equally, that if humanistic or even nihilistic atheism reliably brings about goodness and prevents evil, then none of its denials of the existence of God amount to any reduction in the fullness of God's actuality. And it follows, finally, that if and where *any* other worldview is found to be better at producing good and preventing evil than the theology I am calling "the theology of theopraxy," then the theology of theopraxy, by its own criteria, would have to remove itself from consideration, at least at that time and place and among those people. And remove itself happily, since there would be other philosophies which better prepared people for the very theo*praxy* that its theology aims at encouraging.[57]

History has shown, however, that theism in the hands of its enthusiasts—Jewish, Christian, and Muslim—has been no more reliable at producing goodness and preventing harm than atheism has been in the hands of *its* enthusiasts, especially when either was joined to political power. We cannot know whether adopting the perspective offered in this book would make things better or worse. This is what we need to find out. Could subscribing to the theology of theopraxy turn people toward doing harm, toward evil? We will reflect upon this important question for the rest of this chapter and over the next few.

Now, SOME critics would blame neither theism nor atheism for the harms done on their logic, but only extreme enthusiasm *for* them. It's neither religious faith, they say, nor religious skepticism, that does the harm, but *extremism* in the defense or execution of either.[58] It's unfortunate (they go on) that the angry-prophet tradition in Western religion encourages an intolerance of other gods so absolute that it can easily lead to an intolerance of the *people* who believe in other gods (or in no god at all), as well as impatience with, if not hatred for, any people whose *styles* of belief in the One God differ.[59]

Both Bible and Qu'ran are rich with recountings of God's rewards to complete faith in him expressed a right way, and of his punishment of incomplete faith in him expressed in the wrong way (e.g., through idolatry). "I am the way, the truth, and the life," said Jesus according to John (14:6), "no man cometh unto the Father, but by me." What could alienate Jews, and later, Muslims, more? "Allah is the one true God, and Mohammed

---

57 *Of course, people of different backgrounds will react differently to different formulations of "God" and to different styles of religiosity. The theology of theopraxy is not for everybody, just as Jainism is not, or Zen, or Judaism. Cf. ARGUMENTS 2 and the Preface, p. xx.*

58 *One might mention here both Aristotle's and Confucius' well-known view that essential to happiness is moderation in all things—including religiosity. (One wonders about moderation in moderation itself: ought we sometimes to be immoderate?)*

59 *As many have observed, the First Commandment ("Thou shalt have no other Gods before Me!") speaks of a jealous and mighty God, but not of a God that forbids worship of other Gods as long as we (and those other gods) know their place relative to him, the Lord (of) God(s). Much of the Hebrew Bible is an object lesson in what it takes to avoid the Lord God's anger at being demoted. By the end of the Babylonian captivity, for the Israelites there were no other gods, period, and Judaism became fully monotheistic. Today it is common among liberal Christians and Jews to see God as the maker and harbinger of peace. No anger; no retribution, no jealousy of other gods. I see this as proof of God's evolution with us, and take as further evidence the demise of cannibalism, the abolition of slavery, the rise of women's rights and human rights generally, the coming of environmentalism, animal rights, and vegetarianism. Still to come: the end of poverty and war.*

his only true prophet."[60] What could alienate Christians and Jews more? "For thou art a holy people...and the Lord hath chosen thee...above all the nations that are upon the earth" (Deuteronomy, 14:2). What could alienate Christians and Muslims more?

Atheism is far from innocent of extremism too, as Mao Zhedong and Joseph Stalin proved. Atheists are often radical in their opposition to all religious faith, which they see as nothing more than exploitable superstition, the "opiate of the masses" as Marx famously put it. Belief in God was so sure an indication of weak-mindedness that it needed to be stamped out, like an unhealthy addiction.

If we were not living at a time of conflicting religious fundamentalisms—in particular, war and near-war between Jewish-Christian fundamentalism (with Jewish nationalism) on the one hand, and Islamic fundamentalism (with pan-Arab nationalism or Islamism) on the other, watched over by a multitude of atheists, agnostics, New Agers, deists, and secularists powerless to effect reconciliation using purely humanistic or "spiritual" ideas—we would not need to spend the next eighteen pages on the question. (The problem deserves a thousand, of course...if they would help.) But here is the important question for us: if extremism in the advancement of different forms of theism *or* atheism is the culprit, could the theology of theopraxy support an extremism of its own, and thus "go bad"? For example, might a person become a good-deed *fanatic*, and do harm? Might some subscribers to our theology, believing themselves to *be* God, go on justice-dealing rampages, or figuratively drown themselves like the legendary Good King Canute who moved his throne to the beach and commanded the tides to stop? And what if they have truly bad (in the sense of stupid) ideas about what "good" is?

Forewarned is fore-armed. But let us be hopeful too. Might there be something in the DNA, as it were, of the theology of theopraxy that moderates extremism automatically? Could it help make peace among the adherents of different faiths?

---

60 *I could not determine the provenance of this common article of Islamic faith.*

11 : How religions go bad (1)

A GOOD framework for discussion is provided by Charles Kimball in his 2002 book *When Religion Becomes Evil*. From a range of historical examples, Kimball adduces five "warning signs" that a religion is sanctioning if not actively promoting evil. Each sign, he notes, issues from an otherwise innocuous, even helpful, religious doctrine being pursued to extremes. Here are the five signs: when the religion-in-question starts...

- making absolute truth claims,
- advocating blind obedience,
- establishing an "ideal time,"
- believing that the end justifies any means, and
- declaring holy war.

In this chapter and over the next few I will argue that the theology of theopraxy is less likely to exhibit any of these signs than the three Abrahamic religions have been. Of course, theopraxy is not a religion. Nor are there data as to how the *theology* of theopraxy, as a set of ideas and maxims, would develop in multiple hands and minds. But we should at least look for the seeds of trouble in the propositions upon which it rests.[61] We start with Kimball's first sign, namely:

Making absolute truth claims. Thinking that one knows—or that one's leader knows or knew—the absolute truth about God and what God wants from humanity, forms the foundation of all religious intolerance: the opinion that one's own religion is right and others' wrong, one's own path true, and others' false.[62]

Now, "God is the good we do" is an absolute truth claim, and so we are obliged to ask whether it could become a problem if taken to heart.

---

61 *A note before going on. In principle, defense of enthusiastic belief in X can take two forms. One can argue (1) that X is such that transition from enthusiasm to fanaticism would be highly unlikely (for example, X could be* moderation*); or (2) that X is such that extreme enthusiasm for it could have only slight or no bad consequences (for example, X could be the belief that bagels taste better than rolls). I will use both kinds of defense on behalf of the theology of theopraxy.*

62 *The assumption behind this indictment, of course, is that God is not one who himself doubts, is not one who finds many religions acceptable, not just your own. When it comes ›*

The answer, I think, is no. We can believe absolutely that God is the good we do without believing absolutely that we know what the (absolute) best thing to do is, and we would disavow anyone who habitually, or on God's authority, said they knew *beyond question* what particular act, now, would be best. For the truth is that many alternative actions can be equally good in a given situation, and many more actions good-*enough*, especially given that one can never be sure of the long-run consequences of any action. One simply does one's level best, taking other people's opinions into account, and then tries to develop safety nets and "plan B"s in case one turns out to be wrong.

The theology of theopraxy also claims that doing good reliably, like maintaining a high batting average in baseball, is a skill that people can develop in different degrees. This advocates patience as well as moderates expectations as to how much good any particular person can do. Luckily, all good-doing is God: "big" good-doing (like saving a hundred lives) and "little" good-doing (like opening a door for a package-laden stranger), expert good-doing (like performing surgery on a newborn) and non-expert good-doing (like assuring a friend she's not fat). Which is why God is *all good,* as tradition has it.[63]

Alas, "God is the good we do" could become fightin' words even with nobody claiming to know exactly what the good is. For example, conservative believers could see (correctly) that "God is the good we do" implies that God is *only* the good we do, and object strongly. They might tolerate that God is *also* the good we do, but not *only*... Shall we remove the implicit "only" in "God is the good we do" and make them happy? They

---

‹ to fundamentalist Judaism, Christianity, and Islam, therefore, Kimball's warning is apt to be on target. All three accept the authority of prophets who knew or saw God directly and found him "as advertised," i.e., almighty, all-knowing, and all-good, a "person" without doubts, final in his judgment, to whom the future is known, and who is angrily critical of other faiths. Among world religions, Buddhism, Unitarian Universalism, Baha'i, and Zoroastrianism are notable exceptions. They see God as happy at the diversity in theological conceptions. They promise neither instant cures for what ails us nor salvation for a few dollars. In the words of Hegel: "Those who 'seek the Lord' and assure themselves, in their uneducated opinion, that they possess everything immediately instead of undertaking the work of raising their subjectivity to the cognition of truth and knowledge of objective right and duty, can produce nothing but folly, outrage, and the destruction of all ethical relations." (Cited in Robert Williams [1997, p. 32]).

63 I hear a song: "All things bright and beautiful/All good deeds great and small/All things wise and wonderful/The Lord God is them all." (Modified from "All Things Bright and Beautiful," words by Cecil Alexander, 1848, inspired by Genesis 1:31: "God saw all that He had made, and it was very good.") Ah, if only sentiment were enough.

might also prefer "God is *in* the good we do." Shall we put the "in" in? (see also EXPLANATIONS 1)

No in both cases. For such concessions would walk away from what the theology of theopraxy wants us to face, which is the untenability of believing God to be all-good as well as all-knowing and all-powerful in any literal sense. Our theology asks people to see God's omniscience and omnipotence for what they are: not facts, but, as I offered in EXPLANATIONS 8, assertions evolved to magnify our subtler ethical intuitions, to endorse them, and to give us the courage to act upon them. To be sure, believing that God is all-good, all-knowing, and all-powerful reduces the uncertainty we feel about our ethical judgments: when at a loss, we can simply give over to God, invoking, perhaps, a passage from the Bible. We can let the consequences of our actions be taken out of our hands and put into God's, and so reduce our dread of regret. (If we try for outcome X but it does not come about, then God must not have wanted X to come about—and it was for the best that it did not.)

But we have to wonder: surely there are less metaphysically bedevilled and less exploitable ways to give ourselves the courage to do the right thing on the one hand, and to alert us to our limitations on the other.

IF MAINTAINING that God is (only) the good we do could rile conservative believers, it could also rile atheists. "Why bother with 'God,'" they could ask, "when the God believed in is so contingent, so unmighty, so human?"

We can reply: The reconciliation of faith with reason is of such importance, and the quest for it so old, that both theists and atheists should reconsider their premises. Believers should re-think what they mean by "real" and what they mean by "God" when they assert that God exists; and atheists should do the same when they deny that God exists. The theology of theopraxy offers a middle way: a way for God to be real and also "not-real," to exist and also "not exist" (see EXPLANATIONS 4). I believe it can reconcile differences at a basic level for a good number of people.

Finally, we should note that a quarrel between the theology of theopraxy on the one hand and both conservative theism and atheism on the other, would be only theological, which is to say, only theoretical. For at the level of practical action, and in the vast majority of cases, the theology of theopraxy has no quarrel with what would count as good behavior for believers or atheists. After all, the identification and enumeration of human virtues is not unique to any single religion or philosophy. Nor is the ideal of the love of life—the love of *all* life. The way to avoid widening the conflict, therefore, is to concentrate on belief's outcomes, not belief's contents.

This pragmatism is one that the theology of theopraxy shares with religions and philosophies as diverse as Judaism, Confucianism, Utilitarianism, Zoroastrianism, Ethical Culture,[64] and modern liberal democracy. No other religious philosophy, however, raises that pragmatism to the level of the holy. In the end as at the beginning, it says, God is the good we *do*, not someone or something whose existence we can only argue about.

---

64 *Ethical Culture is a small religious movement in the U.S., founded by Felix Adler. This from his book* Creed and Deed *(1887, pp. 2, 3): "We perceive that every attempt to settle problems of faith has thus far signally failed, nor can we hope for better results in the future. Certainty even with regard to the essential dogmas appears to us impossible. We do not therefore deny dogma, but prefer to remit it to the sphere of individual conviction with which public associations should have no concern. Far from believing that the doctrines of religion as commonly taught are essential to the well being of society, we apprehend that the disputes concerning the 'author of the law' have diverted the attention of men from the law itself, and that the so-called duties toward God too often interfere with the proper performance of our duties toward one another. It were better to insist less upon a right belief, and more upon right action. In order to find a common basis whereon good men, whether believers or unbelievers, can unite, we look to the moral law itself, whose certainty rests in the universal experience of civilized humanity."*

12 : How religions go bad (2)

Making absolute truth claims, continued. We still need to consider whether belief in the truth of such maxims as "God is the good we do" or "God is in our hands" could some day cause harm beyond provoking intellectual disagreement.

Well, first consider this: an avid subscriber to the theology of theopraxy would have to be an existentialist and a romantic, a believer and a skeptic, a traditionalist and a revolutionary, all at once. This is a complex position to hold, to say the least, but it has the following advantage: any tendency to extremism with regard to one of its components would be counteracted by a commitment to another component, likely its opposite. Our theology is self-moderating (some would say: conflicted). Moreover, the complexity of thought involved does not lend itself to easy imitation and thus to rapid propagation in the general population.

So far so good (and bad): the theology of theopraxy is for smart people.

Alas, overly-facile renditions of it could emerge nonetheless, renditions of it that might encourage extremism in certain people. And this would be unfortunate. Consider the following two scenarios, the first mostly an irritation, the second potentially more dangerous.

Do-goodism. The thought that one is *doing* God when one is doing good can be quite heady. Dizzy with the importance of their every action, some people could become annoying to live around: meddlesome, self-righteous, overly earnest and critical. We call them "do-gooders" already: people who *insist* on doing what they think is the higher good at every turn despite other possibilities and judgments. For example, friends and family members who refuse to ask for the help they need because that they "don't want to be a burden" or think you should offer them help "more genuinely"; people who never park over a yellow line because it would be *wrong;* people who *like* running about in constant service to others, "innocently" spreading indebtedness. And so on.

This is not to say that all do-gooders are responding to religious impulses. There are other reasons for behaving in this obsessively law-abiding, holier-than-thou way. But insistent do-goodism has at least this saving grace: it is self-limiting. For as soon as the insistence itself is understood as blocking or undoing the good intended—it stops in embarrassment. The mission might continue, but another way is sought. "Live and let live" becomes the more credible motto, at least until the next reminder.

Add social authority to do-goodism, however, and one has paternalism of the most irksome sort, i.e., permanent, and with *prima facie* impeccably moral intentions or the law on its side. And this can slide into:

Hubris, which is such arrogant, violent pride in one's own moral and creative powers—or, if not in one's own, then in one's tribe or humankind's—that it comes to rival or eclipse God's (as traditionally conceived).

Hubris is no less dangerous in secular contexts ("I *am* France!" cried de Gaulle) than it is in religious ones, where it is blasphemy to presume oneself in any way to *be* God.[65] But pointing to secular hubris is not yet a defense of theopraxy, and blasphemy is what every traditional Christian, Jew, or Muslim hears in epigrams like "Whether or not God exists is entirely up to us," "God is the good we do," or "God is in our hands."

How can these worries be assuaged?

Only by knowing more. For let there be no mistake: the theology of theopraxy does not claim that any person can *be* God, or ever was God, or ever will be God; only that some of their deeds are, have been, and will be (cf. EXPLANATIONS 12). When God is the good we *do*, no one can say, "I am God" or "We are gods," only that "I do God" or "We do God," happily allowing traditional believers to add "-'s will."

Moreover, and more importantly, the God that subscribers to theopraxy believe they (and others) bring into being with their good doings is not the all-powerful God of the Bible. Traditional believers are right: human beings cannot be Lord over God and at the same time mean, by "God," the Lord God of the Bible and Qur'an. But subscribers to the theology of theopraxy are right too. God (in the theology of theopraxy) has none of the Biblical/Qur'anic God's infinite powers and attributes in the first place—powers and attributes that it would indeed be presumptuous, not to say dangerous, for any human being or group of human beings to claim for themselves.[66]

When God is believed to be nothing like the sun, nothing like a king or warrior, or judge-on-high, nor even the Ground of Being or some such ultimate thing, but rather more like a candle flame, a whisper of conscience, a tender gesture, a favor for a stranger unreported and unre-

---

65 *For Christians, Jesus might be exempt from the charge, although even the Gospels avoid direct statements of Christ's divinity. Jesus never says "I am God" in so many words.*

66 *Do I hear "gotcha!" from some readers? "...so you admit that theopraxy's God is not really God!" For my answer to this challenge read on, and see* ARGUMENTS 3 *and* 23, REFLECTIONS 11 *and* 14. *Although theopraxy argues against it in principle, the danger of believing oneself to be God lies more in* what kind *of God* one believes oneself to be *than in thinking of oneself as God at all.*

marked-upon, a flow of deeds and thoughts as rippling and balanced as a dance upon water...what large thing is there for hubris to attach itself to?

Then too, believing that we *all* enact God equally when we do good does not make me very special or powerful: it makes me just another worker in the field, as it were, "lifting the sparks."[67]

A theopracticing person saying "I do good, and thereby 'make God,'" is rather like a musician saying "I play the violin and thereby make music." As I wrote in DECLARATIONS 7: "Wherever and whenever there is a choosing of good over bad, of beauty over ugliness, of truth over falsehood, and life over death... *there* is God and only there, as fugitive as the moment, ready to become a reality enacted." God is in everyone's hands. In the theology of theopraxy, one might say God is neither Father nor Son, but rather more like the Holy Spirit or *Shekinah:* the divine presence that penetrates, informs, and issues from the human heart one situation and one deed at a time. But unlike the Holy Spirit or *Shekinah,* this "spirit," this presence, has no fountainhead, no radiant unitary source, no point in the Beginning whence it emanated. Because of this, theopractitioners do not imagine themselves connected to an all-powerful Creator who works His will through them. Instead, they imagine themselves modest but always-significant sources of good themselves, like fireflies, God present and accounted for by every glowing deed.

This is the Good News of the theology of theopraxy.

THERE ARE those who will say: "This is all very nice; very poetic. But what you are describing is not *God* as anyone today understands the word. It is something else. Why don't you find a new name for it? 'God' is taken."

We can reply: There is no question of finding a new name for good-being-done. It is God. Our aim is precisely to challenge older ideas of God with newer ones, to contest the meaning of the Name.[68] Who, what, when, and how God *really* exists is the question that needs answering in a way that best produces what all believers in God say God wants: the end of involuntary suffering, more beauty, justice, and truth in the world, more enjoyment, peace, and goodwill among men and women and all living creatures...in a phrase: our continued evolution as a moral species.

---

67 *This is a medieval image of our proper task on earth, authored by Rabbi Isaac Luria. See* REFLECTIONS 18.

68 *Of course, no word is owned, as I have said. Nor is any word in the dictionary— much less "God"—immune from drift in its usage and meaning over time. See also* REFLECTIONS 14.

13 : How religions go bad (3)

WE MOVE on now to examining the theology of theopraxy for the second of Kimball's warning signs that a religion is turning to evil, namely:

Advocating blind obedience. As Kimball points out, when any person, ideology, institution, government, or business begins to demand blind obedience, the potential for evil-doing is greatly multiplied.

Now, obedience is far from rare, even in freedom-loving America. It's demanded from soldiers in the army. It's required from patients in hospitals, students at school, employees on the job, and drivers on the road. But these kinds of obedience are "sighted" rather than "blind," because their ends—survival, health, education, a salary, safety—are objectively measurable and endorsed by those who obey. But the obedience that certain religious sects (for example) demand from their followers tends to be of a different sort, not just because the ends are often unconfirmable (for example, reward in Heaven), but because the obedience has a different purpose, namely, to conceal the weaknesses and exploitative intentions of the institution's leaders and/or to deflect attention from contradictions in its governing doctrine.

Moreover, unlike other forms of obedience, the boundaries of religious obedience are not clear. What would/should one *not* do for God? What heinous act can *not* be framed as a test of faith? Certainly when trust in leadership becomes so great that facts about it, which would normally be disturbing, are dismissed, or when submission to irrational doctrine is demanded as a payment for the social or material benefits of membership, one has the very formula for blind obedience. And this can lead to disaster.

There is a parallel distinction between rational faith and irrational faith. Rational faith is a positive response to uncertainty when a decision must be made whose outcomes can and will be judged. Irrational faith is faith that systematically ignores or denies contrary indications, that legitimizes irrationality in principle, and/or that precipitates outcomes that cannot (or will not) be judged. The two obediences, sighted and blind, usually follow from the two types of faith: sighted obedience from rational faith, blind obedience from irrational faith. I want to argue that the theology of theopraxy, in so far as it involves faith, involves rational faith, and insofar as it asks for obedience, asks for sighted obedience. How so?

THE FAITH that the theology of theopraxy asks for is rational because it privileges knowing over believing when knowledge is available, and because it submits itself to judgment of the consequences of belief. If one's beliefs about God do not issue in better actions than otherwise, then it is wrong belief, not just morally, but also scientifically.

Thus, one can be a theopracticing Jew or a theopracticing Christian, a theopracticing Muslim, Hindu, Buddhist, Taoist, or Jain. One can attend services, read sacred texts, sing, pray, light candles, kneel, meditate, even preach because one judges on the available evidence that these are morally creative acts, constitutive of the God they nominally serve. An understanding of the theology of theopraxy might allow people to embrace their home religion in a deeper and more existential way than they were capable of before. This embrace would not be a simple return to faith or a "born again-ness." For once one has understood the meaning of theopraxy, once one has glimpsed its theological implications, one is unlikely to practice one's religion naively, without interpretation. Its precepts will have become true in a different, richer way. Goodness-of-deed will have become the point, not doctrinal correctness. Actions in everyday life will count, not avowals of faith on special occasions, nor fluency in prayer, nor practicedness in ritual. Subtlety of conscience begins to matter, not degree of moral conviction; knowledge of the world, not just knowledge of one's trade and the Bible or Qur'an.

With the theology of theopraxy showing the way, one finds oneself living and breathing the ethical core of the religion in question *and* being watchful for its corruption. One finds oneself loving its peculiar time-soaked images and stories for how they encourage us to protect, promote, and dignify *all* life, while being wary of those images and stories that do not (and many Bible stories do not).[69] One sees religion's rituals as demonstrations of the joy and solemnity of the ethical life, as shapers of community tolerant of other communities, as mechanisms for commitment and recommitment to virtue, as expressions of gratitude for life itself, as reminders of what is at stake. And one remains watchful that these performances—otherwise of no worth—do not de-evolve into rote or pageantry for its own sake.

Now going to the mosque "because it's Friday," the synagogue "because

---

69 *This author, for example, has trouble with the Passover Hagaddah (traditional prayer-book) for the way in which it gloats over the ten catastrophes—the ten plagues—that befell the Egyptians. Others may not be able to bracket away the sexism inherent in all three major Western religions, indeed in all old religions, Western and Eastern. One way to alleviate these feelings is to realize that the Bible is very much a book of cautionary tales.*

it's Saturday," or church "because it's Sunday" represents sighted, not blind, obedience. The compulsion is gone. In its place is self-determination.

"In all great undertakings," wrote Paul Valéry, "tradition, in the true sense of the word, does not consist of doing again exactly what others have done before, but in recapturing the spirit that went into what they did—and would have done differently in a different age."[70]

---

70 *Paul Valéry,* Notebooks, *quoted in Joseph Epstein (2003).*

14 : How religions go bad (4)

THE THIRD of Charles Kimball's warning signs of a religion becoming evil is its **establishment of an ideal time.** What does this mean?

In all three major Western religions, it is common to dream of a future better than the present, to look forward to an era of universal peace, prosperity, and justice. Orthodox Jews await the coming of the Messiah to bring it about. Conservative Christians expect the second coming of Christ, the battle of Armageddon, and a thousand-year reign of peace to follow. Muslims long for the prophesied worldwide Islamic state where all aspects of life—economic, commercial, military, spiritual, social, and familial—come together seamlessly under Islamic law, and none lack faith in Allah. Most believers are happy to wait for these "end-times," drawing comfort from the belief that they are promises that came from God. Others are less patient and take it upon themselves to precipitate the new age—the ideal time—in their own lifetimes.

According to the theology of theopraxy, we should have some sympathy for the latter group, which is at least pro-active. It wants to *make* the world a better place. But we should be wary of propounding an "ideal time" achievable in any real time frame after (or because of) our deaths, or anyone else's, or by means of any single world-event. There is no expectation of such in the theology of theopraxy. There is only the commitment to make today better than yesterday and tomorrow better than today, indefinitely, and by small increments. Subscribers to the theology of theopraxy set no deadlines, expect no showdowns, relish no Armageddons, and long for no final reckonings before God. They pursue incremental evolution, meaning life of greater quantity, variety, complexity, and degree of organization here, and here, and here, and here...

Open-ended evolutionary gradualism of this kind may lack apocalyptic drama. But it defuses the urgency created by visions of imminent consummation, an urgency that easily comes to involve the trampling of others in a rush toward what is actually a myopic and fevered vision without the novelty, loveliness, or surprise that true evolution generates.

Which brings us to Kimball's fourth warning sign:

15 : How religions go bad (5)

Believing that the end justifies any means. Whenever a key event, place, or religious or political doctrine "in effect becomes an end, some people within the religion become consumed with protecting or achieving that end... and zealous believers become blind in their single-minded defense of it."[71]

Perhaps the best example of this is the exclusion of followers of other religions from sacred sites. In India, Muslims and Hindus have massacred each other over a disputed site in the city of Ayodhya. In Israel, dozens of sites are contested by Muslims and Jews, especially in Hebron (al-Khalil) and in Jerusalem. Rights to their stewardship, as well as the right to exclude others from access have come to stand for the legitimacy of entire nations, in defense of which any sacrifice is thought to be justified.

Our theology has no sacred sites—not historically, for obvious reasons, but also not in principle. Everywhere a person can go is potentially sacred, since God can come into being anywhere and everywhere good can freely be done. God does not wait at churches, synagogues, or mosques to be called. Nor does God hover over memorials. In appearances that are as spontaneous as they are short-lived except in memory, *God takes place* in classrooms and hospital rooms, on quiet streets and far off villages, in parks and basements, in cars and on trains and on planes, in office buildings, bedrooms, kitchens, and dining rooms. There is no need to memorialize "contact" with God and then hallow the place where that happened since "God taking place" is not so rare and momentous an occasion. You are probably bringing God into being right now, or were just moments ago.

This is not to say that God comes to life everywhere equally easily or often. There are some places that by virtue of their design and history and purpose are more conducive to ethical actions within them than others. What typically goes on in these places is important too, of course. A jail is not a school; an abattoir is not a nursery. But other things being equal, their physical design and condition can make a difference. Clean streets, watered gardens, and painted walls say something about their owners and about what has been achieved. Spaces that are naturally lit and harmoniously proportioned are dignifying rather than demeaning, as are rooms that are functionally and comfortably fitted out and cared for. They affect

---

71 *Kimball (2002, p. 129).*

the mood of everyone in and around them, putting people subtly on their best behavior. These environments increase the chances of God "taking place" there, and the programming, financing, designing, building, and maintaining of them are in themselves good-doings.

THE DEFENSE-UNTO-DEATH of sacred sites is not the only example of religion putting ends before means. Another is the defense of religious identity, even of faith itself.

If you worship a God capable of killing non-believers, then you or your descendants will someday kill non-believers. If you worship a God capable of killing for "his" ends at all, then sooner or later you will kill for your ends (although you will say it was "in His name").

The truth is, however, that immoral means never justify moral ends, and vice versa: moral means never justify immoral ends. "Thou shalt not kill," means *God* shall not kill either, notwithstanding Biblical evidence to the contrary, and notwithstanding Qur'anic urgings to convert or kill infidels. According to the theology of theopraxy, God is our not-killing. A given war might be justified (perhaps it is a war of self-defense), but it can never be a "holy war," which term, in the view of our theology, is an oxymoron. A theopracticing Jew, Christian, or Muslim will find no reason in his or her faith to stumble people of other faiths on account of their beliefs or to harm any creature whose life is no imminent threat to their own.

This brings us to the fifth and last of Kimball's signs of a religion's turn to evil: declaring holy war.

16 : How religions go bad (6)

Declaring holy war. Until recently, the term "holy war" referred to the Christian Crusades of the 12th Century, sometimes to the French Wars of Religion in the second half of the 16th century, and to the conflict in Northern Ireland in the 20th. From late 20th century onward, however, the term "holy war" became largely identified with Islamic fundamentalism and *jihad*—a word used equally by Palestinians in their struggle with Israel and Al-Qaida in their attack on all things American. Given the state of the world at the time of this writing, I should like to concentrate on this last sense of holy war.

Islamic scholars like to point out that "holy war" is a careless translation of the word *jihad*. As one scholar writes: *"Jihad* has the literal meaning of exerting our best and greatest effort to achieve something. It is not the equivalent of war, for which the Arabic word is *qital."* As the same scholar explains, *jihad* simply means fervent effort:

> Jihad *has a much wider connotation and embraces every kind of striving in God's cause. A* mujahid *is one who is sincerely devoted to his or her cause; who uses all physical, intellectual, and spiritual resources to serve it; who confronts any power that stands in its way; and, when necessary, dies for this cause.* Jihad *in the way of God is our struggle to win God's good pleasure, to establish His religion's supremacy, and to make His Word prevail.*[72]

This passage is intended to allay fear and clarify the meaning of *jihad*. One cannot help but take note, however, of its talk of supremacy, or of its condoning of coercion and self-sacrifice-unto-death for the cause.

What cause? There are two, said the Prophet Mohammed, and therefore two forms of *jihad*, the greater and the lesser. The greater *jihad* is overcoming carnal desire in oneself. The lesser *jihad* is spreading the truth to other nations that "There is no God save He, the All-Mighty, the Wise" (Sura 3.18). It is this second, lesser *jihad* that may well involve action on the battlefield.[73] One wonders whether Mohammed looked to the Bible's Joshua for inspiration. After all, the Israelites did not take Canaan with

---

[72] *This and the following quotes are from the official* Discover Islam *website, www. dislam.org. Actual authorship is not given.*

[73] *Ibid. Here are the actual words: "The lesser jihad, which has usually been taken to mean fighting for God's cause, does not refer only to the form of striving done on battle* ›

sweet words. And lest you think there are no encouragements to violence in the Christian canon, consult Matthew 10:34-39, John 8:24, and 2 Thessalonians 1:7-9.

From a theology of theopraxy point of view, there is something admirable about *jihad* taken to mean sincere effort in the cause of making God happen ("making His Word prevail"). After all, waiting for God to do something *for* us runs counter to the idea of God being in our hands.[74] But the theology of theopraxy offers a path to more peaceful evolution, and away from war, because it does not identify *obedience* to God with moral decision-making. Moral decision-making, if it is genuine decision-making, represents obedience to no-one. It is a free action. It is our taking responsibility for doing good either "just because," or as an expression of our love for God, but certainly not out of fear of or submission to "him."

Here is the crux of the problem. If God is almighty and all-wise, as God is considered to be in all three Abrahamic faiths, and yet we must act without waiting for God to approve of our every action, then we need pre-approval from "him," preferably for whole classes of action. Where is this pre-approval to be found? Why, clearly: in the pages of our sacred books, in the words of God's prophets. But this *modus operandi*, when used to exclusion, is precisely what prevents our own ethical intuitions from evolving. If we cannot serve God in our own modest way and know that that service is authoritative (or rather, authorial), then we will never do better than our ancestors. Having read, having listened, and having thought about the good, having come to see God *as* good-in-action (whatever else God may be), we realize that serving God in our small way *has* to be enough. For this is how God acts: modestly, joyfully, without

---

< *fields. The term is comprehensive. It includes every action done for God's sake." Other apologists make the distinction between Islam, the revealed-truth-and-peace-loving religion, and Islamism, the political ideology, which alone is prone to using* "jihad" *in its most militaristic meaning.*

The real problem, it seems to me, is that Mohammed preached justified violence, which is to say, violence in self-defense, where room was left for taking other religionists' insufficient faithfulness to the One God in their traditions to be offense enough. Thus were the Messenger's followers to act against Jews, Christians, and Muslims who were not good Jews or good Christians or good Muslims, where "good" by definition meant showing complete submission to the rule of God as expressed in following the dicta of their true prophets: Moses, Jesus, and Mohammed.

In short, Islam's lesser jihad *is against "infidels." And who is to make the judgment of "infidelity"? Why, Islam's leaders of the day, as backed by the holy Qur'an. Hassaballa (2006) and Closson (2006) are representative of the difficulties of the argument.*

74 *This is not to say that we would not wait for a situation to develop or mature before acting. Good timing—kairos—is an important part of successful good-doing.*

cataclysm or violence, through you and me deciding on the best thing to do for *all* life, and then, counting ourselves neither first nor last, *doing* it.[75] Holy war will never be fought by soldiers who believe this.

THE THEOLOGY of theopraxy respects all religions, not just out of good citizenship, but because it operates at a meta-level. It is a "meta-religion," if you will. And as such it may well serve as a bridge between them, as a place of common concern. What religion, after all, is *against* good-doing?

But, human nature being what it is, we must finally consider the possibility that being identified as a "theopractitioner" could some day, somewhere, be seen as subversive. In some communities, a theopracticing Jew, Christian, or Muslim (see EXPLANATIONS 21) might come to be perceived as a person with divided loyalty, and therefore a potential traitor. And this in turn could lead to witch-hunts, tests of true faith, the requiring of special oaths and so on, precisely because differences in dress, speech, and behavior between true believers and theopracticing believers would be all but non-existent.

Should we be concerned? Absolutely. It would not be the first time that paranoia has turned trust of the brother into fear of the alien—the alien all the more menacing for bearing an uncanny resemblance to the brother. It happened to the Jews of Germany in the 1930s; it happened to the Muslims of Sarajevo in the 1990s.

Perhaps the best way for subscribers to the theology of theopraxy to avoid this eventuality is to be frank if asked about the nature of their faith. I say "if asked" because most congregations neither ask about nor care what their members *truly* believe, on the principle that this is a private matter, and unprovable in any case. (Besides, they themselves do not want to be similarly challenged.) In secular contexts the question doesn't come up. But in certain towns and neighborhoods it might be best to stay away altogether from religious communities that put great stock on "true belief."

THIS ALL but concludes my discussion of whether the theology of theopraxy is as vulnerable to going bad in the hands of its enthusiasts as the great religions have been in the hands of their enthusiasts. I hope to have shown that it is not.

---

75 *Martin Luther's proclamation of a "priesthood of believers" consisting of ordinary people (over against the Church's priestly hierarchy) was a first step in transforming responsibility-to-Church into responsibility-to-God. The next step is personal responsibility for God, which is what we are arguing for here. See* EXPLANATIONS 18.

Of course, by way of a solution to the whole problem, there is also es-chewing strong beliefs generally—beliefs about anything, that is, except the inadvisedness of having strong beliefs. Paradox aside, this solution would surely have some power to prevent evil (as would removing from religion any attachment to a sacred site and any trace of a mission to per-suade others of its truth, and so on). But the result of eschewing strong belief *per se* could also be to render the religion-in-question harmless though insipidity, or through turning it into a completely private affair with every believer a container of pent-up, inexpressible convictions they are too afraid to act upon.

There is a better way. Better than strong belief in a strong God, better than weak belief in a strong God, and better than weak belief in a weak God, I suggest, is *strong belief in a weak God*—in a God who needs us in order to be realized, a God who is only good, who loves all all-life-loving life, who is easily thwarted, who is manifest as a pattern of actions we can cause as well as witness.[76] This is what the theology of theopraxy recom-mends.

It's a matter of education. Strong faith in a strong God, I suggest, is called for by people who since childhood have been taught to fear "the evil all around" or "the devil in themselves." To people who feel they could succumb at any moment, meeting strength with strength recommends itself as the best strategy. At once atavistic and familiar, the conclusion is inescapable, given the premises. Hence the number of born-again believ-ers in prisons. Hence the courage of religious zealots—Jewish, Christian and Muslim—which is not really courage but fear: fear of a reproving God, fear of evil, fear of themselves, fear of going to hell and/or anxious-ness to reap reward in heaven. And what happens when evil *wins* and we sin grievously? Why, then we can turn to a massively *forgiving* God. And so it goes, ricocheting between extremes.

Strong faith in a weak God, on the other hand, is suited to people who feel the goodness within themselves.[77] It is for people who, for one reason or another, and probably since childhood, have little fear that evil (or the

---

76 *This makes it hard to use standard prayerbooks, especially Jewish ones, which are satu-rated with the most extravagant glorification of "Our Lord, God, King of Universe" you can imagine. To read this, or the Qur'an, and think to yourself "actually, this is a weak God made glorious by the praise" takes concentration. One of the advantages of prayer that draws from the New Testament is that praise of God per se is diluted, sublimated, into praise of Jesus, who cuts a figure more powerful, in a way, than God, for being less powerful than God. Cf. EXPLANATIONS 12. The danger run, of course, is idolatry. Cf. RE-FLECTIONS 13.*

77 *This is not quite the same as "feeling good" about yourself.*

devil) could overwhelm them at any moment, who do not believe that they presently need—or soon will need—forgiveness of a large sort, and who think that good could prevail if they just put their minds to it, or if *we* did. They may be wrong of course. And they may be in need of forgiveness rather more often than they know. But the criticism some would level against them—namely, that in the face of large evil ("a Hitler" for example) they would lack the passion to resist or the confidence to win, because they had no strong God on their side—is not accurate. The path of non-violence is born of quiet confidence, confidence not in the thunder-like power of a God who will smash the evil-doer, but in the rain-like power of unaccountable human goodness to soften the hardest hearts.[78]

As I discuss in REFLECTIONS 7 and in ARGUMENTS 20 and 21, the theology of theopraxy is not for everyone. For its propagation it cannot turn to fear, but must rely on the moral example of its subscribers and on the attractiveness of the ideas you find in these pages.

---

78 *And then too, violence, when necessary, needs no kind of faith, strong or weak, in any kind of God, strong or weak, to justify it or cause it. Self-defense is reason and motivation enough.*

17 : Five wise sayings

It is our choice of good or evil that determines our character, not our opinion about good or evil.

—Aristotle, Nicomachean Ethics

Without virtue, God is a mere name.

—Plotinus, Enneads, II, 9 (33), 15, 39

If anyone were to show me that apartheid is Biblical or Christian, I would burn my Bible and cease to be Christian.

—Archbishop Desmond Tutu, 1984.[78]

Who is wise?
He who learns from all men.
Who is mighty?
He who controls his passions.
Who is rich?
He who rejoices in his portion.
Who is honored?
He who honors others.

—Ben Zoma[79]

Who shall do the good? And when?
"If not me, then who?" answered Rabbi Hillel,
"And if not now, then when?"

WE REALIZE that what is an existential question for us is an existence question for God. God did not give us freedom on any simple, one-way understanding of "give," i.e., God to us, done! Rather, we realize, freedom—our freedom—is prerequisite to God's existence. God must be chosen. Once we understand this, God gives us freedom redoubled.

---

78 *Cited in John Hick (1989, p. 67).*

79 *Ben Zoma,* Pirkei Avot *("The Sayings of the Fathers"), 4:1. Also from Pirkeh Avot: "Good deeds are better than wise sayings."*

18 : Ludwig Feuerbach:
God as projection

The argument that God is a *projection* of human virtues onto and into the universe—making God, in a sense, a creation of human beings—was common among European intellectuals of the 19th century.[81] It was a view most fully worked out and most forcefully propounded, however, by the German philosopher Ludwig Feuerbach. "Only from man," he wrote, "does God derive all his determinations; God *is* what man *desires* to be; namely, his own essence and goal, imagined as an actual being."[82]

This sounds like the theology of theopraxy. But it is not.

For Feuerbach, the idea that God was a projection was both a liberation and a disappointment. The liberation was from the church of his day, whose power to define and impose moral behavior in God's name was already fatally weakened. The disappointment is harder to locate and more interesting to ponder. It can be seen in the very choice of metaphor: "projection." After all, compared to existing as an energic, agentic, autonomous and intelligent *being*, existing as a *projection* could only mean existing passively, as a mere projection, as a shadow in Plato's cave, a chimera, a memory, or a desire...in short, an illusion without self-determination. Compared to God of the Bible—the One who put the sun and moon in the sky, the One who vanquishes armies with a blink, the One who "giveth life and taketh it away"—a God that is a human projection is as good as non-existent.[83]

Of course, to think poorly of human projections, to call them "mere" or illusory, is to betray a rather low opinion of humanity *qua* humanity at the outset, not to mention a lack of understanding of the depth of the concept of information. (This Feuerbach could not possibly have had, as it is a modern idea.) In the truly humanist view, anyway, humanity is anything but pathetic—not at the outset, and not ever. Humans

---

81 *Susan Neiman (2002, p. 214).*

82 *Ludwig Feuerbach (1986 [1843]), Part II: "Critique of Hegel," Section 29. Feuerbach's projection theory would find a prominent place again in Sigmund Freud's 1927 account of religion,* The Future of an Illusion. *To see Buber's I-Thou schema prefigured in Feuerbach, see Part III: "Principles of the New Philosophy," Section 41.*

83 *Of course, if God projects "God"—with writing on the wall, in pillars of fire, in visions of angels—that's fine. But if a human is the projector, "God help us."*

are wondrous beings, and although many of our projections are indeed flimsy and mistaken, many are not. Laws rule. Chess is real. The tears we shed at movies are not false.

Indeed, the phenomenon of movies is especially instructive given how close-to-literally *projection* is involved. While the images on the screen are physically diaphanous in the extreme—mere patterns of colored light—the coordinated skills and painstakingly developed technologies that put those images on the screen are very real, and very much a marvel. To call a movie merely a projection of light on a screen and therefore not real, is to see only the last stage of what is actually a very real process of *production*. It is also to overlook the value and reality of *patterns* of behaviors, of gestures, of words, of images, light, sound...action.[84]

The theology of theopraxy asserts that God, similarly, is no mere human projection but a great human production. There is a world of difference between the two formulations.

BEFORE FEUERBACH, Hegel, his teacher, had made his own arguments about what I want to call not the projection, but the *production* of God. It was Feuerbach who reduced "production" to "projection." For Hegel, God comes into being (as Absolute Spirit) by a lengthy succession of *aufhebungen*, meaning "upliftings" or transcendences, in the course of natural and human history. Absolute Spirit was no mere projection, no mere pipe dream or imagined thing, but a non-material entity, vast and subtle, produced by historical events and then becoming, itself, instrumental in shaping—producing—other events. Absolute Spirit—or God—struggles to realize itself ("himself") in life: creat*ed*, creat*ing*, and perdurable, both responsible for and growing with human civilization. *"Ohne Welt ist Gott nicht Gott,"* he wrote. ("Without the world, God is not God.")[85] With his theory of God as a projection, Feuerbach was subjectivizing,

---

84 *On God as a pattern, as a "configurational entity," see* EXPLANATIONS 4.

85 *G. W. F. Hegel (1966 [1876], p. 148). This is not the only way to read Hegel's theology. In* Wissenschaft der Logik *more than* Die Phänomenologie des Geistes, *Hegel posits divine Being as eternal in essence and pregnant with potential, realizing itself progressively through historical time to appear, ultimately, as the phenomenon of human being. On this rendering, there is a unity between human Being and divine or Absolute Being, the former being a manifestation of the latter and yet the latter depending for* full *realization on the former. But God's "full realization dependency" on human being, to my mind puts humankind in a productive role at least half the time, as it were, and more so if we deny to God (or Absolute Spirit) priority as "Ground of Being" or "Potential" and use instead the model of evolutionary emergence for God in actuality. For guidance in understanding Hegel here, I have depended on Daniel Jamros (1994).*

indeed overturning, what Hegel thought quite real. Feuerbach's was an atheology, Hegel's a theology.[86]

The theology of theopraxy and Hegelian philosophy agree in this much: (1) that God's very existence is bound up with intelligent and conscienced human life, and (2) that the relationship is that of mutual dependency. Our theology, however, does not see God or Absolute Spirit, either created or creating, as a superior entity located somewhere (or everywhere) in some other dimension. It offers no World Soul hovering over humanity like the breath of a crowd on a winter morning. Although stimulated by speech and text and the witnessing of exemplary behavior, in the theology of theopraxy the idea of God occurs to, and in, individual human beings, and becomes actualized *as* God only in their actions. Everyday behaviors that preserve, honor, and promote life in everyday space *are* God's form and substance, in full, each time. No oversoul is required, and no "under-soul" either, no "source," "beginning," or "ground."

---

86 *Hegel's theology, both through Feuerbach and directly, was to have a strong influence on Jean-Paul Sartre and Pierre Teilhard de Chardin, and through the latter (mixed with Buddhism) upon many New Age religions and spiritual movements in the present day. Tracing these influences is beyond the scope of this book.*

19 : From Feuerbach to Buber

PRESENTING FEUERBACH to an English audience in 1855, Marianne Evans (soon to write as George Eliot) argued that the traditional form given to "the love of God" has the unfortunate effect of setting God *between* man and man. It had come to the point, she wrote, that God

> *...instead of sharing and aiding our human sympathies, is directly in collision with them;... instead of strengthening the bond between man and man by encouraging the sense that they are both alike the objects of His love and care, thrusts Himself between them and forbids them to feel for each other except as they have relation to Him.* [87]

More to be trusted, Evans went on, is the love between people that takes place without reliance on divine inspiration or divine intermediation. Those who show love, sympathy, courage, and fairness do not need God, and they do not need religion. Practice these virtues and you somehow already "have" God, or, if not God "himself," then what God wants. Following Feuerbach's lead, Evans was taking Reformation arguments to the gates of Protestantism itself: not only did Church dogma and priestly behavior get in God's way, *but so does God* (or at least, the God of Protestant Christianity in her day). Nietzsche was to agree.

SOME FIFTY years later, the German-Jewish philosopher Martin Buber, who was a student of Feuerbach's and a scholar of Hegel, wrestled with the same thought. Is the Judeo-Christian God a human projection, and a counterproductive one at that? This could not be! In his seminal work, *I and Thou* (cf. also ARGUMENTS 2), Buber offers an alternative:

God is the eternal *Thou*, the Ur-Thou as it were, who looks at us from all people, creatures, and things we treat as having subjectivities and interests of their own. Deeper than sympathy and prerequisite to love, the *I-Thou* outlook betokens *respect*—respect borne not out of fear but out of recognition of the equality of the other's being to our own. This is why, for Buber, God should never be theorized as a (or the) generalized *It*, i.e., as some impersonal "system of forces" that created the world, or

---

87 *Alan Jacobs (2000). A view similar to Feuerbach's is propounded by the British radical Christian theologian Don Cupitt for whom "God is the sum of our values, representing to us their ideal unity, their claims upon us and their creative power" (1988, p. 122). In later books, Cupitt's view turns more Taoist/Tillichian. There God becomes a sort of Fountain of Being.*

as Nature. This would be deism. To regard God as in any way an *It*—i.e., without his own subjectivity—is to miss encountering him. To regard God as having instrumental value to us (say, in enforcing obedience to moral rules, or providing ultimate justice) is also to miss encountering him. Although God can be spoken *of* in the abstract, God is not God until God is spoken *to* in the depths and fullness of another creature's *being* being addressed in, grammatically, 'the second person,' which is to say, as "you" or "thou" (German: *du*). For Buber, God is the eternal *Thou* behind all immediate *Thou*-s.

Indeed, God is the entity with whom *only I-Thou* relations can be had, and *in* whom, in some sense, all earthly *I-Thou* relations take place. This is how Buber puts it:

> *Extended, the lines of relationships intersect in the eternal Thou. Every single Thou is a glimpse of that. Through every single Thou the basic word addresses the eternal Thou. The mediatorship of the (eternal) Thou of all beings accounts for the fullness of our relationships to them—and for the lack of fulfillment. The innate Thou is actualized each time without being perfected. It attains perfection solely in the immediate relationship to the Thou that, in accordance with its nature, cannot become an It. ...Men have addressed their eternal Thou by many names...* [88]

Buber takes theism about as far from deism as it can get. For Buber, God is radically personal. God is experienced in authentic relation with other sentient beings and not in general prayer or in contemplation of the design of the world. And yet, by positing God as the generalized or absolute *Thou*, Buber retains an element of Platonism still. Like the Form of the Good, God—whole and One—waits in eternity. He waits for us to approach and *encounter* him through ethical, compassionate, desireful relations to others. Most actual human relationships only dimly approximate an encounter with God, and few can deliver it "full strength" for any length of time. Nonetheless, there is no other way.

Here the theology of theopraxy has a worry. For if human relationships can deliver, as it were, an encounter with God, then they can come to be seen as a means for having that experience. The *I-Thou* relation itself then becomes an *It*, which is related to "in an *I-It* way." And this has to weaken Buber's program. [89]

Cast in Buberian terms, the theology of theopraxy would offer this instead: God is produced in and by the *I-Thou* relation itself, with both

---

88 *Martin Buber (1970, p. 123). Kaufman translates* Thou *as* You *throughout. I prefer "Thou."*

parties chemically necessary for the reaction to take place.[90] When being in an *I-Thou* relationship with another creature becomes a doing, a concatenation of actions and interactions that make the relationship live and life-promoting, it produces God; it is God. The *I-Thou* relationship must express itself in words and deeds, it cannot be a theory or a feeling alone, and it cannot be thought of as a means to an end. This is why I say that humans *produce* God in their relationships *with* the world and each other, not just *project* God *onto* the world.[91]

This is not the conclusion that Buber draws from his own schema. He did not set aside his belief in a transcendent, autonomous, Creator-God, approachable "in person" in persons. Buber had found a way to weave God into human social life and yet leave God above and beyond that. For Buber, *I-Thou* relationships are like windows onto God—windows that allow participants in, but not observers of, the relationship sightings of God's visage, God's radiance, God's throne (metaphorically, of course). Nevertheless, the idea that people *produce* God by how they act in relation to one other and to other creatures is, I believe, inherent in the assertions of *I and Thou*, a book that was both a critique of Feuerbach's "projection a-theology" and a concession to it. Perhaps this is why Buber remains such an attractive figure in modern religious debate, beloved by Christian "God is love" theologians, and by existentialists, religious humanists, Unitarians, and Reform and secular Jewish thinkers alike.[92]

---

89 *In Zen Buddhism, acolytes are constantly advised not to strive for enlightenment, because the very striving for enlightenment gets in the way of achieving it. In a similar fashion one might advise a Buber follower: if you want to meet God in an I-Thou relation, forget about meeting God. Buber might agree, pointing out that approaching the I-Thou relation pragmatically, as an -It, would automatically reduce the other party, and oneself, to an -It, and thus destroy the very possibility of an I-Thou relation forming, or continuing.*

90 *Hegel thought Geist was produced in this way too. See Note 5.*

91 *Wrote Freud: Religious beliefs are nothing more than "illusions, fulfillments of the oldest, strongest, and most insistent wishes of humankind" (1961 [1927], p. 30). The theology of theopraxy argues that this does not make God merely human, the "universal obsessional neurosis of humanity" (ibid.). And nor does it make humans ipso facto divine. Why? Because, again, God is neither the "I" nor the "Thou" in a relation but the very I-Thou relation itself, wherever and whenever it appears and supports life.*

92 *For example, in a passage from* The New Being *(1955) which both identifies God with love and goes further, Paul Tillich writes:*

"'He who abides in love abides in God, and God abides in him' (I John 4:16). God's abiding in us, making us His dwelling place, is the same thing as our abiding in love, as our having love as the sphere of our habitation. God and love are not two realities; they are one. God's Being is the being of love and God's infinite power of Being is the infinite ›

IT WILL be difficult for orthodox believers of any tradition to accept that people produce God by their relationships and their actions. But once they understand that the assertion intends no blasphemy there is room for tolerance. The theology of theopraxy is happy to be cast as a peculiar religious philosophy that helps set up the conditions under which the Creator-God of the great monotheistic religions could reasonably be thought to exist and act. A devout (but open-minded) believer could say to a subscriber to theopraxy: "Look, if you *want* to believe that man produces God, go ahead. You'd be wrong. But God won't mind, just so long as you do His will." And the subscriber to theopraxy could say to the orthodox believer in return: "Look, if you *want* to believe that God created the universe from nothing, sees all, does all, metes out justice, hears prayer, speaks to prophets and/or manifested himself in Jesus, go ahead. Just do good." Anyone who observed the everyday actions of an exemplary theopractitioner would see only a dignified, humane, courageous, and loving human being who might be of *any*, or no, standard religious persuasion.

Truth is, however, and as I have said a few times now, it remains to be seen whether the theology outlined in this book can yield a kind of faith less prone to co-option and corruption than traditional faiths have been, and a way of life in this scientific age more likely to preserve, honor, and promote all life. I think it can. And I think that the God of Abraham, should he exist as described, would be pleased if I were right.

< *power of love. Therefore, he who professes devotion to God may abide in God if he abides in love, or he may not abide in God if he does not abide in love. And he who does not speak of God may abide in Him if he is abiding in love. And since the manifestation of God as love is His manifestation in Jesus the Christ, Jesus can say that many of those who do not know Him, belong to Him, and that many of those who confess their allegiance to Him do not belong to Him. The criterion, the only ultimate criterion, is love. For God is love, and the divine love is triumphantly manifest in Christ the Crucified."*

This in similar vein from Rabbi Harold Kushner (1992):

"God is found in the incredible resiliency of the human soul, in our willingness to love though we understand how vulnerable love makes us, in our determination to go on affirming the value of life even when events in the world would seem to teach us that life is cheap."

20 : God as production

MANY ACTS of production are aimed at creating larger, longer-term, or more complex goods than we could produce by ourselves: a factory, a building, a business, a movie, a research paper. We often call these goods *projects*. So, by analogy, we might ask, is God (according to the theology of theopraxy) a human project the way, say, the elimination of global poverty is a human project, or the construction of a trans-Atlantic tunnel is a human project? In other words, is God the result of a social, collective effort? Will we have "produced God" only when God's Kingdom is realized?

It would seem that if subscribers to the theology of theopraxy are willing to say that human beings produce God at all, they should be willing to say that producing God is a collective project—the greatest project of all. But they are not, this for reasons that have wider implications.

There are problems with construing God as a social project. Chief among them is the problem of free-riding. When God (or "his" Kingdom) is seen as a collective effort, free-riding becomes a major temptation. People begin to let *others* do the work (pray, be devout, do good deeds) while slacking off themselves. Free-riding is not a problem for the theology of theopraxy alone, of course. It can readily be found operating within traditional religious frameworks at both the family scale, where, typically, a grandfather's or mother's religiosity is felt to "cover" everyone else in the family, and at the larger social scales, where, typically, a charismatic leader-cum-holy-person is allowed (or is elected or is authorized by higher authority) to represent everyone else *to* God and to pray for them in both senses of the word "for."

The solution to this kind of free-riding, as Martin Luther saw, is to make communion-with-God a *personal* project. In this way, individual success or failure at communicating with God would have clearly *personal* consequences. No longer would a caste of priests represent ordinary people to God in return for material support. Rather, how fate shone upon an individual would depend on his or her relationship to God, a relationship that was in *their* hands, and of course God's, to establish and maintain.

This was progress. Unfortunately, Luther's strategy, by its very logic, weakens feelings of co-fatedness or mutual dependency, and thus reduces enthusiasm for projects that really do require everyone to pull together in order for anyone to succeed. After all, if the only relationship that counts is the relationship between an individual and God, why not "go it alone"? Partial, failed, and even dangerous solutions to this problem have been many—for example, propounding that it is God's will that you cooperate with others.[93] But the problem remains: how can group spirit be fostered while championing an entirely private relationship between each individual and God?[94]

If it ought not to be done by seeing God as a common project or by saying God (as traditionally conceived) wants us to work together, what remains? This: we could realize that undertaking certain real, earthly, projects—eliminating poverty, say, or restoring a woodland, or going to Mars—can give rise to God over and over again if, and as, working on these projects lengthens and enriches individual lives and/or reduces involuntary suffering, both as they are done and as a consequence of having done them. Here we produce God without making *God* the project or a

---

93 *This solution takes more doctrine and more organization. And so it played out historically. Keeping communities together became the job description of the new priestly class: namely the new Protestant prayer-leader, preacher, minister. For example, absent the Catholic ritual of confession, one of the methods used was to inculcate in the flock a sort of mutual policing: a constant concern for one's neighbor's salvation, this out of love for them and not (ostensibly) on account of any worry about them "letting down the team." Thus do evangelical Protestants to this day exhort each other to seek Jesus more fervently; thus do they (say they) feel sorrow rather than anger at another's spiritual laziness or moral backsliding. In short, Luther's "priesthood of believers" is kept together by a glue that has little to do with an obligation to contribute to a single holy project.*

In Judaism, where a personal relationship to God is also encouraged and rabbis are seen not as people's representatives to God but as prayer-leaders and scholars, the presence of ten Jewish men over thirteen years of age—a minyan—*is nonetheless required for certain religious ceremonies to proceed. This simple rule underwrites the continuing importance of communality in addressing God, and the idea of seeking God in the fact and nature of human community.*

In Hasidic Judaism, echoing the story of Sodom and Gommorah, there is this appealing belief: that at all times there has to be a minimum of thirty-six good people living in the world in order for it to be saved from destruction (by God). The catch: no one knows who these thirty-six good people are; including the good people themselves. How can you free-ride if you might be one of these people, the one who would make the count thirty-five if you did not live up to your obligations?

94 *Take religious war, for example, or any kind of war in which God is invoked. In war, as in competitive team sports and business, intense cooperation within the group is required with near zero-tolerance for free-riding. How, then, are we to link the idea of dedication to a common social cause to the notion of a personal "account" with God? Within the traditional religious world-view, it can be done only one way: by asserting that God himself wants victory or success to go to the believer's side and will reward self-sacrifice to the cause in proportion to the heroism of the sacrifice, if not in this world, then in the next. The logic of jihad is no different. I do not need to spell out its unfortunate consequences.*

projection, *and* without claiming that God will reward us (individually) for showing solidarity.

Whether we act together or act alone, God is the good we do contribution by contribution. Cooperation simply amplifies the good we can do individually.

To be sure, enjoying the fruits of others' labors is one of the most rewarding experiences of living in community, as is being the recipient of generosity or being witness to another person's unforced decency. These are free-rides of a sort, where the element of *quid pro quo* is suppressed. One simply receives. With maturity, however, the desire to provide the same experiences for others starts to exert itself, the desire to "give back," to add some of one's own labor to the tide of good happenings, to help a stranger just because. One acts to bring God about oneself.

IN *Being and Nothingness*, Jean-Paul Sartre elaborated the distinction between two modes of being: being-*for-itself,* and being-*in-itself.* Humans (and perhaps some higher animals), he said, exemplify being-for-itself. They "look out for themselves" and they look out for favored others. They want things. They have projects. They know they are alive and they fear they will die. Inanimate objects and most lower forms of life, on the other hand, just *are*. They have no ambitions; they offer no justifications; they are content in their own existence no matter how "long" or "short" or "rich" or "poor" that existence might seem to us. Incapable of deception, they exist authentically "in themselves." The physical universe exists in just this way, and so, we must think, does God, who lacks nothing, who is his own foundation, who just *is*. Tragically, quixotically, being-in-itself is what humans long to partake in too, says Sartre, but cannot:

> *(T)he ideal of a consciousness that would be the foundation of its own being-in-itself by the pure consciousness it would have of itself...is the ideal which can be called God. Thus the best way to conceive of the fundamental project of human reality is to say that man is the being whose project is to be God. Whatever may be the myths and rites of the religion considered, God is first "sensible to the heart" of man as the One who identifies and defines him [i.e., man] as His ultimate and fundamental project.* [95]

Humankind's tragic project, says Sartre, is to *be* God, just as it is God's

---

95 *Jean-Paul Sartre (1956) excerpted in Guignon and Pereboom (1995, p. 336). My capitalization and italicization for emphasis. If God is free, Sartre also said, then humans cannot be. Since man is free, then God cannot be, and therefore cannot be God. This argument is easy to rebut in our terms. See ARGUMENTS 7.*

project, we tragically think, to identify and show us what it means to be divinely human. Both projects are doomed, for we cannot be God, and God, if he is, *just* is.

Now, some might say: "How could anything said about God by so well-known an anti-theist as Sartre be anything but flawed, and perhaps deliberately so?" The theology of theopraxy is sympathetic to Sartre. But it disagrees with him on one crucial point. To wit: Man's project, properly, is not to *be* God but to *bring God into being* over and over again by their free moral actions, and so to continue creating/evolving God in human history. For God is humanity-creating as well as humanity-created, where, by "humanity," I mean not human beings as a species, but the opposite of "*in*humanity." God's project, to use Sartre's phrase, is not to produce humankind but to produce *kind humans*—actual ones, just as our project is not to *be* God but to give God life in ours. And there's nothing tragic or doomed about either project.[96]

---

[96] *Two notes: Abraham Joshua Heschel (1976) argued that God calls to humanity through his prophets. It is God who beseeches us to come to him, to obey his laws, and so forth. Heschel privileges the ancient search by God for human beings (God's calling to Adam in the Garden of Eden, waylaying Moses, addressing Samuel) over the modern search by human beings for God (in order to ask for blessings and favors). Which way does the search really go? In the metaphorics of the theology of theopraxy one can say it goes both ways. God and human beings find each other, in acts of co-creation, co-evolution. God is humanity-creating just as humanity is God-creating. Humanity, one might say, is "theogenic."*

A second note: The Book of Genesis gives two rather different accounts of the temporal order in which Adam and Eve were created relative to the rest of nature. On the first account (Genesis 1:24-27) humans follow mammals (who follow birds and fish) implicitly as improvements upon mammals. How do we know they are "improvements"? Because Adam and Eve, unlike the animals, are created "in God's image" and given dominion over animals the way God has dominion over them (and everything else). On the second account, Genesis 2:4-8, Adam is formed from dust—i.e., from the bare physical elements—and only later are plants and animals introduced for Adam's (and later Eve's) sustenance. Our theology leans toward the first account because it is closer to the modern evolutionary story—almost uncannily so—and because it supports the notion that God is who/what made humans humane, meaning better-than-animals, meaning self-aware, capable of guilt, foresight, and logos. God is humanizing. Now add back the historical fact that human beings long ago dreamed up Genesis and we have this: that God is humanizing and humans sacralizing; God is ethicogenic, and humans theogenic." (See also EXPLANATIONS I.)

21 : Irreligious goodness

WHILE THE atheist can point to the millions of people around the world who do not believe in God—much less the Biblical God—and are nonetheless good citizens, honest businessmen, and loving family members, the enthusiastic believer must wonder how this is possible. It ought not to be. If God (or Allah) does not sustain and develop these people's morality, then who or what does? The believer must conclude either that God loves and takes care of all good people, regardless of their faith, religiosity, or actual religion, or that the word of God has filtered through to them by other means (for example, through laws and customs, literature, movies, and other cultural products from which *direct* reference to God might have been stripped but in which the word of God is heard nonetheless).

Both of these options represent a liberal position. Christian and Muslim fundamentalists have a harder time of it. They must wonder why atheists, agnostics, and followers of other religions are not precluded—*by God*—from success and happiness in this life simply for not believing in God the right way.[97]

Our theology, for its part, need not belabor an answer as to how irreligious, non-believing people can be as moral and happy as religious ones, if not more so. It can argue that many belief systems deemed "not really religions" by Biblical/Qur'anic standards, actually *are* religions and have functionally equivalent theologies. Confucianism, for example, has no God, but rather The Way of Heaven as its transcendent moral principle. The Way of Heaven is not a Being or a Creator, and yet its precepts are instantly recognizable as ones endorsed by God. Taoism similarly speaks of The Way, The Way of Tao. And while Buddhism has Brahman as the supreme spirit, it is rather casual about who and how many gods there really are (their multiplicity being a remnant of ancient Hinduism), and about which god is responsible for what. Buddhism prefers to focus attention on the importance of "right" conduct, speech, living, and thought, at the individual level. According to the theology of theopraxy,

---

97 *Of course, in the face of unbelievers' success and happiness, many resentful believers draw comfort from asserting that the infidels will get their comeuppance in the next life. I omit mention of Jewish fundamentalists not because there aren't any, but because it is not an article of Jewish Orthodoxy that God disfavors non-Jews or unbelievers. If people are good people, that's good enough. God loves them too.*

God is alive and well in all these formulations insofar as they lead people to actions—to "ways"—that preserve and promote all life.[98] Ditto most secular moral philosophy, from Plato to Kant and beyond.

In the West, a great deal of religious law, based at one time on mystical encounters with God and associated with acts of moral courage in God's name, has made its way into secular law. (I am thinking here of Abraham, on the advice of an angel, drawing back from murdering his son Isaac, of Moses at Sinai bringing down the tablets of the Law not once but twice, "outlawing" stealing, adultery, lying, etc., of Jesus forgiving his persecutors. There are many other examples.) Across the span of time delineated in the Hebrew Bible, a dozen kingdoms came and went that instituted religious law as civil law with greater or lesser success. By the fourth century C.E. and the Christianization of Constantine, Hebraic law, Christian salvifics, Greek philosophy, and Roman statecraft had fused into a single code, which was itself to evolve in European history into modern times. This is why such ideals as universal human dignity, the rule of law, the rights of conscience and the pursuit of happiness, essential to both the American Declaration of Independence and the American Constitution, can so easily be traced back to Judaic law.[99]

Indeed, so thorough has been the emulsification of religious insight into the body of civil and criminal law, that the modern atheist can claim that *being good* is entirely a secular matter and something self-evidently to be desired. In the modern, post-Enlightenment state, or "civil society," being-good is ninety-nine percent achieved simply by living within the law, being polite, and minding your own business. The remaining one

---

98 *Rodney Stark (2003) makes a similar point. The supernatural component of a religion, Stark shows, is not always where a society's moral code is located. In many, the gods have nothing to do with the (human) good. The move from many gods to one God, and from gods that care not much to a God that cares a great deal how we behave, was the innovation of the ancient Israelites. Stark does not argue as I do, however, that God is actually located wherever that moral code is acted upon. In the theology of theopraxy, the transition from gods-not-caring-about-the-good-no-matter-what-happens to God-being-the-good-as-it-happens is complete. Relative to this, Western religions still retain elements of paganism. As I have said in various ways throughout this book, the seeing of apparitions, the witnessing of supernatural events, the having of experiences of oneness with the universe or of overwhelming awe and humility at the size, creativity, destructiveness, implacability of the universe...experiences which have long been interpreted as essential for religious faith, are all "looking for God in all the wrong places." They are category mistakes, as philosophers like to say. For God is in your hands right now, rather more like a butterfly than the starry sky.*

99 *See Milton R. Konvitz (1978). The founders were highly conversant with the Old Testament.*

percent is achieved through the exercise of secular virtues like patience and hospitality, for which one should just read Aristotle. Promises and threats by a supernatural entity like God are not needed, and possibly never were.

The theology of theopraxy agrees: promises and threats by God or gods are not necessary. But there are a number of weaknesses in the atheist's view, nonetheless.

First, it is rather uncharitable. It is rather like calling one's teachers at high school *dummies,* now that one is a sophomore in college.

Second, atheists tend to underestimate the amount of religious sentiment that remains in their own hearts (let alone in the law), deposited there in geological layers by parents, teachers, literature, and popular culture long before they had a choice in the matter. At the same time, they overestimate how literally, how naively, most self-described believers believe in God, which is not very literally or naively at all.

But third, and saddest of all, is how atheists overlook the truth right under their noses, which is that God is the good *they* do too. If the project of the Enlightenment was to disengage morality from God, the hope of theopraxy is to weld them together again: no God without morality; no morality without God. This is because God (on any model) need not be invoked or believed *in* in order for God (as "he" really is) to be present.[100] Nevertheless, once God *is* mentioned in the context of doing good, and on the understanding of God that our theology tries to provide, certain gates open. These gates may not open onto visions of Heaven or of the Almighty radiant upon his throne, but one does suddenly feel connected, in reverence, to the hundred-thousand-year-long *quest* to distinguish life-perpetuating and life-ennobling behaviors from life-destructive and life-demeaning ones, to codify and perpetuate the former and forestall the latter in a world becoming ever more complex, and to *make* life meaningful, not just find it so, in acts of scientific and artistic imagination, in deeds of justice, love, generosity, and so forth, which are just those acts that perpetuate and ennoble all life. These acts become more than natural, more than reasonable, more than good in the everyday sense. They become holy.

No individual is obliged to adopt this quest as their own, of course. Nor is anyone who adopts them obliged to defer to historical notions of divinity, or theopraxy's, in order to do so. Religions are not cast in stone. They change and can be changed.[101] Their spirit has many forms. They

---

100 *This runs directly counter to Pauline Christianity. See for example Paul's Epistle to the Hebrews 11:6.*

can be accepted in part or in full.

No, the question is not "can we do without God as conveyed by this or that religion?"—clearly we can—but another: "can we do without God?" The atheist needs to explain why people commit themselves to supererogatory (beyond-the-required) quests like the ones I have listed, and why that commitment so often expresses itself, and perpetuates itself, through religious language, religious life, and religious beliefs.

The answer, I think, is not that obvious. Others have written about religion from an evolutionary point of view, the basic argument being that religion as an *institution*, like art or education, evolved for certain reasons: to keep populations socially structured, to make people patient in the hope of eventual justice, to persuade kings to accept limits on their power, and so on. This evolutionary perspective is a good one as far as it goes: it argues backwards from results. At the operational, day-to-day level, however, another perspective on the question "why God? why religion?" is called for. Here, clearly, the demands we place on each other are one source of goodness (hence religion's long insistence on promise-keeping and on "do unto others..."), but a certain emotion of which we are all capable, I suggest, is the other source of goodness—the emotion

---

101 *John Shelby Spong (2004) is especially eloquent on this score:*

"Christianity has changed throughout history dramatically. There was a time when the Pope was married, when the church taught that to invest money for interest was a sin, when slavery was allowed, and when critical thinkers were burned at the stake. The Church did not develop the doctrine of the Incarnation until the fourth century and the doctrine of the Holy Trinity was not fully developed until the fifth century. We once taught that Adam and Eve were real people, that Moses wrote the Torah and that David wrote the psalms. None of these ideas still has credibility in the great academies of Christian learning.

"We now know that the Virgin Birth entered the Christian faith in the 9th decade of the Christian era, that neither Paul nor Mark had ever heard of it. All of this leads me to assert that Christianity is not a fixed system that was born at the first Pentecost and might die in the 21st century. Christianity is a way people journey into the mystery of God. It is a process not unlike the ocean; it never changes its substance but it ever changes its form. People who want to defend or protect Christianity have always defined it in such a way as to make an idol out of their definition.

"An idol always dies. A channel through which the living God is ever revealed never does. Christianity may be transformed but it will not die. Its forms, its creeds, its doctrines, its dogmas, all of which are the products of human creativity, are always mortal. There is no ultimate unchanging truth that anyone possesses. There is only subjective experience to which people apply explanatory words.

"So enter the stream of history that has been called Christianity and allow it to carry you in ways you cannot imagine into the mystery of God, but don't expect the forms of Christianity, developed in human history, to be immortal."

of *gratitude*. This is worth discussing in more detail. Gratitude may be where religion, as the binding of oneself to God, begins (leaving open exactly what "God" means).[102]

---

102 *This is as good a place as any to report that several readers of this book while in manuscript remarked upon the similarity of its ideas to those of Emanuel Levinas, especially Levinas' notions of the "passing of God" in human acts of goodness, the idea of "divinity's trace" being left in human "inventions" such as justice, the importance of the emotion of gratitude (which I am about to discuss), and, with Buber, the locus of God's "face" in face-to-face encounters. This may well be. I have at various times tried to read Levinas and have, in my own estimation, failed. This is why I neither summarize Levinas in the main text nor quote him with any confidence. Yes, I have seen "my" ideas whirl by in Levinas, dressed in metaphors of disturbing loveliness. But they always disappear into the crowd before I can call out to them...only to reappear sentences or pages later in a new garb, and with new qualifications that make me doubt I saw them in the first place. I congratulate those who interpret Levinas for non-specialists, like Oona Ajzenstat (2001) and Alain Finkielkraut (1997).*

From my reading of Levinas first- and second-hand, however, I gleaned this: For Levinas, and consistent with Lurianic Kabbalah, God's uncanniness is absolute, majestic, irreversible. God's withdrawn-ness from the world is complete (cf. REFLECTIONS 18): so complete that even saying "God" is idolatrous, so complete that the only evidence we have of divinity is not any presence but our own (moral) actions, which again and again trace out—which "are"—his ever-vanishing, always-being-washed-away contour. (Cf. REFLECTIONS 21 on Exodus 33, one of Levinas' favorite passages too). I concur with Levinas's conclusion (if I have it right), but not with his lead-up to it or his "explanation." My own view is opposite and complementary to Levinas', with all due respect to his status as one of the twentieth century's great philosophers. It is also far more mundane. The uncanniness of God's presence, in my view, lies precisely in God's extraordinary availability, God's nearness, God's unremarkability. God is all around, plain as day. Indeed, when God is every act of decency, kindness, courage, and creativity, not "his" absence but "his" taken-for-grantedness is the problem, not "his" gone-ness but "his" forgottenness. The tragedy is that it often takes a slide into darkness to miss God's light.

22 : Gratitude

WHILE THE will to *live on* is built into every animal, just as the capacity to feel fear and relief is built in too, only human beings, it seems, have the capacity to feel gratitude for the fact of being alive. What brings on this feeling?

It arises all but automatically after one has narrowly escaped death. It arises almost as automatically when good fortune strikes or when feeling extraordinarily healthy and confident. And it happens, if less elatedly, when one reflects on just a few of the myriad coincidences upon which one's life depends: one's parents' meeting just when they did, there being just the right amount of oxygen in the atmosphere for life, and so forth.

Now, gratitude is an interesting emotion in that it requires two objects: that for which one is grateful, and that *to* which (or *to* whom) one is grateful. Without a *for* and a *to*, gratitude is an undirected and incoherent emotion, a welled-up feeling in search of an origin and a point of application. Here monotheism steps in with remarkable efficiency, offering the most general object to be grateful *for*, namely *everything*, as well as the most general object to be grateful *to*, namely *God*. We are to be grateful to God for everything. The cognitive simplicity of this instruction, I submit, accounts in good part for the breadth of monotheism's appeal.[103]

The theology of theopraxy, however, asks for more—or rather, it asks for more detail. If some person or institution gives you help when you need it, you ought to thank *them*, not go over their heads as it were and thank God instead.

Consider: when "grace" is said before beginning a meal in a devout Christian household, or similarly, when a blessing is offered over the bread and wine in a devout Jewish household, or bismillah ("In the name of God...") is said in a Muslim one, the actual travail of the cook as well as the labor of the household's breadwinner are set aside. Instead, God is thanked directly. And thus is the humblest meal made miraculous, thus does it take on the structure of a gift.

But this practice, though well and good, does not remove the obliga-

---

103 *Unfortunately, gratitude's antipode, anger, has a similar structure: one is angry at X for Y. Now, let X = God and Y = everything, and you have a formula for the atheism felt by disillusioned romantics and victims of injustice, as well as "good reason" if not for doing evil, then for opting out of the moral life. This is another reason why it is better to be more precise in both praise and blame.*

tion to express gratitude to the people to whom gratitude is actually due for what they actually did: the people who picked the grapes, who prepared the meal, who polished the silver, who put the roof over our heads... people by the score, known and unknown to you, by whose ordinary and decent actions this meal comes to be at this table, this night.

Thus is God truly thanked.

23 : What difference
the theology of theopraxy?

America boasts the highest *per capita* church attendance of any country in the world. The majority of Americans, when asked, profess belief in God—"God" meaning anything from an abstract higher power to the Trinity or Allah.

Among them there are many people who are kindly disposed toward religious teachings and practice, who appreciate its aesthetics, and might well go to church, synagogue, or mosque quite regularly, but who have serious reservations nonetheless. They are apt to feel dissatisfied with literal or "true belief" in God as God is described in the Scriptures or Qur'an. They believe in God, but in a way that is unclear even to themselves. They are convinced that science provides more plausible explanations of things, better medicines, and sounder advice in general than religion does. They are convinced too that when it comes to crime and evil, the law of man as interpreted by the courts is a safer place to put their trust than the Law of God as interpreted by priests, preachers, mullahs, or rabbis. They worry that religious enthusiasm can lead to great harms, as history has shown, but they know that radical secularism/atheism is no guarantee of morality either. On the spectrum of faith, they find themselves roughly in the middle, slightly on the believing side of "agnostic." By affiliation, they might be Reconstructionist or Reform Jews, Unitarian Universalists, or Religious Humanists.[104] They might also be "regular" Protestants, Catholics, Jews, or Muslims, keeping their doubts to themselves and being observant for the sake of their children or parents. Or they might have

---

104 *See the on-line journal* Religious Humanism *at* www.americanhumanist.org/ hsfamily/rh. *A brief overview of the movement by Mason Olds at* www.humanistsof utah.org/1996/artapril96.htm, *claims John Dewey as its leading light. (Along the same lines, see also* The Society for Humanistic Judaism *[www.shj.org/] and* The Center for Cultural Judaism *[www.culturaljudaism.org]* I am not aware of an Islamic correlate.)

What distinguishes the theology of theopraxy from Religious Humanism? Religious Humanists are humanists who are emotionally fond of their religion's practices and aesthetics, but not of their religion's (or any's) theological claims. They are atheists "good without God," who uphold religious tradition out of sentiment or respect for the wisdom still contained in it (i.e., despite all the "God talk"). Subscribers to the theology of theopraxy, on the other hand, may or may not follow an observant religious life-style, but they believe that God really exists. They have the "strong faith in a weak God" this book tries to describe (ARGUMENTS 16). I bother to say this because Dewey might have agreed ›

no religious affiliation at all. According to surveys, people like this form roughly 14% of the world's population, and perhaps a much greater fraction if having theological reservations disqualifies one from being called an adherent to a named religion.[105] Bishop John Shelby Spong calls them "believers in exile" and counts himself among them.

Here is the radical question that comes from the perspective of the theology of theopraxy: might believers in exile be, or become, more ethical than either true believers or true atheists? And if this were the case, why might that be? Because of their generally-higher education levels and/or concomitantly higher incomes? Or might firm belief in an indeterminate-in-form but good God, together with the selective, less-than-convinced practice of religious ritual, be the combination that is most productive of ethical behavior?[106] Perhaps the common-sense moderation that prevents most people from becoming crusading fundamentalists on the one hand or scornful atheists on the other, is the same moderation that maximizes the production of *good*, and therefore of God.[107]

I AM writing in the main for those good people who find themselves unable to explain why they are neither true believers nor true skeptics, who

---

< *with our theology more. As Olds writes: "Dewey employed the word God to designate the process whereby the actual is transformed into the ideal, but his friend and colleague Corliss Lamont maintained that Dewey used the term to avoid offending the sensitivities of friends who were theists. However, the word ('God') caused such controversy that (Dewey) repented of having used it." The theology of theopraxy has no such qualms.*

105 *See* www.adherents.com/Religions_By_Adherents.html#Nonreligious

106 *Aristotle would surely endorse the proposition. One would like to cite the "Middle Way" of Buddhism, but that speaks of another dimension of moderation: the one lying between the extremes of asceticism and self-indulgence.*

107 *Take this as possible evidence: of the hundreds of individuals and families who hid, fed, and sheltered Jews from the Nazis in the 1930s and '40s—often for years at a time and at enormous risk to themselves—few were especially devout or church-going. Official statistics are hard to find, but see Gay Block and Malka Drucker (1992), Eva Fogelman (1994) and Sir Martin Gilbert (2003). It seems that most did what they did because they thought it was the right thing to do, or out of simple, direct compassion. Neither Oskar Schindler nor Raoul Wallenberg nor Chiune "Sempo" Sugihara, to name three well-known "righteous gentiles," were religious at all. (This is not to say there were not many devout religious rescuers, like the Ukrainian priest Father Emilian Kovch, who died at Majdanek concentration camp in Poland for his saving of hundreds of Jews. When nuns and priests were rescuers, however, it was usually on condition of conversion to Christianity. This was the case with Kovch.) These people did the "only decent thing." They did what they thought had to be done, "what anyone would do," safe in the knowledge that saving life was an unalloyed good.* >

are sure God exists, but equally sure that God does not exist like the Bible or Qur'an says God does, or like a long-gone Designer. What difference could it make to them to subscribe to the *theology* of theopraxy, which is, after all, a matter of the intellect?

If I might address such people as "you," dear reader, the difference the theology of theopraxy could make is this: relief to learn that your decency, generosity, courage, reasonableness, and ordinary care for others, enacted, *is God*—the real thing, the one and only God, who has been God all along. No longer need you feel incapable of *real* faith, or, for that matter, of *real* skepticism. No longer need you feel tentative about who or what or how God is. God is in your hands today just as He has always been in your hands and everyone else's. The God to whom the theology of theopraxy tries to open our minds is not some pale shadow of the God of true believers, however much they may say so. Nor is your God so overdrawn and contradictory a character that atheists can mock belief in "him." You know that God is not a static entity; you know that God becomes more excellent as we do, and, God-willing, continue to become.[108]

Rather than weak belief in an infinitely powerful and capricious God, you realize that, for the price of accepting a touch of personification, we can have strong belief in a loving and reasonable God: one who, because "he" *depends* on the best in us, *brings out* the best in us; one who, because "his" dignity depends on us, dignifies us; one who, because "his" maturation is our responsibility, makes us more responsible.

This is a God we can love.

You might hesitate to embrace completely the idea that God is the good we do. You may find it hard to accept that we *enact* God rather than just listen to "him" because your disbelief in the literal truth of Biblical portrayals of God has induced in you a skepticism about *all* truth claims about God. This is understandable. Perhaps you have been persuaded to disqualify yourself from any claim that "God is in your life" because you were unable, and remain unable, to commit fully to Christ or Halakha (Jewish law) or Shariah (Islamic law). There's also a chance that a college education has taught you to identify religion so completely with

---

< *Spend time with this literature and one is led to this thought: that strong belief in a "weak" or at least unknowable God who works only through free people may well describe the actual religious belief-state of the majority of decent human beings for the greater part of history.*

108 *Of course, believers today would say "not God, but our understanding of God changes." Most, however, are loathe to admit that current understandings will be superseded. See Jack Miles (1995), Karen Armstrong (1993), and Regis Debray (2004).*

untruth—with over-simplification, superstition, exploitation, and backwardness—that you are prevented from seeing the truth you are living now.[109]

And that truth is this: certain realities are *created* by humans, and not found under the microscope, at the end of a telescope, *or* in a divinely-written book given once and for all. *Music* for example, *mathematics, art, tennis, democracy,* even *the Sabbath*. Where are these things? What

---

109 *There are "hard scientists" who are orthodox believers, of course, and who seem to unite the sides I have described in a more striking way. But the way they pull off this trick more often than not is by pronouncing Nature's mysteries still so vast, and man's effort to unravel them so unlikely to succeed, that there is still a place for God in a quite traditional sense (e.g., as the personally addressable Creator of the universe, the all-knowing giver of freedom and dispenser of final justice). There are other scientists, indeed probably most, who follow some version of Whitehead and Hartshorne's "process view": the idea that the whirring universe as a whole, and God, are essentially one and the same thing. Theirs is an essentially pantheist (or panentheist) theology, which, I think, is quite incapable of offering a moral code even as it supports the virtues that flow from feelings of awe (e.g., respect, patience, modesty, and so on).*

Other scientists, and notably Albert Einstein, hold fast to God being the Creator of the universe in all its beauty, subtlety, and complexity, while denying the existence of a personal, addressible God or a God that cares one way or another about human ethical behavior. Ethics is man's business, physics God's. "My religiosity," said Einstein, "consists in a humble admiration of the infinitely superior spirit that reveals itself in the little that we, with our weak and transitory understanding, can comprehend of reality. Morality is of the highest importance—but for us, not for God." (Helen Dukas and Banesh Hoffman [1979, p. 123]). We recognize here the deism of most scientists, which we discussed in EXPLANATIONS.

Now here is Einstein again, at the Conference of the American Association for the Advancement of Science meeting in 1934: "In their struggle for the ethical good, teachers of religion must have the stature to give up the doctrine of a personal God; that is, give up that source of fear and hope which in the past placed such vast power in the hands of priests. In their labors they will have to avail themselves of those forces which are capable of cultivating the Good, the True, and the Beautiful in humanity itself. This is, to be sure, a more difficult but an incomparably more worthy task" (Anon [1941]).

Permit me to offer that Einstein's "more difficult but...more worthy task" is what the theology of theopraxy attempts. Using a reversal he might have appreciated, it propounds that it is precisely from the human effort "to cultivate the Good, the True, and the Beautiful" that God issues. The phenomenon we call "God" emerges from idealism's effect on human life, something like the way "gravity" emerges from mass and energy's effect on spacetime. The physical universe without us in it, or some moral beings somewhere, would be Godless, a vast and pointless exercise in applied mathematics. As a large asteroid hurtles toward earth, the profound indifference of the galaxies to our welfare and to life in general cannot be accommodated by confident talk of God's beyond-human-understanding power or wisdom, nor does acceptance of it lead to any virtue but humility. Is it paradoxical or simply obvious that theopraxy's God, as it were, not Einstein's, explains why Einstein was moved to write passages like those above?

are these things? "Fabrications" all; fabrications, every one of them. They exist nowhere as self-sufficient entities and yet everywhere they are being enacted or experienced. The same is true of God. God exists only when and where God is being enacted or experienced. God is an *activity*. Like artistic truths and political truths, religious truths are true because they refer to the realities created by human actions bound by *(ligare)* fealty to the goodness of God. The theology of theopraxy adds this: that the reality of *good actions* is the very substance of the God who is said, conventionally, only to inspire them.

If you understand this, then you see that believers are right and atheists are wrong: God exists and is great! But you also see that God exists and is great in rather different senses of "existence" and "greatness" than most expect. God exists "only" as good-doing, when we do it, and because we do it. God is great because performing God is supremely worthwhile at all times. God is great because, as easily as "he" can be stopped here and there, God cannot be stopped forever or everywhere—at least, not until the last human being has taken his or her last breath and all higher forms of life are extinguished. God is great because five thousand years of worshipping God in personified form have made God an idea and a force to be reckoned with in human affairs.

It follows that not a word of the Upanishads, the Qur'an, the Torah or Mishnah or the Gospels—and not a word of the theologians and philosophers on the subject of God, happiness, justice, beauty, truth, or virtue since—has gone to waste, flawed though history might have shown some of them to be. Nor have any of the works of religiously inspired artists been unnecessary. The primordial yearning to understand, master, or conform to the reason for life's goodness continues.

24 : Theopraxy

IN ALL three Abrahamic religions a tension exists between the relative merits of "faith" and "works." Here is the question simply put: which is to be more valued, strong and complete faith in God ("faith"), or good deeds and accomplishments ("works")?[110] Although most believers would agree that having both is best—i.e., strong faith *and* good works—the fact that we can so easily separate the two raises the problem of priorities in cases where both are not equally forthcoming.

Fundamentalists tend to take the position that good works *cannot* proceed from insufficient or faulty faith. Even when it *seems* that good things are being done, as when an atheist helps a beggar, the lack-of-faith in the doer will eventually come through like bad paint from under good to ruin the deed's ultimate effect or to make it unsustainable. Better is it, then, to do the wrong thing for the right reason than the right thing for the wrong reason. This position is held partly tautologically (because actions taken without proper faith are not good *by definition*), and partly out of faith of a more epistemological kind. For when the long-run outcomes of an action can always be said to be not-yet-evident, it is impossible to prove that a deed that seems good really is good. Everything good now might turn out bad hence. And vice versa. Rather, then, have a "pure heart," pray, and hope. Only from the pure heart will good deeds issue. How do we know? Because a pleased God will see to it. (Cf. also ARGU-MENTS 2, Note 8.)

The theology of theopraxy holds the opposite view almost exactly. Doing long-run good by *any* means that exclude short-run harm, on whatever theory, holding whatever beliefs and motivations, is "good enough for God," which is to say, good enough for God to come into being. Sensitivity to outcomes is our moral obligation. Foresight is a gift not to be spurned. *One cannot ask God to turn faith into works for us: the conversion is ours to handle.*

How one comes down on the "faith versus works" question says a great deal about the kind of God one believes in. Together with Judaism and

---

110 *Of Jesus' disciples, Paul was most invested in making the distinction between faith and works, privileging the former over the latter. In most contexts, Paul's use of "works" refers to "works of law," meaning home and temple ritual-keeping, doing what the letter of the Law says must be done. In other places, "works" seems to mean physical doings generally: constructing, carrying, healing, feeding, and so forth. Our discussion focuses on the second meaning.*

Confucianism (and within Christianity, closer to Catholicism than Protestantism, broadly speaking), the theology of theopraxy leans strongly toward valuing works over faith. But it is the only one that goes so far as to identify God with good work, or more precisely yet, with the *activity of doing* good works. Correct faith—even correct understanding of the theology of theopraxy—is neither necessary nor sufficient, just helpful. Nor is faith acquired by God's grace, unless by "grace" one means coming to a point in one's meditations when the idea of God as our good-doing suddenly strikes one as obvious, as having been true all along, and feeling, with that realization, liberated and commissioned at the same time.

The theology of theopraxy is the only theology that recommends doing good on the grounds that the practice of good, and God, are the same thing.[111] God is constituted by *praxis:* by carrying out moral, ethical, life-promoting and life-saving actions—not in principle, not in the abstract, not in memory, not in visions, not in prayer, and not in plan, but in moment-to-moment activity.

When God's being is God's doing, and God's doing is our good-doing, then God's very existence—God's being—is nothing more and nothing less than our good-doing. This is the argument of the theology of theopraxy.

---

111 *Among the books of the New Testament, the Epistle of James (which Martin Luther famously denigrated as "an epistle of straw") comes closest to taking this position. The other writers side strongly with faith as the road to salvation, especially John and Paul. Interestingly, James was Jesus' brother, at least purportedly. Mentioning Jesus by name only twice, James' chief concern was the practice of moral behavior in the everyday, which he called* true religion *(James 2:1-9). I bring up James only to note, first, that the privileging of "works" in Christianity has some scriptural basis, and second, that in the view of the theology of theopraxy, God and James' "true religion" are one and the same thing. Where most would say that one cannot have religion without God, the theology of theopraxy says you cannot have God without religion, if that means* true religion*, which is nothing more than moral* praxis. *For a compatible argument from a Christian theologian, see Lloyd Geering (2002).*

BOOK FOUR

Reflections

1 : Godliness

THE THEOLOGY of theopraxy accepts the Godliness of Jesus. It accepts also the Godliness of Gautama, of Socrates, of Moses, Mohammed, Mohandas Ghandi, Albert Schweitzer, Raoul Wallenberg, Nelson Mandela, and Mother Theresa. But more importantly, it accepts and applauds the Godliness of the many hundreds of thousands of good people whose names we do not know: people on battlefields who ran out under fire to recover the wounded, people in concentration camps who shared their rations or volunteered to do others' work, people who risked their lives or careers or reputations for justice later, people who provided shelter for persecuted strangers or who gently pushed down the gun barrel next to themselves, people in hospitals and churches and schools and universities everywhere, healing, teaching, searching; the repairman at midnight fixing a downed wire; the woman who feeds strays; the brother who lets his brother go first; people down the street and up the street and perhaps in your home right now who again and again find themselves to be sources—in ways that perhaps surprise even them—of creative moral action.

The vast majority of these good people's lives were not recorded and never will be. Accounts of what they did are lost to time. But the effects of their deeds live on: their sacrifices, their creativity, their integrity, their acts of fortitude, kindness, sagacity, and unbidden generosity have slipped silently into the stream of life's goodness for all.

God came into being through each one of them.

2 : The changing image of God

THE GOD that Nietzsche pronounced dead never lived—never lived, that is, as the three great Western religions pictured God to "live," namely, everlastingly, transcendentally, all-wise, all-powerful, and ever-attentive to his Creation. Rather, says the theology of theopraxy, God has always lived in and as the good that people do. *This* God is far from dead. This God has lived as long as good things have happened at our hands.

What of the disappointment people might feel that God exists only in human action? How could the image of good-doing—so simple, so modest, so variable and fleeting, with so many gestures and faces attached— ever replace the singular image of God of the Bible and Qur'an, God resplendent, Creator and Provider, magnificent and merciful? Can the phrase "doing God's will" even make sense without belief in the existence of such a kingly God?

Yes. Because the God-that-is-the-good-we-do is the God that emerged a hundred thousand years ago or more from the human capacity to reflect, speak, plan, and empathize, to feel remorse, and to feel gratitude— gratitude not only to the one who just helped you, but to the unseen causes of one's whole life.

Yes, because this is the God that roughly twenty thousand years ago, in the guise of many gods, gave complex order to the universe, and humankind a role in it.

Yes, because this is the God who spoke to Abraham and stayed his hand over Isaac and so began raising humankind out of barbarism.

Yes, because this is the God who, a thousand years later, evolved into the single, personified but incomprehensible source of all life, goodness, truth, and power, worthy of ultimate regard—regard higher than that deserved by any god, sage, or chief, and higher than Nature herself.

Yes, because this is the God who, stripped of superstition and false strength, today stands revealed as all or any one of a million acts of goodness being carried out each minute by people who are free to do otherwise. This is the God whose instruction to us by example, and from behind the many masks we have made for "him" to speak through, has always been: "Do right and do good. Preserve, honor, and promote all forms and instances of life that do not by their very nature threaten yours.[1] For these are near-dwellers—neighbors. They have the same right to life as you

---

1 *Cf. EXPLANATIONS 6. I discuss idolatry at greater length in* REFLECTIONS 13.

do, and, if human, the same duty to life—all life—as you do. Love them, therefore, as yourself; treat them as you would like to be treated."

Not everyone can form a mental image of this God—"the theology of theopraxy's God," if you will. And this is both a good and a bad thing. Good in that idolatry is made that much more difficult; good in that the formation of cults disconnected from ordinary life is made that much harder. But bad if the trace level of idolatry that seems necessary in order for people to address and feel addressed by God is totally eliminated; bad if the stories long told of God stop making sense. The goal is to reduce that trace to a minimum without eliminating it. The goal is to feel comfortable contemplating God in "his" most resplendent older forms—from Divine Creator to King of Kings to Heavenly Father—and know that these are but traces, patterns in ink and nerve endings that tell of God's arising, passing, and exemplifying what "he" wants; this while knowing too that, in reality, every moment offers up the very fibers of God's being for us to make or unmake "him," to weave or unweave "her," depending on what we say and what we do.

3 : Negating nihilism

Nihilism stands at the door: whence comes this uncanniest of all guests?
...What does nihilism mean? That the highest values devaluate themselves.
The aim is lacking: "why" finds no answer. ...Radical nihilism *is the convic-*
tion of an absolute untenability of existence when it comes to the highest values one recognizes; *plus the realization that we lack the least right*
to posit a beyond or an in-itself of things that might be 'divine' or morally
incarnate.

—*Friedrich Nietzsche.*[2]

NIETZSCHE WARNS of the obsolescence of the biblical God in the
strongest possible terms. With God gone or dead, can we make up another? Can we "posit" God as a projection of our will and desire that
God *should* exist? No, says Nietzsche. "We lack the least right to posit
a beyond," or God, because only *from* God (on the conventional understanding of God) could the right be received to *posit* God. Put this way,
the paradox is evident: if God is dead, we cannot posit God; and if God
is not dead, we need not posit God. Since God is dead, we cannot posit
him, and so "nihilism stands at the door."

But logic, which is cast in language, is not life, which is cast in DNA,
sun, and rain. Reciprocal "creation" is common in evolutionary processes.
Here large-scale cause and effect mingle and loop. A given species affects
the environment in which it thrives and to which it then must adapt.
Species drive each other to invention. "Psychological" preferences for
certain body features in potential mates causes those features to prolif-
erate in the population. Similarly, in the processes of cultural evolution,
people develop ideas—like "justice"—and build them into institutions,
which in turn affect what new ideas and institutions will arise, which in
turn constrain and inspire newer ideas yet—like "rights." In round after
round of increasing discrimination and elaboration, new entities emerge,
including, long ago, gods, and, more recently, God.

Contra Nietzsche, then, positing God is exactly what we have the
right to do, and have done. And God thus posited cannot be thought
of as chimerical. God thus posited is as real as the good we *do* with or
without the thought of "his" existence in mind.[3] Among the rights given

---

2 *Nietzsche (1967 [1878], pp. 7, 9)*

humankind by God-historical—i.e., God now "dead"—is the right, indeed the obligation bequeathed to us in his *will*, as it were, to posit "him" in ever-better ways.

LET IT be admitted: in all areas, people are self-legitimating. By one means or another we give ourselves rights and privileges over other species, not to mention other people(s). But only on the condition of *life's* increase as a whole can the project of self-legitimation proceed for very long. Our life depends on all life, and, increasingly, all life depends on ours. The wheel of evolution spirals upward only because all life wants one thing, namely, more of itself, *more and better life.*[4] What succeeds at effecting this trend we tend to call "legitimate," or soon make so.

Ironically, we cannot ask *why* life wants more and better life and expect an answer. Life *is* that which "wants" more of itself and "knows" how to get it. And what is life made of? From the physicist's point of view, life is nothing more than a set of energy patterns that propagate, promulgate, and otherwise replicate themselves, growing in complexity and degree of organization as they interact with each other over time. Enter biology. From the burgeoning variety and jostle of life-forms on earth there emerges, eventually, an animal that begins to have experiences that it understands as "experiences," an animal that registers its own aliveness

---

3 *I do not mean to imply that all imaginary things can be made real if we act on the thought of them, and certainly not that any of them can be made real exactly as imagined. Unicorns and witches do not become real, as imagined, just because children act like they are. But something else does become real, something uniquely indexed to the thought: certain conversations, decisions, actions, and feelings that would not occur at all, or be what they were, if the thought were not had. God, says the theology of theopraxy, is the kind of entity made real as and when we act well—i.e., ethically, life-promotingly—this on the thought of God in any form, from the most fanciful to the least, or without God in mind at all. All the theology of theopraxy claims is that its picture of God, which DECLARATIONS tried conjure (and almost every page since has too), is closest to who/what God actually is and how he/it actually acts. It remains open to the possibility, broached several times in these pages, that it is (a) quite wrong about who/what God actually is, or (b) that it is right about who/what God actually is, but wrong about the best way to imagine who/what God is. If good behavior is all that counts, then perhaps scientific naturalism's imagery is best, perhaps Christianity's, perhaps psychoanalysis', and so forth.*

4 *This desire for more and better life is the context within which the story of the Tower of Babel (Genesis 11:1–9) could be read as a cautionary tale of too much, too soon, and too presumptuously. But tower-building will stop only when there is no life left on earth. Biologists are wary of talking of plants and animals desiring a better life, of course, but "better" need not mean finer pastries and more opera. It can mean less labor, less fear, more offspring, "sweeter" food, water, or sunshine, greater self-determination, etc., which all have analogs on other rungs of scala natura.*

and finitude, an animal that reflects on what "more life" really means and then on how to achieve it legitimately, which is to say, by using rules that are approved by, or would be approved by, all creatures who want more life for themselves.

Why is there life at all? We need not believe that God intended life in order to justify life. Although God is good for life, life is not justified by God. Life started neither *for* God's pleasure nor *at* God's pleasure. On the contrary, God is justified by life. It is life, specifically *our* life—human life, yours and mine—that God relies upon for "his" very existence. Before we choose God to be our "why go on?", we are God's.

In order for life to continue, then, it cannot be a matter of indifference to actual living creatures whether life should continue. Life has to be preferred to death and pleasure has to be preferred to pain, that harbinger, that warning bell, of life's end. Short-term strategies for survival and replication must be tempered and supplemented by long-term strategies for the same. The *will to live* is the basis for all willing as well as all living. "True religion" among humans is one of the activities that life has evolved to preserve, honor, and promote itself in the long term.

NIETZSCHE GIVES up on radical nihilism because, as devoid of all values as it wants to be, nihilism is itself fully and haplessly the value-laden perspective of a living and longing human being. An understanding of life (or of the cosmos for that matter) from outside of life is not possible. Disillusion is still illusion, as Zen teaches. Nihilism is a picture of life taken from inside of life, as it were; it is a decision *about* living made *by* the living. Far from being objective about the absurdity or meaninglessness of life, the nihilist's analysis is in fact soaked through with self-pity about both, beginning, probably, with disappointments in the nihilist's own life and then drawn to the easy heroism of "living without a/the Father."

For us—as for Nietzsche and Camus—nihilism is conquered when one says "yes" to life for no good reason other than that's what life *is*, what life wants, and one cannot deny at least one's body's complicity in the project. This affirmation in the face of life's lack of grounding in any God above, below, or beyond life itself is the act of meaning-recovery that Nietzsche hoped to teach with Zarathustra, and indeed exemplify himself.

Is Nietzsche's teaching atheistic? Not in the view of our theology, which argues thus: Affirming life in the face its lack of grounding in any God above and beyond life itself gains its *genuinely* heroic aspect not from denying God's existence (any philosophy major can do that), but from the commitment "for no good reason" to bringing about everything good that believers say God wants—life's proliferation, higher consciousness, more love, an end to involuntary suffering...—the realization of which, day by day, moment by moment, is the very substance of God in the first and last place anyway.

One cannot get farther from atheism than that.

4 : Not for everyone

THE THEOLOGY of theopraxy is not for everyone. Like Zen Buddhism, the theology of theopraxy is a mature person's "religion," best adopted by people who have lived a little, who understand the importance of abiding by the law, who have learned firsthand the wisdom of such ancient moral precepts as the Golden Rule, who have experienced love and separation, seen birth and death, who know what it's like to do good, and who have asked at least some of the big Why questions.

Helpful, too, is a genuine respect for what "God" means to believers in one or more religious traditions. One would then know that there is enough overlap among religious traditions to make it likely that a good and wise person in one tradition would be recognized as good and wise in another.[5]

In short, theopraxy assumes, indeed requires, that those who would consider consciously engaging in it have the beginnings of wisdom.

It follows that the *theology* of theopraxy—which is to say, theopraxy's intellectual, reflective side—is not well suited to those in whom the basic principles of morality must still be established: children and young adolescents for example, but also the insane, the deeply ignorant, or the long misled. Here, rather, some moral authority is required in order to inculcate habits of common human decency, at least at first—as a starting point.[6]

Until this foundation is laid, the theology of theopraxy offers little of value, and could even be unhealthy. For example, if one touted to a

---

5 *This is not to overlook ambiguities or differences in the matters, for example, of the rights of women, the duties of parents, or the relative weights given to the virtues. It is only to say that the similarities would outweigh the differences.*

6 *Nor, conversely, is it wise to imprint religion too early. Impressing children (under ten, say) with the agony of Christ or the fear of Allah or God Almighty, is, I believe, deeply unfair to them. "Getting them while they're young" is the strategy of the insecure. All it does is produce atheists—adults in flight from religion—or acolytes, people unable to see the world scientifically or through the eyes of other faiths. To children between the ages (roughly) of two and eight, I believe, morality is best taught on utilitarian and self-interest grounds. Before that it should be presented as self-evident (x is right and y is wrong) through the exercise of simple parental authority. Always, however, and through all ages, teaching others by one's own exemplary behavior is the most effective method. This conclusion is hardly new. But its warrant might be: for witnessing good is witnessing God, and witnessing God is no small thing—as we seem, intuitively, to know.*

morally untutored audience that *God is in our hands* without conveying how, or why, or in what sense this is true, the apparent fictionalizing of God could be taken as an admission that God "doesn't really exist" and therefore cannot have authority.[7] Worse, some could come to see themselves as more powerful than God (and tragically mean God of the Bible). It takes maturity and intelligence of the sort I described in the first paragraph to understand that some fictions are more precious than others, that God is the most precious of them and not a fiction at all as and if we act on it. It takes some wisdom to see that God's being "in our hands" increases rather than decreases our obligation to find out who or what God is.

WHEN THE theologian and rabbi Richard Rubinstein met Swami Muktananda of Ganeshpuri for the first time, the guru said to him:

> *You mustn't believe in your own religion; I don't believe in mine. Religions are like the fences that hold saplings erect. Without the fence, the sapling could fall over. When it takes firm root and becomes a tree, the fence is no longer needed. However, most people never lose their need for a fence.*[8]

Let us ask ourselves, and answer truthfully: "Am I getting along without religion's 'fence' entirely?"

Can my children?

Was the Swami?

---

7 *In truth, what God does not have is power; what God does have is authority—the authority we give. See* EXPLANATIONS 15.

8 *Richard L. Rubinstein (1992 [1966], p. 293).*

5 : Six kinds of prayer

ALL THEISTIC religions sanction prayer of some sort. Here is one way to categorize them.

Prayers differ from each other in *timing* and in *intention*.

With regard to *timing*, there are *deliberate-and-extended* prayers, which usually involve a degree of planning, usually follow religious canon, and are often spoken, chanted, or sung out loud (sometimes in unison) for minutes or even hours on end. There are also *spontaneous-and-momentary* prayers, which are offered without planning, which (need) follow no particular formula, are usually silent, and might last for a few seconds or less.[9]

With regard to *intention*, some prayers (or parts of prayers) are *laudatory*, praising God for his power, mercy, justness, for creating the universe, and so forth. Others *give thanks* to God for making life possible, or for some particular benefit or gift received. And some prayers are *petitionary*, asking God for protection, strength, forgiveness, wealth, health, wisdom, or to take some special action—to intercede—on behalf of one's self, family, or countrymen.[10]

Combining the two timing and three intention alternatives together, we get six basic kinds of prayer:

- deliberate-and-extended laudatory prayer
- deliberate-and-extended thanksgiving prayer
- deliberate-and-extended petitionary prayer
- spontaneous-and-momentary laudatory prayer
- spontaneous-and-momentary thanksgiving prayer
- spontaneous-and-momentary petitionary prayer

Given the familiarity of the first three kinds, I should like to focus on the last three, starting with the last because it reveals something about *sensus divinitatis*.

SPONTANEOUS-AND-MOMENTARY PETITIONARY prayer, I would suggest, is all but instinctual and pan-human. Imagine standing on a curb and crying out to oneself, "Oh please, don't let that car hit that child!"

---

9 *I omit deliberate-and-momentary and spontaneous-and-extended prayers not only because they are rare, but also for simplicity of analysis.*

10 *Some call this type of prayer "intercessionary." Interestingly, the word "prayer" itself comes from the Latin for asking or begging.*

or waiting in a doctor's office for test results and repeating silently, "Oh please, let me not have cancer!" The petition might go out to God, the gods, or the "powers that be." It might go out to Fate or to "the universe as a whole." No matter. It is still prayer. Children and gamblers are well acquainted with spontaneous-and-momentary petitionary prayer; as are soldiers in battle, athletes and fans at sports events, and patients and their loved ones in hospitals...whether they are atheists, agnostics, or believers. In all these cases the desire to change the apparent course of events is so fervent, and what would make the difference between disaster and safety, failure and success is so small, that we feel compelled to invoke every occult force we are capable of imagining in order to deflect fate, this whether or not, at a calmer moment, we really believed in such "forces." Or in God.

Does the existence of spontaneous-and-momentary petitionary prayer by atheists pose a problem of consistency for them? It is commonly thought to. Recall the taunt "there are no atheists in foxholes." But we can say it does not. Helplessness in the face of impending disaster is so strong an emotion that it can throw the staunchest of realists into superstition. To judge atheists intellectually inconsistent because of their atavistic behavior *in extremis* is not entirely fair. All it proves is that atheists are human.[11]

More telling, perhaps, is that spontaneous-and-momentary thanksgiving prayer (our fifth type) can happen after critical events have passed. When disaster is averted even atheists can feel overcome by the feeling of *gratitude*, a gratitude to...well, who? or what? The emotion of gratitude— the desire to give thanks—is real, spontaneous, pre-intellectual, and undirected, as we discussed earlier (ARGUMENTS 22). Within seconds, it seeks a *to-whom* (or *to-what*) in order to make sense of itself. Unbidden, gratitude turns to spontaneous momentary thanksgiving prayer, whether to Lady Luck, Fate, God, or the Universe.

Whereas spontaneous-and-momentary petitionary prayer and spontaneous-and-momentary thanksgiving prayer are common, spontaneous-and-momentary *laudatory* prayer (our fourth type) is exclusively associated with traditional belief. I think this is because few people are moved instinctively, atavistically, to express praise (as distinct from thanks) *in*

---

11 *Although, taking up Pascal's Wager, non-believers could cool-headedly ask, "Given there is nothing we can do, why not appeal to occult powers or heavenly intervention on the minuscule chance there is some truth to these things?"...this is not how they reason at the time, because they do not reason at all. Spontaneous momentary petitionary prayer is the most human expression of hope.*

general. One usually knows to whom praise is due: for wonderful food, the good cook; for an interesting book, an interesting author; for the world as a whole, God the Creator. The atheist has no one to praise for "the world as a whole." Nor probably does he or she want to. Why? For one, because "the world as a whole" has too much in it that is bad and accidental, and for another, praise of God, like praise of powerful people, is often motivated by self-interest. Interestingly, the deist can have praise for the Creator (having just expressed awe at the intricate immensity of nature), but no one to deliver that praise *to*. Fellow human beings can witness it, to be sure, but they cannot receive it.

For its part, and pragmatic to a fault, the theology of theopraxy endorses all forms of prayer that support the doing of good by those who pray, and opposes all forms of prayer that support fatalism, passivity, feelings of entitlement, or lack of curiosity. Certainly, the existence of spontaneous-and-momentary prayer among the faithful and non-faithful—among theists, deists, pantheists, panentheists, atheists, and theo-practitioners alike—speaks of a responsibility-seeking, God-creating impulse in human nature, one that predates formal religion, and that will probably postdate it too. *Sensus divinitatis.*

HERE IS a man, getting on in years, who does not believe in God the way he thinks he should. Depending on who asks, he says that he's an atheist or an agnostic. Every so often he visits a cemetery and lays flowers on the grave of old friend. Then he rests against a tree. If, as he rests, he thinks that *something has been done*, something more—even a *little* more—than the arousal of his own memories and feelings, then he is a believer despite his theological misgivings. If, in the hours and days that follow, he is a kinder person, more patient or more brave in some life-affirming way, then he is a subscriber to the theology of theopraxy, although he might not know it.

Perhaps a stranger saw him lay flowers and rest against the tree. If seeing the stranger see him (although being seen was not his purpose, and although the stranger might mistakenly think him devout)...if seeing the stranger see him does not displease, then he is a subscriber to the theology of theopraxy too.

For something *was* done in that cemetery, something good, something holy, registered in the "book" of the world as having happened in one and perhaps two locations. God is as good happens; where good is, God happens.

Theopraxy would have us do traditional things, but it requires no traditional faith. (Cf. EXPLANATIONS 7)

6 : George Santayana

GEORGE SANTAYANA, in his 1905 book *Reason in Religion,* came close to rendering the essential insights of our theology. Santayana:

> *(T)he doctrine that the physical universe is the creation of a supremely good personal deity is a pictorial rendering of the insight that everything in the world is potentially usable for the enrichment of human life. The Christian story of the incarnation, sacrificial death, and resurrection of Jesus Christ is a way of making the point that self-sacrifice for others is of supreme moral value. It is worthwhile embodying these moral insights into theological doctrine because this vivid presentation, together with the systematic cultivation of feelings and attitudes that accompany it, provides a more effective way of getting across the insights than would a bald statement.* [12]

A Harvard philosopher raised as a boy in Catholic schools, Santayana thought that religious belief was a developmental stage, rather like adolescence, through which humanity was passing. "Religion is the natural reaction of the imagination when confronted by the difficulties in a truculent world."[13] We should give credit, he thought, to the great religions for bringing humankind out of an earlier darkness, but it was time now for religion to step aside for the greater light shed by science, reason, literature, beauty, justice, and other expressions of the best in humanity.

Santayana looked forward to a world without God except in the most abstract deist form, and therefore without God-worship, prayer, ritual, or religion. The theology of theopraxy, by contrast, recommends neither belief in a deist God nor the elimination of religion. It holds that God is *composed by* the very narratives, images, and maxims transmitted by

---

12 *Quoted by William P. Alston (1967, p. 172) discussing Santayana's* Reason in Religion *(1905). Santayana was an atheist or a deist; to the best of my knowledge, he did not decide which. "My atheism, like that of Spinoza, is true piety toward the universe and denies only gods fashioned by men in their own image, to be servants of their human interests." It is this "piety toward the universe" that makes Santayana a deist rather than a true atheist. (True atheists are "a-deists" too.)*

13 *Ibid. Actually, this idea goes back at least to Kant's book* Religion within the Limits of Reason Alone, *where Kant argues that with cultural maturity, people see Biblical stories as allegorical, and start to rely on their own capacity for pure reason, which has the divine in it from the start, and which inevitably leads to doing good out of a sense of duty.*

the religious language that Santayana thinks we can do without, *together with* all the poetry and science that strives to discriminate the good, true, and beautiful from the bad, false, and ugly. I use the phrase "composed by" advisedly because these processes are not God until they are brought into the concrete and "sensuous" world—until, that is, like music, God is *performed* through free human action. God thought of this way is no less demanding of a response from us than the Biblical God. The God that the theology of theopraxy beholds is no abstraction. In all but the darkest pits of hell, God is performed and witnessed directly in a thousand ways daily.

THE IMAGE of God presented in religious canon has its reasons. God's omniscience in dealing out mercy and justice, for example, stands as a model for us and a lesson: to take the largest and most objective view possible in making decisions involving others. But whereas the manifest inconstancy of God's expression of his divine attributes is a mystery to conventional believers, it is no mystery at all to subscribers to the theology of theopraxy: *God's* inconstancy is our inconstancy reflected back upon us. Similarly, God's freely-chosen self-limitations are our necessary limitations reflected back upon us.[14] Infallibility is not an essential attribute of God. The only consistent and necessary attribute of God is goodness-in-action.

Are we consistently good in everything we do? No. Nor does goodness occur everywhere and always, but rather here and there. It follows that God "himself" is *in existence* not everywhere, always, but here and there. So atheists are partly right. When and where evil is being done, then and there God does not exist. Good*ness* defines God linguistically and conceptually; actually-doing-good is what brings God into literal being. Whosoever does "God's will" therefore enacts God's very existence.

God is like a flame lit by us and shining upon us in return. It's no wonder that God has had a human face for so long.

---

14 *See* REFLECTIONS *18.*

7 : Religious reconciliation and theopraxy's Seven Tenets

HISTORICALLY, ATTEMPTS at conciliation between religions have taken two forms. One has been to adopt the liberal ideals of tolerance, fairness, universal human rights, and respect for all racial and cultural differences. When the object is interdenominational Christian unity, it is called *ecumenicism*. When extended to all religions, it is called the Interfaith Movement.

The second form of conciliation has been more philosophical. It entails asserting that beneath apparent differences in ritual and language, all religions *really* worship the same God, i.e., the one and only God in whose eyes, conversely, all humanity is one big family. This view is propounded by Universalist Unitarians, Baha'i, by popular mythologists like Joseph Campbell, by historians of religion like Huston Smith, and by prime ministers and presidents, at least in public, as well as by most Jewish, Christian, and Muslim public intellectuals.

While respecting the virtues of these two approaches (when sincere), the theology of theopraxy looks for conciliation between religions on more meaningful grounds, grounds requiring more than live-and-let-live tolerance on the one hand or veiled assertions of the supremacy of you-know-whose God on the other.

The theology of theopraxy, as the reader well knows, takes a more metaphysical stance: namely, that free moral *praxis* is God. This means that old religions, in their attempt to be modern, should not have to jettison their core rituals and narratives just to make them agree with the latest biological, cosmological, or archeological findings. Nor should they be forced to admit that their beliefs and rituals are merely "useful fictions," which has been the sociologist's view of them since Durkheim (and before that, Feuerbach and Nietzsche). Such admissions would be self-defeating, not to say injurious, for the greater number of their followers, who suspect it anyway, prefer it unspoken, and who are wise enough to see that these "fictions" are to be taken with considerable if not complete seriousness.[15]

---

15 *Most of us think that our ancestors* truly *believed while we "moderns" only try to believe, sort-of believe, or pretend to believe. But our ancestors thought the same about themselves and of their ancestors, all the way back. How do we know that? Well, first,* ›

The theology of theopraxy takes this commonsense acceptance a step further. The core narratives and beliefs of each religion, it says, are genuinely *constitutive* of God-in-idea and often conducive to God-in-actuality. Many if not most ordinary, decent, "half-believing" people are adherents already but don't know it.

LIKE SANTAYANA, John Dewey wanted to "emancipate the religious from religion." And what is "the religious?" In *A Common Faith* (1934, p. 31) Dewey formulates it carefully: "Any activity pursued in behalf of an ideal end against obstacles and in spite of threats of personal loss because of conviction of its general and enduring value is religious in quality."

As we heard it argued earlier (ARGUMENTS 19) by Feuerbach and Evans, Dewey argued that ideals such as love, compassion, justice, and so on could be pursued without belief in supernatural agency, i.e., without belief in God. Of course, Dewey is right: no all-powerful, all-seeing, and all-caring, Creator-God need be posited in order to bring out the best in humankind. And *forcing* people to believe in this God is certainly counterproductive.

But this does not prove that out-and-out secularism is the alternative. Nor does it prove that "natural piety" toward the kind of world science discloses—a prescription which is at the core of deism—is the best of alternatives. There are other theisms—pantheism and panentheism, for example. And there is the theology of theopraxy, which says that the

---

< because classical texts, from Homer on, consistently praise the ancestors for being closer to the gods, or God. But second because anthropological research shows that it is common for people to hold to their society's beliefs provisionally. Even so-called "primitive" people do this, people whom we imagine to be totally, helplessly, sincere, rather like children, and incapable of irony or pragmatism. As anthropologist Dan Sperber (1982, pp. 149–180) argues, primitives, just like sophisticates (i.e., skeptical moderns), are perfectly capable of appearing to believe, of going along, of indulging their myths, of acting as if this or that superstition were literally the case...all the while appreciating the social utility of their fanciful cosmologies and enjoying the entertainment, seduction, and prestige-garnering value of religious occasions. Faith has its uses, and so does the show of faith.

   Most anthropologists have been wilfully naive on this score, says Sperber, taking ritual performances (by primitives) to be always-sincere, and taking what their native informants are telling them is going on at face value—while in fact it is often the informant making things up to keep the anthropologist interested, or for reasons of their own. Two-mindedness, half-belief, irony, and pragmatism—being a grown-up and a child—are pan-human traits. See also Dan Sperber (1975). For an example of anthropology that does do justice to the power inherent in "primitive" myth systems while showing at the same time how those myths are understood poetically, pragmatically, and with good humor rather than naively, literally, and dourly, see Laurens van der Post's writings on the Kalahari Bushmen, e.g., van der Post (1984).

God to whom good and devout Jews, Christians, and Muslims pray, and whom they obey, is real. "He" is just not real in the way the literature of mainstream Judaism, Christianity, and Islam say God is.

How then is God real? declarations 11 tried to convey how in poetic terms. explanations 4 offers a more discursive answer. Here let me reply in the light of what has been discussed since, and offer a first draft of what might be called the Seven Tenets of the theology of theopraxy:

1   God is not a person or thing or principle or spirit. God is activity of a certain sort: the free doing of good, where by "good" we mean that which preserves, honors, or promotes all forms and instances of life.

2   God was not the Creator. Nor is God all-powerful or omniscient. God is the newest and weakest "force" in the universe, a human production, even as God—good-doing—produces humaneness in turn.

3   Freedom is necessary to doing good, and good-doing is necessary to producing more freedom.

4   Science is the friend of true religion, which is faith justified by works.

5   The development of ever fairer and more compassionate laws as well as more broadly life-sustaining social and cultural practices is God's mandate, and our task.

6   Long-evolved religions present powerful and highly specific rituals, images, arguments, narratives, and commandments whose purpose is to effect Tenet 5, and can be respected and practiced without significant alteration when they succeed in doing so.

7   Both the idea and substance of God remain open to evolution.[16]

---

16 *Contrast Tenet 7 with the First Commandment.*

In places in A Common Faith *(1934), Dewey flies close to all the Tenets. For example: "It is the active relation between the ideal and the actual to which I would give the name 'God'" (p. 51). Or "Whether one gives the name 'God' to this union, operative in thought and action, is a matter for individual decision. But the* function *of such a working union of the ideal and the actual seems to me to be identical with the force that has in fact been attached to the conception of God in all the religions that have spiritual content..." (p. 52). Or "In any case...the meaning of ('God' as I would use the word) is selective. For it involves* ⟩

‹ *no miscellaneous worship of everything in general. It selects those factors in existence that generate and support our idea of good as an end to be striven for. It excludes a multitude of forces that at any given time are irrelevant to this function." (p. 53).*

8 : Study and practice

COULD SOMEONE raised completely without religious instruction benefit from the theology of theopraxy, or at least find that it makes sense?

Further to REFLECTIONS 4, the answer I think is: yes. Although theopraxy benefits from an emotional tie to, knowledge of, and respect for at least one religion, it is not a requirement. Most people know what "God" means; even irreligious people. (To say "I don't believe in God" or "I don't go in for all that religious stuff!" is still not the same as saying: "G...o...d? What *is* this word?") Knowing what "God" means does not vouch that one has had a religious experience, of course. But it's a start. Many people disaffected by organized religion will say that they are "spiritual, but not religious." That too is a start.

But the best start is this: nearly everyone, with or without a formal religious background, knows what moral goodness feels like, and this in a powerful and primitive way that probably goes back to early childhood (in experiences of generosity, say) or further back still, to our neural wiring. And because of that, the theology of theopraxy might offer a way *toward* a religious tradition for many non-believers, and a way *back* to a religious tradition for many "believers in exile." By seeing how it is that God is the good we do, both kinds of people are able to see that the narratives and doctrines of traditional religions are less descriptions of historical fact (and thus mostly wrong) than allegories about goodness's historical emergence from barbarism (and thus mostly right), allegories urging us in this always-modern day to realize the potential we have to freely choose and do what is best for all.

How can someone without much religious background but with a strong feeling of what goodness means be awakened to the notion of theopraxy? Can one "train in theopraxy?" I think the answer is yes, in two rather ordinary ways: *study* and, well, *practice* (in the sense of repeated exercise leading to proficiency).

Study: This means learning more about a religion, preferably one's own family's religion. One might attend services, go to Sunday school, read books, talk to parents and grandparents. One might also take courses in comparative religion. The aim is to come to a genuine emotional and intellectual appreciation of the *glory* of God as traditionally conceived. For if the theology of theopraxy is to have something to which to apply itself, it helps to respect the majestic conception of God (or Allah, Brahman, Tao, or the Way of Heaven) that drives all the great religions. In order to transform Scriptural accounts of God into the grounds for autonomous, ethical action without literal belief in that God, it helps to appreciate the passion of the prophets and the wisdom of religious philosophers.[17] After all, an interpreter starts with something to interpret as well as an understanding of what the author or speaker is *getting at*.

No less important is studying the basic concepts and arguments of secular moral philosophy, whose conclusions are rarely at odds with the religion's.[18] There, concepts such as fairness, goodness, justice, altruism, wrongdoing, and so forth are richly discussed (to put it mildly) with a minimum mention of God, or none at all, which exercise itself is salutary regardless of one's intuitions about God's part in all this, or the manner of "his" existence.

Practice: If we are to understand how God is in our hands, we must first know what it's like to have *anything* "in our hands," that is, what it's like for something consequential to be up to *us*. Sadly, not everyone has had this experience. Many are accustomed to seeing themselves only as re-actors, not actors; as responders, not initiators. So the second mode of "training" for theopraxy might be firsthand experience of creative moral action and of creative activity in general. One must learn what it feels like to *make* things (artifacts, drawings, arrangements) as well as make things *happen*: events, occasions. One must learn how to take responsibility both *for* that making, and *to* the thing or event made. One must understand the dynamics of projects done alone or together, as leader or follower, but in either case, one must know what it feels like to turn a plan into a deed by one's own acts, choices, and will.

How might one do all this? Assume a cold start. One could begin with a project in art ("make something beautiful") or in social intervention ("do something good");[19] with gardening ("help something grow"), with

---

17 *These prophets and philosophers need not have enjoyed one-hundred percent belief themselves, though they spoke as if they did. See Note 15.*

18 *"Whoa," I hear you say, "not true! How about the 'issues' of abortion or homosexuality, or chastity, or Darwinism, which seem to divide people cleanly into believers and non-believers?" Well, of course, they only seem to do so to fundamentalists. The difference between people on these issues is not located on the fault-line between theism and atheism. Many secularists are on the same side as fundamentalists—being "pro-life," say, or disapproving of homosexuality—and many are on the other. The same can be said of religionists.*

19 *Nothing will make an unhappy person happier faster than giving aid or joy to another. Why wait till "all else fails"?*

writing ("write something interesting") or even cooking ("cook something tasty"). In all these cases the vagueness of the word "something" is essential, because it forces the trainee to choose what exactly their project will consist of, and then to take autonomous steps toward bringing it about. Later, such projects become self-assigned. There is no lower or upper age limit for beginning this training.

In God, human creativity, morality, and autonomy are one. Life-enhancing action becomes theopraxy. Of the closeness of God-in-practice, in contrast to the remoteness of God-in-doctrine, Moses says to his flock (Deuteronomy 30:11–14,):

> *Surely this instruction which I enjoin upon you this day is not too baffling for you, nor is it beyond reach. It is not in the heavens, that you should say, 'Who among us can go up to the heavens and get it for us and impart it to us, that we may observe it?' Neither is it beyond the sea, that you should say, 'Who among us can cross to the other side of the sea and get it for us and impart it to us, that we may observe it?' No, the thing is very close to you, in your mouth and in your hearts, to observe it.*

With study and practice one realizes how it is that "God is in our hands," how it is that "whether or not God exists is entirely up to us." One comes to appreciate the gravity of these claims and the unexpected grandeur of their modest promise to us: Do good, do it yourself, do it because you want to, and the Heavens will rejoice.

9 : The situation of atheists

ATHEISTS ARE convinced that God does not exist in any objective sense, which is to say, that God does not *really* exist. They believe that people invented "God" in order to motivate each other to be good, to console each other in grief, and so on. At best (they say) God is a moral fiction.[20]

Believers, of course, would never go along with the demotion of God from fact to fiction, although the claim makes disturbing sense. Indeed, it is precisely in order to head off this always-possible demotion of God from resplendent-king-of-the-universe to salutary-figment-of-the-imagination that organized (Western) religion so strongly and insistently perpetuates belief not only in God-objective but in God massively, grandly, objective: Creator of the universe, all glory and beyond comprehension (except that He *clearly* chose Israel, sacrificed His only Son for our sakes, made Mohammed his last and best prophet, etc., etc.).[21]

Say atheists: efforts to impress "God" upon *hoi polloi* using such overwhelming claims do more harm than good. When not serving the powerful or fanning hatred, they cloud reason, obstruct science, and breed passivity.

The atheist's worries are, alas, all too often justified. Having bad ideas of God can have consequences worse than having no idea of God at all. But seekers of the theopracticing life are likely to believe that the *good* done by belief in God has, on the whole, outweighed the harm. Absent religion, we ask, would the same wars, purges, and murders not have been committed for other reasons?[22] We will never know. Perhaps religious differences have always been a cover for installing and then perpetuating ethnic and economic inequalities, a way of legitimating them, of sanctifying them. As the strategies of Joseph Stalin, Mao Ze Dung, Pol Pot and a dozen other anti-religious warlords attest, however, there are many ways other than calling on God to keep the disadvantaged at a disadvantage,

---

20 *In* ARGUMENTS *we remarked upon the development of this critique by Ludwig Feuerbach. It was expressed formally much earlier by William of Ockham. The term "moral fiction" should be credited to John Gardner's 1979 book* On Moral Fiction.

21 *The paradox of the last attribute is not often seen: for if God is beyond knowing ("beyond ken"), then we cannot be* sure *God is/was the Creator, is all powerful, etc., etc.*

22 *Certainly, medieval society was rife with pagan superstitions and magical beliefs—astrology, alchemy, and witchcraft among them. We tend to forget that the relatively austere teachings of the Church were an advance at the time, or at least a simplification. See Keith Thomas (1971).*

the credulous obedient, and the poor grateful for what little they have.

Atheists on the other hand, if they are intellectually honest, are obliged to be grateful for the teachings of Siddartha Gautama (the Buddha), of Hammurabi, Confucius, Lao Tse, Moses, Solomon and the prophets of ancient Israel, of Jesus and Mohammed, Aquinas, Augustine, and Maimonides, to name a few of the classic teachers. Most of their teachings are now written into secular law, into state constitutions, and into the social fabric as everyday human decency, *including the atheist's*. In more recent times, philosophers have wrestled with trying to square religious faith with experience and with science, and in that striving have produced the very body of thought upon which atheists rest their case. Immanuel Kant, Tom Paine, John Stuart Mill, Thomas Jefferson, Bertrand Russell, William James, and John Dewey, to name just a few prominent non-theists of the last few centuries, wrote what they wrote and said what they said embedded in a Christian milieu whose basic moral principles they accepted and by whose narratives they were suitably moved. So were Alfred North Whitehead and Charles Hartshorne.

And if die-hard atheists, trying to circumvent the Bible, were to go back to the philosophers of ancient Greece in search of examples of lives of pure reason, they would come upon Socrates, Plato, and Aristotle paying respect to the gods—*their* gods—smiling and with easy hearts.

Ironically, atheists who really understand the traditions they oppose might be in a better position to reach an understanding of God through the theology of theopraxy than those who are unthinkingly faith-full. But good atheists—already theopracticing—might well be prevented from reaching that understanding by an emotional, personal need to reject their religious heritage. Don't all smart teenagers scoff at the "lies" that civility is based upon? Don't they all smirk at the foolishness of ordinary people (read: their parents and their parents' friends) for not cottoning on to the contradictions of faith or the failings of church leadership?[23] Atheists are wont to believe (1) that *intelligence* and *illusion* are simple adversaries, (2) that in this world there are only material things, energy, and Nothing, (3) that what most people do with their lives doesn't amount to a "hill of beans" in the larger scheme of things (no all-seeing, caring God to tally minutiae), and (4) that commitment to human ideals in the face of life's absurdity is either pointless or misguided.

---

23 *Perfectly illustrative of the sometime arrogance of atheism is Joyce Arthur (1990). See also Dawkins (2006) and Hitchens (2007). For the argument that "intense atheism" is chiefly the result of the atheist's fathers' cruelty, weakness, absence, abandonment, or early death, see Paul C. Vitz (1999), an interesting if unscientific study.*

My point? How frozen in youthfulness these opinions are. For a start, intelligence is no protection against illusion. Indeed, as often as not, intelligence is illusion's sponsor. For another, the category of *information* is far deeper than that of "matter" or "energy." The universe is mindless and stupid—a cosmic screensaver, generated by a line or two of code playing itself out over arbitrarily large dimensions. But the universe is smaller than a pea in the realm of what matters, which is what lies behind every pair of eyes that see, and is vast. And finally: in fact, nothing is more Godly than *creating* meaning in a world that would otherwise be without it.

Tragically, atheists tend not to see the closeness of what they are rightfully calling for—rationality, intelligence, honesty-to-goodness, responsibility, creativity, and courage in an indifferent universe—with what they are inveighing against, namely, a relationship to a God. Theopraxy *needs* no theology to get it going or to back it up, although clearly (I think) it benefits from one. Theopraxy *needs* no faith in God, ordinary or extraordinary, although faith of *some* kind may help. In the view of our theology, atheists undo atheism with every good deed they do, just as believers undo God with every bad one.

10 : The first commandment

"THOU SHALT have no other gods before me." This is the first of the Ten Commandments. Does our theology obey it?

Traditional believers would say "absolutely not," since the "me" referred to here is none other than God who spoke to Abraham, who parted the Red Sea, who appeared to Moses at Sinai, who stopped the sun above Jericho, who took Isaiah and Jesus to his bosom, who guided Mohammed through the angel Gabriel, and so forth. They might also point to Tenet 7 of REFLECTIONS 7 as evidence: "Both the idea and substance of God remain open to evolution." This is not the One God of the Torah, Gospels, or Qur'an! (Nor for that matter is it Brahman or the Tao.)

In its own view, however, the theology of theopraxy does not break the First Commandment. Why? Because it sees God of the Bible (specifically) as a "character" from the outset, demanding, in Exodus 20:3, that no other Gods be esteemed more highly than Himself, and later that Israel have no other God at all, period. But, as many Bible scholars have observed, God changes in name, image, character, and *modus operandi* across the span of the Bible itself: from patriarch to liberator, from liberator to lawgiver, from nearby spirit to remote principle, from mighty creator/destroyer to pan-human father, and thence to love itself. How could it be otherwise? Knowledge grows. History transforms mental as well as physical landscapes. Inasmuch as later Gods (Heavenly Father, Yahweh) supplant earlier ones (El Shaddai, Elohim), the Bible itself, it would seem, breaks the First Commandment.

Of course, one might answer that it is our *understanding* of God that changes, that evolves, not *God*. Or one might answer that God deliberately changes how "he" presents "himself" to us, according to what we are capable of understanding. But these answers come very close to staking out a difference that makes no difference. For if God is unknowable in full (as all traditional believers agree) then God's *im*mutability might be just one more thing we *think* we know about God, but don't.

We might also be wrong about whether we can know God in full. *Perhaps we can.* Insisting that we *cannot* know God in full, rather than betokening intellectual humility, might be a convenient evasion of the responsibility that would surely fall upon our shoulders if we *could* (understand God completely). Perhaps there is nothing *simpler* than knowing God; perhaps we know what God wants all too well. Take away all the "perhaps"s and you have theology of theopraxy's view.

Besides, even if we hold that all of the above understandings of God—traditional and heretical—are given to us by God in the first place, they can still change. For God (as traditionally conceived) need only so will it. God might say: "See how I change!" and change. Indeed, if the Bible is God's word, then perhaps God is already saying that—and changing too.

The possibilities are dizzying.

Intuition tells us, however, that *something* about God must stay constant for God to be God. The question is: what might that something be? You know what the theology of theopraxy answers: it is God's goodness as embodied in our free actions. This is what never changes.[24] Because good actions vary in detail in the way they preserve, honor, or promote life, so too do the specific actions that constitute God vary in detail from place to place and from situation to situation. Here it is a favor offered; there it is a favor refused. Here it is more justice; there it is more mercy. Here it is writing a book; there it is digging a well. This accounts for God's "changeability." But in every case that good is done, God is brought to life.

Ironically, God as the theology of theopraxy wants us to understand God (i.e., as the good we *do*), could safely *be* the-one-God-before-whom-no-others-should-be-had. I say "safely" because all other conceptions of God permit evil to be part of God or God's will. So parsimonious, so to-the-point is the theology of theopraxy's description of God, and difficult to corrupt by definition (for if an action is not good it is not God), that it could well be the best understanding available today of the One God who has been God all along, who does not change what "he" wants or what "he" does. Agree, forgive a bit of personification, and the First Commandment is restored to its rightful place. In fact, suspicion is cast the other way.

You may well find these last few claims a bit much. Set them aside. We can reflect fruitfully on the First Commandment without them, starting with the Biblical understanding of God. (Recall that the *value* of that understanding is not challenged.)

The First Commandment from God to humankind was given as the

---

24 *There are other candidates, of course, for the single most-essential and unchanging attribute of God (as traditionally conceived), the one that makes the others optional if need be: God's omnipotence, immensity, unknowability, justice, omniscience, etc.. One might cite the ten* sefirot *(facets or aspects) of God from the Kabbalah, namely, his Divine Majesty, Wisdom, Understanding, Mercy, Justice, Beauty, Eternity, Glory, Foundationality, and Presence on earth. The Kabbalah insists on all ten being required and co-active in God for God to be God...and then pronounces the* sefirot *altogether inadequate to describe God really, who is the* Ein Sof, *the* Without End, *and beyond human imagination.*

First Commandment from Moses to the Hebrews, to the "chosen people," and only to them. But no less was it the first "demandment" from the Hebrews to God, the chosen One, in return: *"Thou shalt have no other People before us, because of all the gods, You are the One we choose."* That was the pact. That was the contract, the covenant. And covenants work two ways.

Moses' innovation was not without its inherent problems. The God of Israel might be addressed as "Lord (of gods), our God, King of the Universe," but the very fact of God's entering into a doubly binding contract with humans—albeit it with a small group of them—brings God down from ineffability, and down, too, from supreme kingship. Kings don't deal. Kings don't have to keep their word to ordinary people unless they want to. God could overturn anything and everything at will. God can retract any promise and laugh at our consternation. But according to Moses, he would not. *God would consider himself bound.* This was the miracle, the gift above all gifts: the Lord God's protection in return for loyalty and obedience to his laws.

And thus was general moral law brought under contract law, albeit a very special contract.[25] Thus too, by the same token, were *all* contracts given divine spark. All keeping of promises, all acts of honor and loyalty, all fairness, all debate and agreement between men...all justice and good business became part of religion's concern. God would become intimately involved in morality and in daily life.

And so it remained for millennia, until today, when we have a choice: Either God is "dead" and we are guided merely by conscience, nature, and the edifice of law, or God is alive in and as every free act that preserves, honors, and promotes all life or that inspires the construction of new law with that goal in mind. You know which I choose.

RETURNING TO history: on the largest view, says the theology of theopraxy, accepting the lordship of Yahweh was the means by which *a* people, the people of Israel, made a covenant with itself—a covenant between the wise and the foolish and the old and the young—to establish and preserve the ethical life down through the generations of Israel. This is one interpretation. Says the traditional believer of the same set of events at Sinai:

---

25 *Contract law was prevalent throughout Mesopotamia and Egypt at the time. A relatively new invention, contracts rapidly became the preferred way to govern business, family, and diplomatic relations. Moses' innovation (and let us recall his role in Pharoic bureaucracy) was making a contract—a covenant—with God the centerpiece of a theology. For more on this, see Bernhard Lang (2002, p. 384 ff.).*

"Thus was Israel the means by which God made a covenant with himself—promising himself, committing himself—to care for his people, on condition of their obedience to his law." This is another interpretation.

Both are good. But here is a third interpretation: The truth of this event is that the Jews were not the chos*en* people. They were the choos*ing* people. They were not "elect of God," but elected God. (Cf. EXPLANATIONS 15.) They were not God's first choice among peoples, but the first people to choose God among the scores of gods that were worshipped in ancient Mesopotamia and the scores more that were worshipped in Egypt. The Hebrews chose there to be one God, the One who was Lord of all gods, the One who created everything in heaven, everything on earth, and everything in between. The world could no longer be accepted as incoherent, that incoherence blamed on irresolvable conflicts between multiple gods (or, later, substances). It now had *one* explanation, *one* consistency, *one* purpose, *one* set of laws, *one* beginning, and *one* end. It would be centuries before the intuition of oneness would translate into the faith of kings and prophets, and millennia before it would translate into the faith of scientists—who all-too-easily forget its origin.

11 : The unsettled referent of "God"

It MIGHT seem that our theology wants to have it all ways. It wants to combine the skepticism of atheists with the trustingness of the faithful. It wants to ride the five-thousand-year-old horse of monotheism, as it were—to learn from and enjoy its stories, images, rituals, and metaphors—but it does not want to feed the horse, possess it, or be possessed *by* it.

And so detractors might ask: is it fair that the theology of theopraxy gets to *talk* about God but not actually hold to a God any believer would recognize *as God?* Is it exploitative for the theology of theopraxy to assume the pulpit, proclaiming "God is this" and "God is that...", when the audience contains people in whom *any* talk of God blooms with Biblical or Qur'anic imagery? In short, is it legitimate to capture the emotion of one set of beliefs and transfer them to another on the back of similar language?

The answer, I think, is yes.

Many if not all cultural innovations involve giving old words new meanings. Consider how *art* was re-defined in the 20th century. Or *substance* in science. Indeed, hardly a word in the dictionary means what it meant originally, and hardly a word we use today does not benefit from the weight, the shading, given to it by its past meanings. The word "God" is caught up by this process too. "God" has been a contested term for a very long time, not only between religions but also within each religion's own scholarly communities, each of whom use it in respect of the others, borrowing their opponents' meanings even as they propound theirs or new ones. Consider the marvelous Christian construction of "triune" God: Father, Son, and Holy Spirit, or the Kabbalah's Ten Sefirot (or aspects) of God, scholars of which love to insist that this God is actually identical with the One God of Genesis. God's name, image, and preferred *modus operandi* change even across the span of the Bible, as we know.

On the other hand, the meanings of words ought not to be up for grabs with every use of them. We should avoid anything like this Alice-in-Wonderland extreme. And yet we must keep open for debate and for improvement the meanings of words that mean a great deal and continue to give us trouble—words like "value," "fairness," "democracy," "person," "truth," or "justice." These are words whose deeper meanings squirm away from us as we approach them. Indeed, this is why circles of guardians, some quite fierce, gather around certain interpretations of these words, to defend them and to keep them stable. All the more is this true of "God." The theology of theopraxy sets up a new circle, as it were, helping to defend older meanings of "God" against atheism...up to a point, while offering, in the effort to make peace with all, one more thing that "God" could mean in *this* day, in *this* age.

Enough of the analogy.

The debate as to the true meaning of the word "God," which is also the debate as to God's nature, will, character, role, and so on, goes on in theological circles to this day, indeed today perhaps with more sophistication, openness, and urgency than ever before. For thinking people, for spiritual seekers, and for the *truly* devout of every religion, the meaning of "God" is not settled and cannot be. The theology of theopraxy would put a seal on this state of affairs and say: Amen, "God," if not God, is the greatest still-evolving idea human beings ever had.

12 : Beliefs that work

GOD DOES not destroy or kill; "he" only heals. God does not punish or put down; "he" only lifts us up. This is what our theology holds (see DECLARATIONS 9 and 10, and EXPLANATIONS 9). Here we reflect upon *how* God lift us up.

A young man, let us call him Peter, dies tragically. Traditional faith consoles grievers by allowing them to say to each other: "God gave Peter such life as he enjoyed *at all,* and for this we should be grateful." They are further consoled by the belief that God had something larger and better in mind for the long run—a Plan for Peter's family, or for all humankind, which required God to shorten Peter's earthly life.

To David Hume, as to Karl Popper, as to any skeptic, such consolations are deeply problematic, if only because no conceivable actual event could disconfirm their "truth": If whatever happens is God's will, then whatever happens is by definition *good,* and so it must be good that Peter died, that Kennedy was shot, that the World Trade Center came down, that Lisbon had an earthquake, and so on and on.

The theology of theopraxy here sides with neither the believers nor the skeptics. It sides with William James and the pragmatists. It makes room for *beliefs that work,* which is to say, for beliefs that, when acted upon, effect change in the world whether or not they (the beliefs) pass stringent tests of rationality or correspondence with facts.

Not all beliefs-that-work are *good,* of course, as we discussed in EXPLANATIONS 7. The point is that beliefs that work to produce goodness are worthier than better-supported beliefs that work to produce harm. If people derive genuine comfort from traditional belief in God, if they are helped to re-commit to preserving, honoring, and promoting all life (not the least their own) the sooner, then the false ideas about God upon which they rest (i.e., that God knows all, intends all, created the universe, and is wholly good)...are productive *of* God, and in that sense are not false at all.

Of course, there is one consequence that in the long run might be bad for families other than Peter's, namely, perpetuation of the belief that God *causes* inexplicable, unfair and untimely deaths, which belief in turn can support irrational so-be-it fatalism on the one hand, and equally irrational God-will-protect-me risk-taking (which is actually fatalism again) on the other. One ends up with a population divided between the resigned and the reckless.

Best, without a doubt, is holding only to good-doing truths. But there are cases, as I have said, where good-doing falsehoods are to be preferred over harm-doing truths.[26] This is why the theology of theopraxy's understanding of God in the case of grief, say, must be able to offer equal or greater long-term healing and return to life. I think it can, based in part on REFLECTIONS 17 and 18. But if it cannot, or cannot for certain people, then it must concede that for these people traditional faith is better—and *truer to God*—than the theology of theopraxy, at least in the matter of recovering from grief.

The same might be said of petitionary prayer (see REFLECTIONS 5) and prayer in general. To wit: If the effectiveness of prayer depends on the strength and literalness of one's faith in God along traditional lines, and if the theology of theopraxy, which brackets this literalness, thereby undoes that effectiveness, then either the theology of theopraxy must cede (by failure of its own mission) or it must show, with a plausibility at least as great as that which establishes the effectiveness of traditional prayer, that the good that flows from subscribing to theology of theopraxy more than compensates by, for example, lessening the longer-run social harms

---

26 *A dangerous claim, this, that "good-doing falsehoods are better than bad-doing truths," and seemingly very much counter to Kant's Categorical Imperative. But here is how it is meant.*

Tests for "good-doing" and "bad-doing" must be medium- to long-term. It is when short-term benefits are discounted that a strong bias to truth-telling emerges, because in the long run only the truth squares with the nature, with law, and with the course of events. Lies multiply and disrupt the flow of events; they undermine trust, and are apt to be injurious to life. Only upon the truth as it is best known will all people agree to agree. This is why science in general is a moral pursuit: it works in the long term. Morality without the knowledge that science provides is blinder than it has to be.

Tempering one's confidence in such unoriginal pronouncements, however, are certain technical difficulties. For one, "long term" does not specify how long a term is appropriate in any one case: seconds? hours? months? decades? For another, we often cannot predict, or discern afterwards, all the consequences of an action. Most vexing, however, is that untruths—lies, falsehoods, errors, fictions, call them what you will—are often essential to life's ongoing goodness, biologically and culturally, and it is very hard to tell, at the time of their occurrence, which untruths ought to be left to do their work and which not. All art is a lie, for example, albeit framed as such; while all tact and diplomacy involves lies not framed as such. The usefulness of language itself is based on its capacity to cause real responses to non-present realities as well as to known fictions. Misunderstanding is crucial to conversation and creativity both. And as though to make matters worse, we simply could not live if we knew, or had to know, all that there is to know before acting. Ignorance is necessary if we are to avoid paralysis—or be free.

Lest would-be subscribers to the theology of theopraxy despair, be it known that these difficulties beset all moral and religious philosophies. There are many clear goods, nonetheless, and we shall not run out of clearly-good things to do any time soon.

that the same belief might have (as I brought up earlier in the scenario of a population divided between the resigned and reckless).

FOR ATHEISTS, proof of the effectiveness of prayer would not prove that God exists. It would prove only that *faith*-in-God and trust in the *effectiveness* of prayer can make some prayers effective, maybe.[27]

Subscribers to theopraxy cannot be so summary in judgment. The difference between their view and the atheists' is subtle but significant. To wit:

The theology of theopraxy agrees that prayer to God can change things for the better, *and that this is one proof of God's existence*. But it does not go along with the traditional believer's notion of what sort of God is thus proven to exist. Even if it were shown that *only* prayer premised on belief in a singular, all-powerful, all-knowing, all-good Creator-God was effective, it still would not prove that there *was* a singular, all-powerful, all-knowing, all-good Creator-God. It might just as easily prove that the tender and real God who dwells in the human heart and in human hands—that God who is the "newest and weakest force in the universe"—requires, in some people, massive amplification in order to be actualized. But in others, God does *not* require such amplification: we know that for sure. For them, theological hyperbole is counterproductive and off-

---

27 *For example, statistical evidence suggests that religious belief improves the physical health of believers, especially in recovery from injury. But it is uncertain as to whether the cause is belief itself through promoting general optimism and lowering stress ("God will take care of me"), or the relatively temperate and hygienic lifestyles of the faithful, or the social networking provided by church attendance...rather than the response of God to petitionary prayer or in unilateral reward of piety. We can comment in this way: Skepticism about claims as to the last explanation (that God intervenes) in favor of the first few (the social-psychological benefits of faith), e.g., at www.sciencedaily.com/releases/1998/10/981030081243.htm, misses the mark entirely: for it is precisely a more moral, more social lifestyle that indirectly constitutes God. It's no use looking for God elsewhere. For example, "Altruistic Actions May Result in Better Mental Health" is the title of one article, which goes on to read: "People who offer love, listening, and help to others may be rewarded with better mental health themselves, according to a new study of churchgoers..." (From www.sciencedaily.com/releases/2003/10/031020054121.htm.) This is God in action.*

There is no way to know whether people of "better mental health" are more altruistic to start with, but whichever way the causation goes, the theology of theopraxy sees God at work. Certainly, laudatory and gratitude-expressing prayer can make the one who prays feel better, less indebted, self-expressed, forgiven, and so on. Every atheist could concede this. As far as I know, however, there is no evidence of the effectiveness of petitionary prayer on behalf of others, specifically on behalf of people who don't know they're being prayed for. See Raymond Lawrence (2006).

putting, not to mention logically troubling. These people are candidates for the conscious practice of theopraxy, and their prayers, if they do not take a different form, would be offered in a different spirit.

From the perspective of theopraxy one can see that a habitually prayerful attitude toward life is not a good thing. Chronic reliance on prayer in the trust of prayer's effectiveness, or even in the *hope* of its effectiveness, can breed both passivity and over-confidence, a problem we noted earlier, especially when it causes one to be unwilling to devise "Plan B"s on the grounds that if one made such plans it would prove lack of faith in God, *which very lack would cause God not to effect "Plan A"* (which is what one is praying for). This is a test of God, not of faith, and all creeds agree: God will not tolerate being tested.

13 : Idolatry

Thou shalt not make unto thee any graven image, or any likeness of any thing that is in heaven above, or that is in the earth beneath, or that is in the water under the earth: thou shalt not bow down thyself to them, nor serve them, for I the LORD thy God am a jealous God...

—*Exodus 20:4-5*

NO CHRISTIAN, Jew, or Muslim imagines themselves idolatrous. Those that *seem* to worship graven images (I am thinking here of Roman Catholics) are quick to point out that carvings of the crucifixion and statues of Mary are *icons*, not *idols*, designed to be prayed *with*, not *to*.

Relative to such purely metaphysical conceptions of God as Spinoza's *Deus sive Natura* (God-or-Nature), Hegel's *Absolute Spirit,* or Whitehead's *process*, however, all three of the Abrahamic religions are idolatrous to some extent, and are thus, arguably, in partial violation of their own Second Commandment. As though fearful of this possibility, representatives of the three religions like to compare themselves to each other on this score. In the eyes of Protestants, for example, Catholicism represents a lapse into paganism and idolatry. (We have seen how Catholics reply.) In the eyes of Jews and Muslims, however, *all* Christians fall into idolatry, first because prayer directed to Jesus Christ (a mortal) is made equivalent to prayer directed to God, and second, because Jesus is often, and God is sometimes, represented pictorially. Neither Judaism nor Islam permits graphic or sculptural representations of God. Devout Jews may not even spell out God's name in writing or print. Jews find the extreme veneration of the person of Mohammed by Muslims disturbing, close to being idolatrous. (In fact, Muslims do not believe that Mohammed was anything but a man, albeit a prophet. And accordingly, Mohammed himself is never prayed to.)

Lest one imagine that Judaism is free from idolatry, let it be noted that orthodox and Hasidic Jews hold a certain book—the Torah—to be the very tree of life, and treats all physical copies of it with such reverence that they could be accused of religious fetishism if not idolatry, as could conservative Muslims for their extreme veneration of the Qur'an as an object, and their obedience to all-too-human mullahs. Then again, for all three, it is from the pages of the Bible and Qur'an that God speaks; it is in and among those pages that we read how God "sees," that God is "angry," God is "pleased" or "jealous"... What does it matter that these very human images of God are graven in ink on paper rather than carved in thicker wood?[28]

One could also point to the extreme sacredness of several physical sites in the Middle East, from the Western or "Wailing" Wall and Dome of the Rock in Jerusalem to the Qaaba in Mecca.

BECAUSE IDOLATRY quite clearly permits of degrees, the Second Commandment's injunction against idolatry might best be read as a minimizing principle, something like: "Believe in Me as directly as possible, i.e., with as little idolatry as you can manage and still believe." This, effectively, is how it is taken by missionary Catholics, who often defend the Church's use of icons of Christ and the Virgin Mary in certain countries as a significant *reduction* in the number of nature gods, household gods, half-human figurines and totems that would otherwise be worshipped by the locals.

But truth be told, all the great Western religions construct an accessible mental if not physical image of an all-wise, eternal Supreme Being—King of Kings, radiant, glorious in justice and love. And for this, they are all idolatrous. Indeed, when God is addressed univocally as the omniscient, omnipotent, and benevolent governor of the world; when God is petitioned for this and that but hardly ever comes through for reasons of "his" own; when God is thought of as jealous or desiring, or angry or needful of praise and yet cannot be called to account; when God can have a son by a human woman; when God can speak, send messengers, or perform miracles...then arguably we have worship more idolatrous—for being so blind and so anthropomorphizing—than the worship of a wooden statuette, which at least can be thrown out the window.[29]

What a mess we have made of our image of God under cover of being metaphorical.

One wonders, on the other hand, what would happen if religions ever succeeded in eliminating the idolatry within them completely; that is, if they eliminated *all* human-made and human-like images of God, verbal as well as sculptural, musical as well as graphic. Would religions become so intellectualized and/or intuitivized that their moral force would be

---

28 *The copy of the Torah housed in the tabernacle of every synagogue must be a single scroll, hand-scribed in ink, and without error from beginning to end. On high holy days and on the Sabbath in Orthodox synagogues, it is bought out for use in prayer with great ceremony and care, with worshipers coming forward to press kisses transferred from prayer shawl to its tassled velvet casing, with a bow. This quasi-idolatry is weekly practice. If there is no idolatry among Reform Jews today, whom their more-Orthodox brothers would call "secularized" or "hardly Jewish," we can say it took four thousand years to make it so.*

drained? Would personal accountability to anything more than the law-of-the-land be harder to sustain? Would spontaneous feelings of gratitude for everything go undirected, without name-able recipient? Would ancient religious texts and their "naive" struggles to conceptualize God be swept away in scorn? Would one be left with nature-worship, albeit in the modern form of Buddhism-tinged deism or "process?"[30]

One hopes not, although for many it already has. We should consider the possibility that for a religion to be religion, and for "God" to refer to God, *some trace of idolatry must remain*, like the impurity in an oyster around which a pearl grows. The challenge is to allow sufficient idolatry—but no more than is necessary—to grow around our *sensus divinitatis*, without becoming its focus instead. We shall explore one way this can be done in the next chapter.

---

29 *Moshe Halbertal and Avishai Margalit (1992) essentially agree; but distinguish between* anthropomorphizing *God, which the Bible definitely does throughout, and* idolatry, *making and worshiping a sculptural or graphic depiction of God, or stand-in for God, which the Second Commandment definitely forbids. Anthropomorphizing involves creating* mental *images of God (king, husband, judge...) and are permitted. Halbertal and Margalit also note, however, that the definition of idolatry has changed over the centuries, bringing anthropomorphizing God increasingly under the rubric of idolatry. We are part of this trend.*

30 *Only in their most mystical moments do Judaism, Christianity, and Islam "allow" God to be dissolved completely into Creation, immanent and non-entitative, created and creating, and thus come close to "process." (cf. REFLECTIONS 20).*

14 : Keeping the good name

CONSIDER ZEN Buddhism. Flourishing in Japan from the 12th century on, Zen (for short) goes back to 6th-century China, where it was known as Ch'an, and before that, to the very beginnings of Buddhism in India.

Now, in every Zen temple or monastery to this day there sits a statue of the faintly smiling Buddha, usually made of wood, sometimes covered in gold leaf. Acolytes bow briefly to this image of the Buddha before and after sessions of meditation and on entering or leaving the building. Incense is lit at its feet. And yet Zen is renowned for its irreverence to doctrine, for how little quarter it gives to theology, much less idolatry. When asked "Who was the Buddha, really?" the Zen master Unmon famously replied: "A shit stick!" To the same question the master Tozan replied: "Three pounds of flax." How is this paradox in attitude accommodated?

For a start, it reminds us that Siddartha Gautama, who founded Buddhism around 500 BCE, aimed to reform Hinduism, which was an ancient religion already. In particular, he aimed to rid Hinduism of its transcendentalism and supernaturalism as well its support of the caste system. Buddhism was to be down to earth. It was to be socially just. Enlightenment was to be sought in right living, i.e., moral, rational everyday life, not in violence or passivity, not in hedonism or asceticism. Serenity and moderation were the virtues to be cultivated. Of course, centuries of institutionalization turned the Buddha's insights into an elaborate religion, with prescribed rituals and doctrines and more doctrines erected upon those. Much the same became of Jesus of Nazareth's attempts to return Judaism to its covenantal roots.

Zen today is not a religion, and does not claim to be. In cleaving to the original meaning of Buddhism ("Buddha" means "one who is awake"), it lays down no commandments, offers no elaborate moral code. Rather, Zen is a *way;* it is a way of doing things, all things, a way of looking at life and of being alive. By its meditation practices, its mental exercises *(koans),* and participation in artistic endeavors, Zen offers a path toward sudden *satori* or enlightenment, which does not mean escape from life, but being able to live spontaneously and freely while living within the moral frameworks provided by the environing religion. It is from those environing religions—Buddhism, Taoism, Confucianism, Shinto—that some quotient of idolatry seems to remain, and in particular statues of the Buddha.

So far so good. But we still haven't limned exactly why Zen devotees bow to them.

Truth is, no Zen devotee is devoted to Zen. This would be attachment. No Zen master feels obliged to put his hands together and bow before Buddha, but he does so anyway, and he does so without inner conflict. In general, we find masters of Zen both polite and brusque, both a bit selfish and a bit altruistic, just as you and I are...but with a difference that comes from not being agonized about it. They know that it's as much in their nature to be ethical as it is in a bird's nature to fly. Gracefulness is the prize: spontaneous appropriateness, ungrudging respect where it is due, and a lightness of being that is perfectly aligned with life's actual transience and absurdity.

In the mind of the Zen devotee, then, the seated Buddha is no God or idol, but simply a respected inheritance from an ancient religion, and a reminder of the man, not God, Siddartha Gautama, who long ago discovered how to live free—free not from suffering, but from suffering about suffering. Like the temple itself in its design and atmosphere, one does not dwell on this fact, but rather, *in* it.

LIKE ZEN Buddhism, the theology of theopraxy offers no detailed moral prescriptions or proscriptions of its own. It leaves these to the environing religious, philosophical, and cultural traditions, as well as to individual creativity and conscience, *insofar as they carry out the general mandate to preserve, honor, and promote life in all its forms.* (Cf. EXPLANATIONS 6)—insofar, one might say, as they support right living. Theopraxy entails no distinctive lifestyle, no manner of dress, diet, or aesthetic, except, perhaps, a tolerance for complexity and serendipity, because these qualities are the *sine-qua-non* of evolution.[31] Zen also does not require that you leave off from practicing the religion of your family or past, since it cultivates an attitude that allows one to see ritual practices as not-serious in the way they advertise themselves to be.[32]

The theology of theopraxy is not Zen Buddhism, of course. But it

---

31 *Complexity, that is, in amounts that reflect and promote the complexity of life itself. It may seem strange to inject aesthetic/stylistic concerns here, but like it or not, styles have moral overtones, and sometimes, in execution, moral consequences. A subscriber to the theology of theopraxy would have to be tolerant to many a culture's tastes in music, art, architecture, poetry, cuisine, and so forth, and would be naturally suspicious of styles that embrace and ideologies that promote universal asceticism. The theology of theopraxy suggests we enjoy color, spontaneity, subtle orderings, reflexivity, generosity, lux, calme et volupte...these things over efficiency, distillations, self-denial, or simplicity simpliciter.*

32 *To my mind, Alan Watts was exemplary of a Christian Zen Buddhist. See especially Watts (1974 a and b). Many American Zen practitioners and teachers today are Jewish, e.g., Philip Kapleau (1967) and Barry Magid (2002).*

asks for the same embrace of life, including life's traditionally religious dimensions, without succumbing to unnecessarily idolatrous beliefs and without imagining that there is a rigid relation between correct *ritual* behavior and God's approval. In obedience to the Second Commandment, it leaves the images that fill prayerbooks and sermons in place but behind. It leaves these picturings of God behind for the feeling of God as the good we do anywhere, any time. It leaves them behind for knowing God as an image-less *activity*, rather clumsily called "good doing," the fruits of which are all around, in every bridge that stands while cars roar over, in every bell that rouses the sleepy shop owner. Although it is more difficult to form a singular picture of this God than it is to form a picture of a King on high, or even of a ghostly spirit, it is not impossible, as I have tried to demonstrate.

Theopraxy begins with seeing God first *in* and then *as* the otherwise unaccountable goodness in human eyes, words, and actions, first *in* and then *as* the choosing more life for the least of creatures when one could easily do otherwise, or the taking of a course of action that benefits others at least as much as oneself. It ends with understanding that God *is* not where good-doing is not—and that God's presence, therefore, is up to us. God is at the core of the theology of theopraxy; not God of the Bible and Qur'an, as I have said many times, but a distillation of "him" that yields us, finally and merely, God's goodness and God's name. To change this God's name from *God*, or to call God *"It"* in the attempt to avoid accusations of anthropomorphizing or of "poaching" on religion, would be to break the thread of the ancient quest to know God, to find God in human history rather than in the stars. "God" is a good name and the right name for what religious seekers are after, preserving, in the theology of theopraxy, that faint trace of idolatry that must be kept for a religion to be a religion and for "God" to refer to God.

The theology of theopraxy, I submit, is monotheism at its least idolatrous. It is theism at the last stop in the line of abstraction that ends in God disappearing into the indifferent "Process" or "Ground of Being" from which God emerged but *in* which and as which God has no existence at all.

THE GREATEST of all early-modern Jewish sages and the founder of Hasidic Judaism was Yisrael ben Eliezer of Okop, which is in the Ukraine. By the time he was thirty-six, in 1734, he had become known as the *Ba'al Shem Tov,* which means the "keeper of the good name." It is easy to miss the profundity of this odd-sounding appellation: "keeper of the good name." For what the Ba'al Shem Tov kept from semantic harm, what he exemplified by his actions and transformative stories, was the name of the good, the *good* name of the good, which is: *God.*

Hasidism is a movement focused on the joy of living the ethically good life and accepting the possibility—no, the necessity—of an intuitive personal connection to (the Biblical) God in His fullness and mystery to do so. The Ba'al Shem Tov taught, of course, within the framework of the theological language available to him. Like all great sages, he used the metaphors and images of his milieu to point to deeper truths. Like all mystical teachers he was unafraid of apparent paradox, unafraid of saying "dangerous things."

Now, among the Ba'al Shem Tov's most paradoxical and dangerous sayings is this: "the Evil is the throne for the Good."[33] I close this chapter with an attempt to understand what it could mean.

The phrase ends a passage in which the Ba'al Shem is lauding the real-world one-ness of God, which includes evil things too.[34] Were his an ordinary theology, we would be forced to accept that evil is in God, and God in evil, as deists, vitalists, and process theologians must. But the Ba'al Shem's choice of the *throne* metaphor is crucial to understanding his meaning. After all, a throne is the *place* of the king, not the king himself, who occupies it, who sits in it, and who is the emanator of justice. A throne without a king is just a big chair, or an abstract "position." The throne awaits the king, then, and becomes a throne only upon his arrival.

In the same way (and now I make the transition to the theology of theopraxy), God, who is goodness *in action,* acts most strikingly where God is most needed—which is upon the bad, the indifferent, the chaotic, the rigid, the ill, the dying, the dark. God does not act conspicuously where God's redemptive action is not needed, where everything is already all goodness, light, and life. In those places God is already in place, as it were, and at work, and it takes gratitude to notice. To say God's place is in evil is analogous to saying that a nurse's place is in a hospital.

"The Evil is the throne for the Good," then, is a paradox—a dangerous saying. But its paradoxicality dissolves when we see God as—when we see that God *is*—redemptive action, that God is the "transformative doing" that can happen equally and identically and completely everywhere

---

33 *Ba'al Shem Tov, "Instructions in Intercourse with God," translated by Martin Buber (1958, p. 208).*

34 *"The indwelling Glory embraces all worlds, all creatures, good and evil. And it is the true unity. How can it then bear in itself the opposites of Good and Evil? But in truth there is no opposite: the Evil is a throne for the Good." Ibid.*

there is good to be done, and is done—which is to say, everywhere life can be preserved, honored, and promoted, and is. "This is the mystery of the oneness of God," said the Ba'al Shem Tov,

> that at whatever place I, an insignificant bit, lay hold of it, I lay hold of the whole. And since all teaching and all Commandments are radiations of His being, so he who fulfills any one mitzvah [commandment from God]... by this single mitzvah lays hold of the oneness of God, and thereby holds the whole in his hand as though he had fulfilled the entire Torah.[35]

In short, God, whole in every part, is to be king in every soul.

---

35 *Op cit., p. 191. My words in brackets.*

15 : More on idolatry

YOU MIGHT hear this said some day: "Religion says: God created humans. The theology of theopraxy says: humans created God. This the worst idolatry I've ever heard!" What might we reply?

First, "humans create God" is too brief, by half, to encapsulate what the theology of theopraxy asserts, which is that God evolves in and along with humankind. Humankind evolves as it advances the work of God, and God evolves through the better acts of humankind, in a rough but ultimately upward spiral of mutual development, of "co-evolution." Human beings and God create each other.[36] This is a much more complex picture.

Second, the God that (the theology of theopraxy says) we actually create is *not* God-the-Creator, God of the Bible, as we have discussed a number of times.

Then too, to say that "humans create God" does not yet say *how* we do this or should. It is certainly *not* through carving little statues and worshipping them. Here the theology of theopraxy and the Abrahamic religions agree. But nor is it through elevating certain people to Godhood and worshipping them instead. Here the theology of theopraxy, the Torah and Qur'an agree. No, God is realized in and through the *doing* of good. All who follow this Way are of equal stature, in kind, if not in degree. Here the theology of theopraxy sits alone, with a few helpful images to meditate upon: hand-cupped flames, fireflies, games...

Third, and finally, we can reply to those who, like St. Anselm, maintain that God cannot be conceived (of) by humans *at all,* with the implication that anything definitively said of God is idolatrous for being, inevitably, *wrong.*

Such worries can be laid to rest. The theology of theopraxy has not "cracked God's code." No theology has. God is not done with us, nor we with God. God will change with us, and we with "him." But we can do better, logically, ethically, and morally, than we are doing now when we invoke God, or pray, or debate theological questions. We must continue to try to conceive of God as He/She/That who/which (choose two) acts

---

36 *Religion's traditional emphasis on God's temporal and causal priority is strategic. It improves the behavior of the credulous and naturally dependent. Theopraxy's emphasis on the converse is strategic too. It improves the behavior of the non-credulous and naturally independent.*

in through, by, and *as* human beings acting on behalf of all life every-where. This idolizes no person and no thing.

Says the theology of theopraxy: one can conceive God completely (as in 'give rise to') without conceiving *of* God completely (as in 'figure out in totality'). God is an activity recognized instantly by those who have freely done and known good themselves. It confounds those who have not.

16 : The burning bush

Now Moses...came to the mountain of God, even to Horeb. And the angel of the Lord appeared unto him in a flame of fire out of the midst of a bush: and he looked, and, behold, the bush burned with fire, and the bush was not consumed. And Moses said, I will now turn aside, and see this great sight, why the bush is not burnt. And when the Lord saw that he turned aside to see, God called unto him out of the midst of the bush, and said, Moses, Moses. And Moses said, Here am I. And He said, Draw not nigh hither: put off thy shoes from off thy feet; for the place whereon thou standest is holy ground. Moreover He said, I am the God of thy father, the God of Abraham, the God of Isaac, and the God of Jacob. And Moses hid his face; for he was afraid to look upon God.

— *Exodus 3: 1–6 (King James Bible)*

HERE GOD speaks directly to Moses from a bush that burns but is not consumed. This well-known image is telling for two reasons (aside from the fact that God is speaking at all): first because it reports a contravention of the laws of nature (flames consume what they burn, bushes don't talk), and second because the event is extraordinarily timely and consequential. It reports, therefore, a *miracle*, which in turn authorizes the message (cf. EXPLANATIONS 20).

Distracting, I suggest, is the "bush." What kind of bush was it? we naturally want to know. (Or at least *I* do.) Was it really a tree? Then too: how exactly was it burning? With hot flames, all crackling and smoke? Or was it just radiant with its own sheer presence?

And why does God choose *ventriloquism* in the first place? Why not speak to Moses from thin air, or as an inner voice? Shades of idolatry? Or why not from a stone or a bird rather than a "bush"? Is it because these things do not typically *burn*? Excuse the pun, but I think we are getting warm.

Let us not focus on the speech or the bush, then, but on the burning itself, for these are flames, we are told, *that do not consume*. This is the heart of the trope.

NOW THE theology of theopraxy, not very originally, uses the image of fire, of flames, as a prime metaphor for how God can exist in the same way anywhere, be complete there, and yet be particular to a location. Also as an image of how goodness seems to radiate from certain acts and certain people as holy light, as halos around them, as shining brows, twinkling eyes, and so on.[37] So here, possibly, is another lesson of the burning bush story: not that God *protects* from conflagration the things and people he values (which God does elsewhere in the Bible, e.g., Daniel 3:22-27), but that goodness-in-action is like a flame that produces warmth and light without destroying its host. This flame is generative rather than consumptive. It is a giving without a taking. It is a making without a destroying. Quite inverse to ordinary fire, we might call it (un-originally again) *sacred fire*.[38]

Let us go one level deeper into the poetics of Exodus 3:1-6, a level at once more scientific and more religious.

Ordinary fire is the energy released when the molecules of complex and organized matter, like wood, break down into simpler and more disorganized molecules, like carbon ash and carbon dioxide, by a heat-generating and heat-perpetuated chemical reaction. The heat (and light) given off by the natural burning of wood can be understood as the energy of sunlight, stored by the tree over several years in a library of hierarchically structured molecules, rapidly being liberated.

Sacred fire is ordinary fire's entropic (not to say metaphoric) complement. It emits from processes that convert lower, less complex-and-organized systems (like piles of soil, water, and sunshine) into higher, more complex-and-organized ones (like cells, trees, and people). Sacred fire does not consume but *produces*. It is the fire that glows from those who turn ashes into trees again, who turn ruins into beauty and death into new life. It is fire that speaks, fire that teaches—an image of Logos—and it is fire that can be seen only by those who are ready to see it.

Sacred fire produces the light of God. It does not consume its source. It has no remote source of fuel. Neither singular nor fierce, the light of God is like the light of fireflies, of hand-cupped matches, of shining brows, of inner illuminations, of kindnesses between sons and daughters, of humble neural bushes sending sparks into the void.

---

37 *The New Testament is replete with references to the holy light that radiated from Jesus; especially the Gospel of John. One scientific explanation: the involuntary dilation of the viewer's pupils when seeing the object of their adoration.*

38 *The image of sacred fire, of course, is common in several mythologies. In the Bhagavad Gita, Chapter 7, Verse 9, the Lord says: "I am the brilliance in the fire." The Celts believed in keeping the sacred fire, which they never let die. In synagogues to this day an "eternal flame" flickers over the ark and is never turned off. Holy fire is a favorite image too in Hasidic Judaism: as "lifting the sparks" is a metaphor for doing the good, and thus restoring God's unity.*

17 : Starting with "as if"

IF YOU believe in God in the conventional way, then you believe that whatever happens happens because God intended it to or permitted it to. Good fortune enjoyed by the wicked, like bad fortune suffered by the righteous, only *seems* random or perverse. For in truth, behind all events there is a larger order and a larger purpose, which is God's Plan, which is unquestionably for the good. This belief has soothed many a troubled heart. It has helped many a soul accept—indeed embrace—what in fact they had no choice *but* to accept. This is to its credit. Unfortunately, it is an effect based on a false belief.

Now, you may not agree with this judgment, which is the atheist's bitter critique of faith. But rejecting the atheist's critique does not undo the plain fact that the belief that God has a Plan has persuaded many a person to accept what they had no need to accept, should not have accepted, and would have done better to try to change.

What does the theology of theopraxy offer that helps in this matter?

When faced with an especially absurd or unfair event, it suggests adopting an "as if" strategy, at least to start. We should decide to act, and then act, *as if* there were a God as described above—i.e., a God who planned the event and thus has given it meaning already—but a God *who is mainly interested in the event's effect upon you, and in what actions you will take because of it.*[39] God can be who *will* turn this otherwise senseless event into the *beginning* of a meaningful and life-enhancing sequence of events *through you.* Once embraced in this future-oriented context—as the beginning of something rather than the end—the event will be absurd no more, and the question of whether or not God planned it in the first place becomes less important.[40] In general, when the idea of God

---

[39] *Says the true believer: "Yes, and God planned your reaction too! That was part of it from the beginning." Such arguments, like so many involving God, are irrefutable, as Karl Popper pointed out, and thus without empirical content. In the last chapter of this book I will argue that the "as if" strategy, thought of as an "as if strategy" is only a first step toward theopraxy.*

[40] *Analogy: Here is a happily married couple, both members of which like to believe that their in-fact-chance first meeting was planned by a higher power. This is undeniably a wonderful feeling. But they know that it was their subsequent, together-made happiness that is lending meaning to their first encounter retrospectively, redeeming it from chance, as it were, rescuing it from orphanhood. Let their love falter, however, and suddenly their first meeting will seem less fated.*

gives meaning to what is otherwise meaningless, then God becomes more than a remote and impassive First Cause, capricious in "his" oversight since. When we redeem the random events of the world by *making* them the beginning of a sequence of non-random events that serve life, God becomes actual. God becomes what God has always and only been: life increasing itself through conscious human action.

It is here, at this last turn in the road of faith, that the subscriber to the theology of theopraxy takes his or her leave from the traditional true believer. God is in our hands because good is. The past has always to be redeemed by turning the present toward a better future. The present is always a juncture, a switching station.

We are not the first to think along these lines. Within Judaism, we come upon the concept of *tikkun olam*.

18 : Tikkun olam

WHAT DOES *tikkun olam* mean?

Tikkun is a Hebrew word that means *repair, healing,* or *uplift. Olam* means "the whole world." Its context is a striking world-creation myth penned by Rabbi Isaac Luria in the 16th century and known as *tzimtzum* ("self-withdrawal" or "self-contraction").

In this myth, God is imagined as holy light, a light that once filled the universe so fully that God and universe were co-terminous: they were One. Then, in the act of divine will that appears to us as Creation, God withdrew or contracted himself from all to part, leaving reality as we see it: differentiated, in constant movement, with shade and shadow, solid and void, both a remainder and a reminder of original perfection. Why did God do this? In an act of canonical, self-sacrificial love, it was in order to leave room for the stars, for the earth, and for us, that we might be; and at the same time to give us a purpose. And what is that purpose? It is *tikkun olam*. It is to repair, heal, restore, lift up, and return whatever is broken and whosoever is fallen to a position of blissful original unity with God: like sparks back to the mother fire, like shards back to the unbroken window.

A magnificent vision, this, both esthetically and ethically. Creation is seen as a withdrawal of God from the universe, a Fall that precedes the Fall described in Genesis where disobedience to God results in God's bequeathing humanity a life of labor in a world without steady divine protection. And yet this first withdrawal—*tzimtzum*—was not a punishment but a gift...the gift of everything you see around you, the pebbles, the stars, life itself.[41]

The Creation sequence imagined by Luria stands at the logical extreme of the idea of an original paradise. The story of *tzimtzum* tells us that

---

[41] *I have already remarked (ARGUMENTS, Note 37) upon the similarity between* tzimtzum *as a cosmogony and the theory of cosmic inflation by Alan Guth (1997). Might Guth have read the Zohar? One can also compare Luria's metaphorics (or is it metaphysics?) to the Hindu and Buddhist doctrine of the transcendental world soul, Brahman, of which every individual soul,* atman, *is a fragment, destined to return to Brahman in ecstatic reunion. In Hinduism, this happens when the* atman *escapes the cycle of death and rebirths and melts, sinless at last, into Brahman in a final death. In Luria's vision, the "raising of the sparks" is done by virtuous deeds, in living acts of reconstruction. Death is not the solution. Might Luria have read the Bhagavad Gita? Might Teilhard de Chardin have read Luria?*

before there was "reality" at all, before there were "waters" to hover over or voids to form, there was only God, God in full, perfect, and without end *(ein sof)*. Material and energic reality, heaven-and-earth, the cosmos...is already a fallen state, and a partially abandoned one. Depressing? Not at all. For Luria's vision is also a future-looking one inasmuch as it delineates an obligation to bring about a future unity and perfection, not in theory but in *reality*, a restoration of God on the one hand, but a new configuration of the facts of existence on the other since Creation cannot be undone or reversed.

This obligation, this call to action, is what gives Luria's vision an ethical force that transcends NeoPlatonism. God's willful contraction of himself in order to leave room for the world as we know it is to be matched by *our* willfully applying ourselves *in return*—in return, that is, for our very existence—to innumerable gift-like acts of ethical care and creativity: *tikkun olam*, the "making-good" of the world. Our charge is to "lift the sparks" until the world is made whole and holy again, illumined in every quarter by God's light—indeed consisting of God's light again, but differently.

Whether or not we accept this charge, of course, is up to us. We are free. The reward to future generations will be the nonpareil experience of ecstatic self-dissolution into unity with God; but, as much to be desired and undoubtedly the whole point of the image, the reward in our lifetimes will be the living of *a meaningful life until then*. Could one ask for more? To Isaac Luria and the many sincere readers of the Kabbalah to this day, the answer is: No.

THEOPRAXY IS less ecstatic. It does not promise mystical unity with God if that means eyes closed in bliss, individuality gone, desires expunged and consciousness flooded by light or love or the hum of the universe. Nor does its theology offer the good eternal life in heaven. No, God is simply the good we do when we do it, which is not always, or with the same intensity or success. Which means—personification permitting—that God feels like what *we* feel like, and we feel like what *God* feels like, when we do good.[42] You are as united with God as you will ever be when and where you pick up a child to get a drink from a tall faucet; when and where you resist the temptation to slander; when and where you make a difficult choice that favors the lives of many over the

---

42 *Two things to note. First: doing good does not always "feel good" in the hedonistic sense. Often doubt persists, and often there is pain. When there is pain, however, it is "good pain," worthwhile pain, bearable pain, consented-to or welcomed pain, life-preserving, life-honoring, and life-promoting pain.*

few, or when and where you make something better than it has to be "just because." In the view of theopraxy, God is not who or what *tikkun olam* is directed at. *Tikkun olam* is who or what God is, God "himself," God in person(s), God in action.[43]

I feel sure Rabbi Luria would not quibble: *"Tikkun (olam)* is a collective task,"* he wrote. *"A divine spark is attached to each prayer, each charitable act, each moment of goodness. If a person fulfills her duty and strictly follows the ethical path, that spark is restored to its source in the divine realm. To assist another is to do God's work. To redeem one person is to redeem the world."*[44]

< *Second: when I say God feels like what we feel like and we feel like what God feels like when we do good, I am not referring to God of the Bible. For otherwise we would feel all-powerful, all-wise, all-knowing, all-good, personally responsible for the entire universe, and deserving—no, demanding—of worship...which we clearly are not and should not, even when we do good. Rather, I am trying to make a statement of what I believe God (according to the theology of theopraxy) actually "feels like," which is a far more modest thing: to wit, pleased without being proud, clear-conscienced without being ignorant, warmed without being overheated, glad to be alive and grateful-in-advance for the opportunity to do good again. In short, I am trying here to describe what the-good-we-do feels like to the one who does it. I would not presume to know what God of the Bible feels like to Himself, if that even makes sense. Personification here simply short-circuits.*

43 *"One hour obeying God's commandments in this world, is more glorious than an eternity in the World to Come." (Talmudic saying quoted, unattributed, by Meir Y. Solo-veichik [2003, p. 41]). In Zen Buddhism, which is not explicitly theistic or ethical, as we have discussed, enlightenment is not intended to remove you from reality so that you can live in a bubble of personal bliss. It is intended, rather, to help you engage life-at-large without illusions, to be open to all things but incorruptible. Of particular interest in this regard is the Zen allegory of "The Ten Cow-Herding Pictures." Here enlightenment (satori) is pictured as a lone cow that has wandered away from the herdsman and gotten lost. The first seven pictures depict the process of search (starting with the realization that one has lost the cow at all!). By the eighth picture the cow has been found and ridden. The ninth picture is blank: there is no cow, there is no herdsman: even enlightenment is transcended. In the tenth, our herdsman joins the life of the marketplace—ordinary life—in joy. See Daisetz T. Suzuki (1986, p. 363 ff.).*

44 *Isaac Luria, in Joseph Dan (1986) as cited by Gail Hornstein (2000, p. xvi). I wonder whether these are Luria's exact words. Did he mean to imply that it takes everyone's effort to redeem one person?*

19 : Man in God's place?

ACCORDING TO Pope John Paul II, secularism "puts Man in God's place."[45] This is a very bad thing. Does the theology of theopraxy "put Man in God's place"? Is it just secularism masquerading as religion?

No. And no again. To believe that "God is in our hands" is not at all to believe that humans *are* God—still less that *I* am God, that *you* are God, or that *he* or *she* is God. When God is the good we do, as our theology holds, we are not only responsible to God, but responsible *for* God, as discussed in EXPLANATIONS 18. Responsibility for God is half the meaning of God's being "in our hands."[46]

No person is God, no creature, and no thing. But we all have responsibility *to* God and *for* God's continued existence. Even if a few zealots overly pleased with the good they had just done thought for a moment they *were* God, they would not imagine that they had become God-of-the-Bible, almighty creator, and so forth. The God that theopraxy strives to bring into being is a sparkle.

The way God is portrayed in the Bible, and that conservative clergy are committed to perpetuating, is but a way to impress people with the power of goodness, lest they discover that goodness, in fact, is the youngest

---

45 *In August 2002, Pope John Paul II visited Cracow, Poland. Here is the report of* The New York Times: *"Frequently man lives as if God did not exist, and even puts himself in God's place," the pope said. "He claims for himself the Creator's right to interfere in the mystery of human life," he added...referring to a range of issues that clearly included abortion, cloning and euthanasia. "Rejecting divine law and moral principles, he openly attacks the family."*

"...The blame for this," (the pope) went on to say, lay partly with "the noisy propaganda of liberalism, of freedom without truth or responsibility." In his homily, he deplored the way that modern civilization "wishes to determine life through genetic manipulation and to establish the limit of death." ...He said people were trying "to silence the voice of God in human hearts" and to "make God the great absence in the culture and the consciences of people." He spoke of previously unimagined dangers in the world, a phrase that seemed to encompass new implements and methods of warfare as well as the expanding frontiers of medicine. "Man lives in fear of the future, of emptiness, of suffering, of annihilation.." Frank Bruni (2002, p. A3.)

46 *The other half of the meaning is that God exists as what good we actively* do—*make happen*—*by our actions, by our "hands." I do not propose that God is in the good we make happen, which is like saying God is in nature, or in the love we have for one another, and so forth. This is only a first approximation to the theology of theopraxy's proposal, which is that God exists as the good we make happen.*

and weakest 'force' in the universe dependent upon them for its propagation and so lose confidence in the ability of goodness to prevail.

But times have changed. Religions must change too, as well as the content of the faith that undergirds them. In this secular and scientific era, with human beings massively empowered by technology, it is not any New Age religion, nor any return to the "tried and true" of orthodox religion that will work to bring God back to life (in both senses of that phrase). It is the theology of theopraxy's understanding of God, I submit, that stands the best chance of re-awakening "the voice of God in human hearts," and of "making God the great *presence* in the culture and consciences of people" that God needs to be.[47]

---

47 *John Paul II, quoted in Bruni (2002), op. cit.*

20 : Guidance from God, firm and gentle

ALL BELIEVERS expect guidance or direction from God. Some expect that guidance to be firm; others expect it to be gentle.

Firm guidance or direction is easy to recognize. God presents "himself" to you in a vision or dream; or God speaks from nowhere; or from a fire or mist; or God temporarily undoes the laws of probability or of physics on your behalf. After a period of prayer, you might wake up one morning to find yourself resolved to do something you have never done before or even considered doing before—something good, something great!—and you know exactly how to go about it. Or out of the blue a weight feels lifted from your shoulders, and a chronic fear, obsession, or tiredness vanishes like smoke. Or in a jam, you find that you know things you never knew you knew, that you have strengths or talents you did not have before. In all such cases God most definitely demonstrates his power and his interest in *you*.

Gentle guidance or direction from God is harder to detect. God's "signs and wonders" are not as obvious, not as impressive. Very likely your patience will be tested. God might speak to you through anyone, in words that do not at first seem wise, or in actions that do not at first seem helpful. Like the philosopher, you are "condemned" to living in doubt, each evening sifting through the events of the day as though for gold: "Was God trying to tell me something there?" But you know you cannot be *too* meditative on this score because, like a warrior, you must often act while still uncertain as to whether you are doing the right thing, as to whether you heard God aright—or at all.

It would seem that the believer who expects firm guidance is in better position, psychologically: less confused, less doubtful. But, in fact, the expectation of either type—firm or gentle—has its problems.[48]

For example, if you expect firm guidance or direction from God, you might well spend too long waiting for it—waiting, say, for deliverance

---

48 *The Bible often seems to want to have it both ways. Here, in an emblematic passage (1 Kings 19:11–13) God heralds his imminent presence with a show of strength, but actually manifests himself as a "still small voice" which, like the voice of conscience, is hearable only after the storm of emotion has passed through: "The Lord said, 'Go out and stand on the mountain in the presence of the Lord, for the Lord is about to pass by.' Then a great ›*

from the wrong job or a harmful relationship. You might hold on to damaging beliefs indefinitely because you think yourself unauthorized to change them without a clear indication from God that changing them would be good, and what beliefs to change them *to*. Advice from friends falls on deaf ears. The maxim "God helps those who help themselves" sounds callow, faithless. You might turn down reasonable offers and incremental opportunities because they do not solve your problem at a single swoop (as God surely *could* do if he wanted to...so he must not want to). In the absence of firm guidance, you might finally believe that the reason for God's silence is due to the weakness of your faith. And so you might re-commit yourself to the religious life, attempting to twist God's arm, as it were; or at least get God's attention by praying harder, getting baptized, changing churches, going on pilgrimages or performing some feat of charity or self-sacrifice. You might also follow some charismatic preacher who will tell you quite clearly what God is saying to you.

Can good come of expecting (and accepting) only firm direction from God and waiting for it? Yes. But only if you resolve to do better in some specific area of your life *while you wait*. Indeed you must be happy to wait, because, as every religion will vouchsafe, God cannot be persuaded, tempted, blackmailed, hurried up, or bargained with. God's judgment as to whom to direct, when, and how, is sovereign; and there is no higher court of appeal.

Expecting and accepting only *gentle* guidance has its problems too. Among them is uncertainty about what God is advising. Worse, perhaps, is developing hypersensitivity to *clues* as to God's will—worse because it leads to a kind of paranoia. After all, if everything could be a sign from God depending on interpretation, how do you know you are *not* hearing God's voice? God can speak through anyone: the bum on the corner, a minister, a child...even your mother-in-law. God might speak in overheard remarks as well as ones addressed to you. Or "his" message might be scattered about in the silent conversation you carry on with yourself all the time.[49] Is this not maddening? One might as well read tea leaves!

< *and powerful wind tore the mountains apart and shattered the rocks, but the Lord was not in the wind. After the wind there was an earthquake, but the Lord was not in the earthquake. After the earthquake came a fire, but the Lord was not in the fire. And after the fire came a gentle whisper. When Elijah heard it, he pulled his cloak over his face and went out and stood at the mouth of the cave. Then a voice said to him, 'What are you doing here, Elijah?'"*

49 *In Book 8 of* Confessions, *Augustine tells that his conversion to Christianity and the ascetic life came during a time of emotional upheaval, and hearing a child in the courtyard* >

And once you have acted, there is always the problem of rationalization after the fact: Wanting to preserve the rightness of your reading of God's will, and the goodness of the advice itself, you are likely to judge *whatever* followed from heeding "his" voice as having been for the best.

And finally there is this problem with gentle guidance: social unreliability. Take chance encounters. If chance encounters are actually arranged by God, then why keep the appointments one has already made? Similarly, if it is God who presents new opportunities at every turn, why fulfill old commitments and contracts? Does God not move in mysterious ways? Lack of confidence that we have heard God correctly can lead us to make safe choices or risky ones, but, in either case, choices to which we are not much, or not long, committed.

To skeptics and atheists the solution to all these problems is simple: "Don't believe in God." For their part, deists can say "believe in God, just don't expect guidance, direction, or advice. God is not that sort of God." Both recommend that we rely for moral direction on reason, law, virtue, utility calculation, philosophy, and ethical intuition. Consult with the wise, they would say, with the ethically trained, with friends. Get educated. Get used to uncertainty.

But the theology of theopraxy is neither atheism nor deism. It is more congenial to the gentle-guidance expectation and would work to combat its attendant problems. The voice of conscience is indeed God's voice, as 1 Kings 19:11–13 and 1 Samuel 3:1–10 seem to suggest. And the advice of good friends is God's voice too. But this faith is tempered with the belief that people have ultimate authority and responsibility for their choices. When God is the good we do and not the good any faraway, all-knowing, all-powerful, and entreatable deity would do on our behalf, we realize that we take the guidance we want to take, and must stand prepared to learn from its outcomes. God depends on our "good sense." God seeks out the same reasonable, far-sighted, and benevolent people that skeptics and atheists would seek out too. God expects us to take the initiative, always.

The theology of theopraxy understands that God's guidance shows up as a feeling that is more often delicate than dominant. But dominant or delicate, firm or gentle, clear or ambiguous, one is never literally in dialogue with any distant powerful being. The latter is a construction that

---

< of a neighboring house chanting *"take and read; take and read..."* He took this as instruction from God through the child to open the Bible at random and read; and so Augustine did, and this changed his life. For the whole story, visit www.takeandread.org.

atheists concede is forgivable—even useful—because "ordinary people" (unlike themselves) are such deeply social creatures that they find it easier to *think* in dialogical, dramaturgical terms, and because ordinary people (unlike themselves) are so dull that they *need* their consciences to speak to them as though it were a universal, singular, and powerful entity "outside of space and time." But the theology of theopraxy rejects the atheist's disdain.[50] Coming halfway back to traditional faith, it says this: that the feeling of "hearing God's voice" or of being guided by signs, which is entirely delusional to the atheist, is not delusional at all. The concept of God, even in its oldest formulations, is neither a mistake nor a waste of time. The voice we hear today might not speak from the clouds and it might or might not speak in the language of the Bible, but from whatever voice or text or action we are persuaded to do good or are shown how, it is God who speaks—or rather, the idea of God that speaks. Where there is good to be done, the idea of God emerges and precipitates in us the desire to realize "him," to bring "him" into actual *being* by our actual *doing*. This, after all, is what it means to love God with all one's heart, not promises of obedience sung to the rafters.

---

50 *For a recent example of that disdain, and its source in immaturity, see Sam Harris (2004).*

21 : Beholding God's presence

GOD ACTS through us and in no other way. This is a fact to which we should become accustomed. The trouble is, of course, that we can never be *sure* that the course of action we have chosen will turn out well, let alone for the best, and never be sure that the voice we listened to was God's. As though representing us all, Moses, in frustration, cries out to God to show himself in full: "Let me behold Your Presence!" (Exodus 33:18–23). And in what is one of the most electrifying passages in the Bible, God answers:

> *"I will make all My goodness pass before you, and I will proclaim...the grace that I grant, and the compassion that I show. But...you cannot see My face... I will shield you with My hand until I have passed by, and then I will take My hand away,* and you will see My back."[51]

I should like to attempt an exegesis of this passage through the lens of our theology.

First: what is the lesson of the above passage? Could it be that we can only *know* we have done good after the fact (i.e., after God has passed by)? That we can know that God *was here*—we can see His back—but not that God is here.[52]

Perhaps. But this cannot be the last word. After all, God is here speaking to Moses in the present tense, as God does repeatedly throughout the book of Exodus. But Moses wants more than disembodied voices, fires, columns of smoke and other signs. He wants to see God. But God refuses, showing Moses instead what God *does:* 'I will make not My figure but My goodness pass before you; I will show you "the grace that I grant, and the compassion that I show," My figure detected only in motion: a sudden warmth over your face, a breeze, and then My vanishing back.'[53]

And so the subscriber to theopraxy, together with the liberal-minded believer, can ask: "When you and I, in good faith, deliberate the good,

---

51 *I have here used the* Tanakh, *in the new JPS translation of the Holy Scriptures according to the traditional Hebrew Text (1988).*

52 *Cf. Lawrence Kushner (1994, pp. 94,95).*

53 *This "passing by" and "breeze" trope is similar to the one in Genesis 3:8; another occasion in which God is heard and felt but not seen. That God's invisibility could be due to his placing his hand right in front of our face(s) is itself an interesting image. Are we blinded by hubris the very moment we even seek His visage? The Bible is more daringly* ›

who is speaking?" and answer: *"God."* Or "When compassion, beauty, and justice are unfolding in the events around, who is 'passing by'?" and also answer: *"God."*

THERE IS more, of course. "No man can see My face and live!" God declares in the same passage (verse 20). The usual interpretation of this verse goes like this: to see God directly, face to face, would be so terrifying an encounter that it would kill a mere mortal. There is another interpretation however, one that is more aligned to the theology of theopraxy's "kinder, gentler" view of God. It requires that I tell a true, not-at-all-religious story, and treat it metaphorically.

It was near the end of a long day touring the architecture of France. My wife and I, with another young couple, were barreling along a tree-canopied avenue in a (very) small Fiat when suddenly, between the golden leaves and boughs whizzing by, I spied a ravishingly beautiful white chateau. "Stop," I cried, "go back. I have to photograph that building." I was sitting in the back of the little two-door and so it took a minute to get out with my camera bag. I ran back along the road, peering through the trees. No chateau! I clambered up on a wall and walked along it, ducking up and down. No good. All I could glimpse here and there, between the leaves, was a patch of white an indefinite distance away (was it a wall?), and then...was it a window, a roof-line? Yes, but no picture was possible here. I returned to the car, defeated. I realized that the only way to see this lovely building from the road was to travel past it at around 40 m.p.h., letting the slivers of view permitted by the dense foliage reveal it over time. Stop to stare, and it would be gone.[54]

And so it is with many things, including God. God is not invisible. But God's shape—God's *"face"*—is visible only as events unfold in a certain way next to us and around us—while God and we are in relative motion, so to speak, past each other. Stop to confront God and God vanishes. Demand that he show himself and you will be met by the sight of the good

---

‹ metaphorical, not to say inconsistent in places, about the consequences of seeing God's face. Exodus 33:11 for example reads: "And the Lord spoke to Moses face to face, as a man speaks to his friend." In our theology there is nothing to fear in meeting God "face to face." Or trying to.

54 *The perception psychologist J. J. Gibson explained how we see a stable three-dimensional world using the highly changeable, two-dimensional images that fall on our retinas in the same way. We detect the invariants (cross-ratio proportions, texture gradients, optical flow accelerations, shearing edges, and so forth) in the flux of images, and those invariants correspond to a stable world and reveal it. Stop the flux, and we literally go blind. See J. J. Gibson (1966).*

already in the world, proceeding without you. We see God through the way the world works and as we work, not in the world as an entity among others. We see only God's ever-vanishing back. And feel the breeze.

22 : God most contingent

God is not some particularly good thing, but the principle of Good. Were He
(per impossibile) *not to exist, no good thing would either.*

Charles Hartshorne, explaining St. Anselm. [55]

THEOPRAXY FORSAKES Anselm's claim, attractive as it is, that God "is
not some particularly good thing, but the principle of Good." Principles
can remain unrealized, and God, to actually *be* God, must be realized in
"particularly good things." So the theology of theopraxy prefers to reverse
the second sentence to read: *"Were no good thing to exist, nor could He."*[56]

Moreover, from the fact that there is some "good thing" happening
somewhere, or that once happened somewhere, or that might yet happen,
it is insufficient to infer that God exists everywhere and always. Contrary
to the traditional view, God forms, God comes into being, where, when,
and as what good is happening, and not otherwise. Just as your lap comes
into existence every time you sit down and vanishes every time you stand
up, so God is capable of appearing and vanishing in a single gesture, depending on what you do. What gives us the impression of God's temporal
duration and independence is that we keep the *idea* of God alive by join-
ing God's more obvious "appearances" together in memory and in hope,
so that God becomes a noun rather than a verb, a principle rather than an
activity, a constant rather than an episodic presence.[57]

---

55 *Here is the whole passage:"(W)hat exists contingently is assembled from elements
which previously existed, perhaps in another combination or arrangement....(But) Greatness, unlike other predicates, does not exist by virtue of Being or Goodness taking on some
accidental form like Greatness. God is not some particularly good thing, but the principle of Good. Were He* (per impossibile) *not to exist, no good thing would either. And
as Anselm's teacher, Augustine, said, God is Truth itself; without Him nothing could be
true. Hence (the phrase) 'without Him' cannot express a possible state of affairs." Charles
Hartshorne (1965, pp. 35-36).*

56 *Anselm is here being a good Platonist and follower of Augustine. The theology of theopraxy, by contrast, is committed to the evolutionary paradigm in which the later-emerged
is often better—meaning more complex, efficient, adapted—than the earlier-emerged.
Theopraxy is also compatible with naturalism and humanism in that there can be values
and virtues in the world without God, but, it says, there can be no God in the world without values and virtues.*

57 *The anonymous author of* Theologica Germanica, *written in 1497 and translated by* ›

Complementary to this abstract in-mind-only presence, however, is the continued *functioning* of good laws, good mechanisms, good rituals, inventions, institutions, buildings, and so forth. These things outlive their creators and persist in good-doing, like desert wells that draw water long after their makers have gone. Inasmuch as they continue in this activity, God becomes "infrastructural." God's presence in these cases is less vivid, to be sure, for its very expectedness—less vivid than directly witnessing or being the recipient or doer of unexpected good for the first time. But open oneself to the notion that God is the good we do dwelling in the what-we-did too, and one is flooded by appreciation if not plain gratitude: for God is to be thanked for every bridge that does not fall down, every tree that was planted in the right place, every joke that lightens our burden, and every sentence of the Constitution.[58]

ANSELM ARGUED that both non-existence and *contingent* existence (i.e., existence that depends on the prior existence of something else) were deficient, and that since God was by definition in no way deficient, God *must* exist, and exist non-contingently, which is to say, necessarily. This argument is part of Anselm's famous "ontological proof of the existence of God."

The theology of theopraxy, contra Anselm, offers that contingent existence is in no way "deficient." In fact, quite the opposite is true: that which is ultimately contingent—i.e., that whose existence is dependent on *everything* else's existence—might well have higher claims to our

---

< Martin Luther in 1516, puts it this way: "(I)f ever man or the soul is to be made blessed... one thing alone must be in the soul. (S)ome might ask, 'But what is that one thing?' I answer, it is Goodness, or that which hath been made good; and yet neither this good nor that, which we can name, or perceive or show; but it (Goodness) is all and above all good things." Here you see me arguing the opposite, even as I agree with this fifteenth-century Dominican, that "(A)ll the great works and wonders that God has ever wrought or shall ever work in or through the creatures...can never make me blessed, so far as these things exist or are done outside of me, but only in so far as they exist and are done and loved, known, tasted and felt within me." (Chapter IX, available online at www.ccel.org/a/ anonymous/theologia/htm/v.IX.htm).

58 *The great medieval Christian mystic Meister Eckhard could not disagree more. For him, deeds, good and bad, are soon covered over by time, lost, effaced...and therefore cannot be the locus of God. Only in the Spirit, which is eternal, does their goodness/badness live on. Medieval Judaism, for its part, developed the notion of the Book of Life, in which all of a person's deeds are recorded. This Book exists in a non-physical realm, is eternal, and is read only by God at the time of judgment. Both of these ideas have affinities to the ancient Hindu idea of karma: a sort of spiritual plenum in which currents of good and bad circulate eternally and influence the fates of all.*

>

ultimate respect than that which is simply originary. The lock that has the most tumblers is the best; the person who will arrive only after everything is prepared is most valued.

And so "The last shall be first...." (Matthew 19:30) might mean something other than, or more than, that losers will be winners when God's Kingdom is come. If free and morally conscienced human life is the latest development in the story of life in general, as naturalists might easily agree, then so too is *God* the last-evolved and most contingent activity in the universe ("the youngest and weakest force..."). "Most contingent" because God depends upon *our* moment-to-moment judgments of good and bad in an increasingly complex world, judgments that can change at a wisp, and because human beings as a species stand as the most developed product of billions of years of biological evolution on this earth, and perhaps in this or any other galaxy. Could the stars exist without us? Certainly. But we without the stars? Not for an instant. That, exactly, is what makes us marvelous and the good we do rarer and more marvelous yet.

The theology of theopraxy fully accepts the ephemerality of deeds. Many if not most deeds do indeed dissipate into entropy, and so must be done again. Only our theology, however, bites the bullet as it were, and conceives of God as episodic too, rather like flame ignited under the right conditions. But it does not, on that account, say that human works that persist in doing good (here is a well still drawing water, here is a church turned into a hospital; here is a business providing legitimate livelihoods) are not also God instanced. They are just much more taken-for-granted, and for that reason harder to see as God. Some flames last longer than others, just as some burn more brightly.

23 : Goodness and freedom

WHEN A mother grouse feigns a broken wing to lead a fox away from her chick, is the bird being *good*?

The answer lies in whether the grouse had any choice in the matter. The action would be good, and an instance of God, if she could conceive of other actions, if the ruse was not automatic, if it was a reflective action taken to preserve her chick's life. Atoms, molecules, bacteria, plants, and worms would be good (or bad) as and if they freely or even half-freely chose to support life (or destroy it). Since they do *not* choose anything, however, they cannot be good or produce God. If they could, then every inch of continental drift, every rainstorm, and every species extinction and stellar cataclysm that led to the present day and to *us* would be good, too, and we would have to conclude that God is Process, death-camps and all.

According to the theology of theopraxy, the distinction *good/bad* only comes into existence with humankind more or less as Genesis 1 allegorizes, i.e., not with Eve's eating of the fruit of the Tree of Knowledge of Good and Evil—this was simple disobedience—but later, when she knew she could have done otherwise and felt shame. In other words, the distinction *good/bad* (as evolved from *obedience/disobedience*, of which many animals are capable) comes into existence with the cognitive capacity to imagine acting in several ways under the circumstances, and then acting in one of those ways because one has decided to. Although some animals might also be capable of this (dolphins? chimps?), to say of non-sentient creatures, of inanimate things, or of mechanical processes that they are good or bad is a projection on our part, where "good" simply means "good for us, or life," and "bad" means "bad for us, or life." These creatures, things, and processes choose neither for life nor against life because they do not choose at all. It requires imagination and some degree of freedom to genuinely choose at all, let alone choose the good.

If I might expand:

St. Augustine taught that God (as most then understood God) gives us the freedom to choose (and do) good. But this freedom, once received, is also why we can choose (and do) bad, or evil. This is one solution to the problem of evil, as we discussed in ARGUMENTS 7 under the rubric of "freedom solutions." What Augustine, as far as I know, did not emphasize, but could have, is that God must also give us the faculty of *imagination*. For without imagination, freedom—genuine moral freedom—is not possible. Without the capacity to visualize alternatives or mentally construct possible futures on our own, there is no choosing except between courses of action, or *fait accompli*-s, set before us by others.[59]

So here is the question: How is our capacity to imagine-and-choose, not just choose, increased? Answer: by honoring, preserving, and promoting all forms and instances of life for a long time. That is, by *doing good* for generations, for centuries. For this is how species and lifestyles multiply. This is how productive encounters between them multiply. This is how options and laws, technologies and knowledge, tools, languages, and ideas are increased, and hence how minds and "faculties" are expanded.

Put another way: God gives us the freedom to do good or bad, yes. But *doing good* (i.e., choosing life) *develops the freedom and the imagination needed to choose God*. "Choosing the devil" remains possible, of course, but that choice chips away at the very freedom to choose the devil again. In the long run, evil is suicidal. Only by choosing God do we keep the freedom to choose again. (Cf. Deuteronomy 30:19-20).

Said less atavistically: goodness is prerequisite to freedom and freedom prerequisite to goodness. Each amplifies the other in cycles. Evolution.

Said again in terms of the theology of theopraxy: Our capacity to choose among self-imagined futures and to commit ourselves to realizing only those futures that seem likely to honor and preserve and promote all life, produces the very space required for God to exist.[60]

---

59 *This is precisely the limited kind of freedom that consumers* qua *consumers have in advanced market economies.*

60 *Note the structural inversion of the* tzimtzum *metaphor presented in* REFLECTIONS *18. Here God does not contract "himself" to make room for everyday reality, but rather, everyday reality, burgeoning with complexity and uncertainty, creates the "extra" space for God to enter.*

24 : Theology of theopraxy as a meta-religion

THE THEOLOGY of theopraxy is not offered as a new religion but rather as a meta-religion (cf. ARGUMENTS 13 and EXPLANATIONS 21). The theology of theopraxy allows one to appreciate and endorse what traditional religions offer, with their language, rituals, and myths largely intact. Thus one can be a theopracticing Jew, Christian, Muslim, Buddhist, Hindu, Confucian, Baha'i, Zoroastrian, or Jain. The intention is to help people admire the beauty, wisdom, and rigor of the founding texts and images of their religious heritage from a new evolutionary vantage point, and to participate in religious life with a new frame of mind.[61] Subscribers to the theology of theopraxy could, for example, form discussion groups within the aegis of the church, synagogue, or temple they regularly attend, depending on its level of tolerance.

Through the theology of theopraxy, one re-adopts a religion knowing of its power to civilize and ethicize and *bring about* the God it idealizes as already there. But "theopractitioners" must also be willing to walk away from any religion that produces harm or endorses evil, no matter how attractive it is esthetically or socially. Indeed, the rational perspective of the theology of theopraxy can tell us when to break rank with an otherwise beloved religion. Goodness is the judge of religion, not religion the judge of goodness, just as William James argued should be the case.[62] And this might lead some to change allegiances.

FOR OTHERS, however, embracing organized religion on any terms is not a viable option. They cannot bear to sit through a regular service of *any* denomination. While they might accept that God is the good we

---

61 *That is, knowing that God is a glorious human construction called for by the very processes of life once they reach human complexity, knowing that God is at once humanity's child and humanity's mother-and-father, with all the responsibilities that these relationships imply. Here, again, "humanity" means "humane-ness" or "pro-life-ness" at an ever-increasing distance above animality. When you realize that God is the good you do—nothing more, nothing less—you realize that good can be done on a large number of culture-specific metaphors and narratives. Such culture-specificity is not just a matter of historical accident; it is also a matter of effectiveness. For example, the cult of Mary empowers mothers, and women in general, in Latin America, but would not do so among Protestants in North America. Religions develop to support, and only gently correct, the >*

do, they also believe that *more* good can be done with *non*-religious narratives in mind than with religious ones. This makes it impossible for them to recite the praises of Lord, Our God, King of the Universe, or of Christ Our Savior, or of the Great and Merciful Allah, even with the best of intentions and full bracketing. For such people, the intuition that God nonetheless *exists* has few outlets for expression. It remains stifled. Does it make sense for them to seek the company of others who feel the same way?

I am not sure. Nevertheless, it is interesting to imagine, briefly, what a "theology of theopraxy meetingplace" might be like, and what one might do there.

It would have to be a place that is clean, well lit, well-considered in design, and yet also, in part, accidental, serendipitous. Here people might join together to do some good thing, to discuss, plan, or review new ways to do good, or to discuss moral theories, theologies, religions, and cultural beliefs with a view to clarifying their actual ethical consequences—i.e., as opposed to comparing their "truth," or assuming their equivalence, or docilely reciting their wisdom poetry.

A meetingplace could be in a hospital or clinic, a construction site, a classroom, a kitchen, an animal shelter, a library, a spa. It could be indoors or out. Since the theology of theopraxy does not venerate nature *per se*, such sites would not have to have, or be given, any sacred value. (No sacred value, for example, would attach to any of the cardinal directions, or to facing Jerusalem or Mecca, to sunrises or sunsets, the North Star, etc.) Perhaps, though, they could be sited at the place some extraordinary good was done, just by way of endorsement and reminder. For example, people might meet where Abraham thought the better of slaying Isaac, or where Oskar Schindler had his clothing factory during World War II. Such places are many, and creativity in finding them would be encouraged. "Here significant good was done," the finder would say, "...and this is what happened." These sites, however, would not be thought of as

---

< cultures that cultivate them in turn. This is an entirely circular process, to be sure, with sometimes nefarious outcomes. But at other times religions work to oppose their dominant environing cultures, and when they do they take on profound evolutionary value. An example of this in recent times is Liberation Theology, a movement emphasizing activism on behalf of the poor, which grew up largely from within the Catholic Church in Latin America.

62 "Our test of religion's value is empirical: its fruits must be good for life....To pass a spiritual judgment upon these states [i.e., religious ecstasies and other mystical experiences], we must not content ourselves with superficial medical talk, but inquire into their fruits for life." William James (1985 [1929] Sections III and IV.)

sacred, and would not to be defended by means any stronger than verbal dissuasion of those who would replace them with worse (cf. ARGUMENTS 15).[63] I could also see just walking around in the world pointing to the enormous deposits of goodwill, good law, and life-enhancing intelligence embodied in commonplace things and events: clean buildings, cars stopping at red lights, couples laughing, people holding elevators for others. Civility is an achievement.

LET ME not go on. This is not a cookbook for a new religion. What I have just suggested can be done by people of any faith, as well as by people of no faith at all. For those who cannot embrace their traditional "home religion" with the renewed understanding offered by the theology of theopraxy, Unitarian Universalism or Ethical Culture might offer the best alternatives.

The truth is: God need not be mentioned or even thought of in order to do good. This is very much part of the theology of theopraxy. *When you freely do good, you are bringing God into being regardless of what you think you are doing or what you say you are doing.*[64] Indeed, there are times and places when mention of God, even obliquely, could be counterproductive to good-doing: during a class at a major state university, for example, or on a government committee. At such times and in such places one should not mention God.[65] But were someone to say that "at such times" (in the previous sentence) ought to be "henceforth," or that "such places" ought to be "anywhere," I would say: you are wrong. There are many people, not just evangelicals and fundamentalists, who *want* to feel connected to religion's long struggle with promulgating goodness, if only to see the drama continue and perhaps be part of it.

Certainly, it is essential that "God," the word, be reclaimed for goodness and for reason, and be freed from exploitation, politics, and superstition. This cannot be done if intelligent, moderate, and rational people abandon the use of God's name entirely for fear of being identified with religion's less admirable characteristics.

---

63 *An interesting book that explores this line of thought in entirely secular philosophical terms is Robert Sack (2003). See also Margaret Visser (2001).*

64 *Christians might refer to Matthew 25:31-46 at this point. Much of the teaching of the theology of theopraxy is there, on the understanding that the "last judgment" is in fact upon ourselves and from ourselves in the final hour of each day, each year, each life.*

65 *I shall withhold comment on the new prominence of "God-talk" in the halls of American government under the presidency George W. Bush.*

IT IS often noted that the word "God" does not appear in the American Constitution. The Constitution's authors were deists rather than theists. Although each in his own way professed devotion to Christianity's moral principles, and although each made honorific references to God in other writings and speeches, their agreement, as framers, was that God's favor of the American people depended not on words of allegiance to God in the language of Christianity (or any other religion), but on the sovereignty of deeds, on the natural appeal of acts of justice and goodness undertaken because they were right in the light of reason. This is not to downplay Madison, Adams, Franklin, Jefferson, or even Paine's deep feelings for God. The wave of anti-Enlightenment piety that was sweeping Protestant Europe and the colonies at the time distressed them all.[66] But one could argue that the faith of the founding fathers was purer than any evangel's, then or now, precisely because it risked applying itself without appeal to a watchful and punishing master.

Martin Luther King, Jr. saw the point. Pastor, preacher, and trained theologian, King nonetheless rationed his references to God and made few references to Jesus in public fora. As his friend Richard John Neuhaus wrote in a memoir:

> *I recall rallies when, in the course of his preaching, King would hold forth on the theological and moral foundations of the movement. The klieg lights and cameras shut down, only to be turned on again when he returned to specifically political or programmatic themes. "Watch the lights," (King) commented. "They're not interested in the most important parts."[67]*

The "most important parts"? Matters of theology and morality can remain most important without professing them to be so. God acts in any case. God acts in specifics. "(T)he most acceptable service we render to (God)," wrote Benjamin Franklin, "is doing good to his other children."[68] I cannot claim Jefferson or Franklin for the theology of theopraxy, of course. Or King, or Mandela. But no other creed than this creed of "deed over creed" takes their message more seriously.

---

66 *Historians call this movement "the first Great Awakening." For an overview, see Brooke Allen (2005).*

67 *Richard John Neuhaus (2002). King owed a great deal to the theologian Henry Nelson Wieman, and Wieman's essentially ethical-creativity understanding of divinity. See, for example, Wieman (1964 [1946]), from which this author benefited a great deal.*

68 *Letter to Ezra Stiles, president of Yale, March 9, 1790.*

25 : Lewis Mumford

Is the sense of divinity, then, a mere figment of the imagination, a radical misinterpretation of the elements man finds in his own nature? No: it is only as an over-ruling benevolent providence that the divine is a figment. Our logic is at fault in assigning God to the wrong end of the cosmic process. The universe does not issue out of God in conformity with his fiat: it is rather God who in the long processes of time emerges from the universe, as the far-off event of creation and the ultimate realization of the person toward which creation seems to move. God exists, not at the beginning, but at the end: we shall not find him, except in an incredible degree of tenuity, in the earliest stages of the formative process; for he first disclosed himself in a self-revealing and identifiable form, only in the human heart, as a truly personal God. ...God, latent in nature, is the ideal consummation of the whole process.

—*Lewis Mumford*[69]

HOW CLOSE this is to the theology of theopraxy! But although our theology proffers that God was not present at the Beginning, and that God emerges first in and from us, it does not think of God as an entity that will arrive, or complete "himself," only when humankind, nature, and the universe are morally perfected. Mumford's theology here shades into Teilhard de Chardin's or Samuel Alexander's. Perhaps Mumford had read Rainer Maria Rilke's "Letters to a Young Poet," which expresses the same idea.

In the theology of theopraxy, however, God is here now, not just getting ready to be here in the future. In the theology of theopraxy God evolves and improves indefinitely, just as we humans do, ups and downs included. Doing God's will and enacting God are the same thing.

A RULER approached Jesus and said, "'Good Teacher, what must I do to inherit eternal life?' And Jesus said to him, 'Why do you call me good? No one is good except God alone.'" (Luke 18:18-19) Mumford regards this passage (and the parallel passage in Mark) as proof-positive that Jesus did not think of himself as divine in any supernatural way.[70] We agree (see

---

69 *Lewis Mumford (1951, p. 71).*

70 *Ibid. p. 106.*

EXPLANATIONS 12). I want to go a little further, however, and imagine that Luke's account might easily have read: "...Why do you call me God? No one is God, except goodness alone," and imagine that Jesus was addressing the ruler as well as his (Jesus') followers. On what Scriptural grounds would I even suggest that? Because of the remarkable specificity of deed over faith with which Jesus goes on to advise the ruler:

> "You know the commandments: Do not commit adultery, Do not murder, Do not steal, Do not bear false witness, Honor your father and mother." And [the ruler] said, "All these I have kept from my youth." When Jesus heard this, he said to him, "One thing you still lack. Sell all that you have and distribute to the poor, and you will have treasure in heaven." (Luke 18:20-22)

How many of us, going beyond the easier fundaments of morality, would sell all that we own and distribute the proceeds to the poor? I venture none. Should we all? Perhaps not. If we take Jesus' words to be universalizing beyond this man, this ruler, even God-loving altruists would think twice about implementing any program of *total* wealth redistribution. No, Jesus, as ever, was interested in voluntarism, not obedience, in redirecting the will, not writing new law. Jesus was interested in actionable faith, in people doing what was in *their* power to do to improve the lives of those whose lives most needed improving. The ruler was presumably in a position to do what Jesus suggested he do: he had wealth and power in superfluity.[71]

Then again, how many people, rulers or commoners, would heed such advice if he or she were not ardently searching for "eternal life" or "treasure in heaven" and believed them possible to have? Fewer today than once upon a time, when faith was more literal? Maybe not. The fact that there are agnostics and atheists today, both rich and poor, who practice charity without fanfare and philanthropy without the promise of heavenly reward, represents moral progress. God is with them anyway. If they were not atheists but subscribers to the theology of theopraxy they would understand that "eternal life" and "treasure in heaven" are but metaphors for the profound happiness available here on earth to those who do good, and do good again, which is God's "will" that we do and God's substance while being done.

---

71 *King surely gets it right here: "God never intended for one group of people to live in superfluous inordinate wealth, while others live in abject deadening poverty. God intends for all of his children to have the basic necessities of life, and he has left in this universe enough and to spare for that purpose. So I call upon you to bridge the gulf between abject poverty and superfluous wealth." Martin Luther King, Jr. (1956).*

26 : "If among the stars..."

Rousseau was the first to propose a natural connection between sin and suf-
fering. Our misery isn't groundless but results from our sins. The relation
between the two is all the more direct for the fact that it requires no inter-
vention from God. We suffer because of our actions, but not through direct
divine punishment. Every sin contains its own penalty as a natural conse-
quence, every virtue its own reward. We are the authors of our own suffering
(argued Rousseau) and could be the source of our happiness—not because
God is keeping score and meting out justice, but because He has so arranged
the world that such justice is a part of the natural order.

—Susan Neiman[72]

WHAT ROUSSEAU could not say is that God is the "arrangement of the
world" whenever "justice is a part of the natural order." Which is not that
often. Says the theology of theopraxy: better than the belief that God
works *through* humankind, which suggests that we are puppets of a sort,
is the belief that God is humankind's working-to-promote-life. This suggests that God's presence is distributed (to use a computer science term),
and everywhere originary (like the same software running on millions of
computers).

Says traditional theology, theist or deist: without God there would
be no people, or anything else. Says our theology: without thinking, acting, doing, free people, there would be no God. This does not make humans gods or the "masters of God" except insofar as each of us can bring
theopraxy's God about, *or not*, right where we are, by our own actions. To
be sure, this idea of God (like any idea of God) can be common property,
belonging to all. Which is to say, as a "meme," this God might succeed
and transcend all individuals. The theology of theopraxy's God shares
with the Biblical God at least these transcendent attributes, plus, of course, that of pure goodness. But it makes God smaller in another sense: in
reality, in action. In reality, in action, it says, God is as weak as a feather, as
a curl of smoke, as a glowing cinder. And yet this unmighty God cannot
be dismissed and will not be extinguished until the last human being dies
and takes with him or her the flame that is good-doing for life's sake.

---

72 *Susan Neiman (2002, p. 47), my parenthetical words.*

God is not an oak, but a willow, not a willow but a reed...not one reed, but every reed, millions of reeds, bending in the wind.

If among the stars there are planets with advanced conscious life upon them, then God is there too. God will have another name, but that name will point to the same fragile but persistent swell of goodwill toward life in general that arises unaccountably, but necessarily, in the breasts of any and all creatures who procreate, live, think, cooperate, and die among each other in an otherwise indifferent, contingent, and overwhelmingly lifeless universe.

27 : God as moral action

In *A Theory of Justice* (1971), John Rawls famously argued that when trying to determine whether a new law is going to be just or fair (for Rawls, justice and fairness are all but equivalent terms), legislators should each ask themselves the following question: "Would *I* be happy to be *anybody*—i.e., anybody chosen at random—in a society the same as ours in every respect except that this law was in effect?" Only if they could all answer "yes" should the law be enacted.

For this strategy to work, several things must be assumed. First, the legislators involved must be very risk-averse, because only this would yield laws in which already badly-off minorities would be *sure* to be no worse off. Second, all the legislators must have the ability to imagine themselves being someone else. Not everyone has this ability.

Nevertheless, Rawls' proposal deserves the attention it has received. It uses natural self-interest to test whether a law will be fair. It encourages small groups to become more representative of the larger group that their decisions will affect. It is a way of extending Kant's Categorical Imperative (which says we should act only on principles we would be happy to see become universal law, binding upon everyone, including ourselves) into the legislative process. And it builds in too the Utilitarian principle that seeks actions that will produce the greatest good for the greatest number, with the proviso that (further) harm come to none.

Why mention Rawls here? Because the theology of theopraxy seems to propose an exercise similar to Rawls'. It seems to recommend that we soliloquize thus: "Let us act *as if* there were an omniscient, omnipotent, omnipresent, and omni-benevolent Creator-God. What would *God* do in this situation?" Or better: "Let us act as if there were an omniscient, omnipotent, omnipresent, and omni-benevolent Creator-God. What would God want *me* (or us) to do in this situation?" The correct answer would surely be a *good* answer, which is to say, one that led us to do the good, which is also God('s will).[73]

---

73 *Using a similar strategy, the 17th-century mathematician Blaise Pascal famously argued that religious faith is rational because it is a good wager. Since we cannot* know *whether or not God exists or whether there is Heaven and Hell, we are all well-advised to act in ways consistent with the belief that God exists and will judge us. Worst that could happen if it turns out there is* no *God? We will have lived a moral-because-God-obedient life. Worst that could happen if it turns out there is a God? He judges us well and rewards* ›

But the theology of theopraxy does not finally adopt the "as if" strategy proposed by Kant and extended by Rawls. Why?

Let me first recap. Rawls does not propose that legislators actually believe that they will wake up one morning and find themselves inhabiting different bodies and living in different circumstances. This happens only in fairy tales. Rawls asks them to make law *as if* it could happen. Likewise, Kant does not ask us to believe that every maxim by which we justify our actions could realistically become universal law. He recommends that we behave *as if* it could and should, and we would be happy that it did. These are thought experiments.

Similarly, one could say that one does not *have* to believe in the Biblical God literally in order to believe it wise and good to act *as if* there were such a God—moreover, a God who prefers you and me to do "his" will rather than to step in "himself."[74] Indeed, this is precisely what I suggested in these pages as a strategy for holding to a religion's rituals and language while holding back from literal belief in the theological assertions that support them. But I also suggested that to do so is to take only the first step in the quest to "live in God."[75] For the problem is that moral actions sometimes demand more commitment from us than "as if" thinking alone can support. The problem is: "as if" thinking is ultimately less compelling than "actually is" thinking.

Consider: Most people think of "as if" thinking as a form of play, important to the fine arts and theoretical sciences, perhaps, but properly trumped by "actually is" thinking, i.e., by thinking based on beliefs that are based on facts and on probable, rather than hypothetical, scenarios. True, we learn from "moral fictions," to use John Gardner's phrase. Aesop's fables make good points. Jesus' parables are marvelous and Proverbs is without compare. But when it comes right down it, legal facts and actual situations are what count.

‹ us with eternal life in Heaven. Our theology complexifies Pascal's Wager (as this argument is known) because by "God" Pascal meant a Catholic God, and because Pascal did not distinguish between thorough-going faith and prudential, as-if faith, which his God might.

74 *This was essentially the view of Christian theologian Don Cupitt in the early 1980s. See John Hick (1989, pp. 200–201.).*

75 *Noting that belief often follows on action, many Jewish and Christian theologians proffer that acting as if God exists is a good thing, but also that it is second best,* preparatory to *believing in God fully (in the traditional way). In this book, acting as if God exists (in the traditional way) is offered as preparatory too, not to traditional faith, however, but to the theology of theopraxy, where we realize that the act is God. As though in agreement, the great Christian apologist C. S. Lewis (1960 p. 123) wrote: "Ask yourself: 'If I were sure that I loved God, what would I do? When you have found the answer, go and do it.'"*

"As if" thinking asks us to accept that what we know to be fiction can—and, in cases like Rawls' above, *should*—have equal sway with what we believe to be fact, and this is a hard sell. Given this commonsense bias toward the real, Kant's and Rawls' propositions can go only so far. People will do only so much on an act-as-if basis. I would venture that people adopt act-as-if proposals only if they are convinced of the merit of the procedure's result on other grounds, such as personal history, old-fashioned religious faith, the Constitution, or more deeply-held convictions yet (for example, the notion that all people are created equal).[76]

If the theology of theopraxy, then, is to engage the law, literature, and liturgy of a religious tradition in a new and full way, it ought not to be by reading religious narratives as only "fables yielding valuable moral lessons." Keeping them at arm's length like this might be a start for atheists and a corrective for overly-literalist believers, but this framing of religious narratives (as is done in Religious Studies, Sociology of Religion, Philosophy and Anthropology classrooms around the world) can lend actual support to only the easiest of moral deeds—like giving a dollar to a beggar or comforting a frightened child. But who would do more, or risk more, because they thought they ought to behave *as though* these stories were true, *as though* God exists, or *as though* there were heavenly rewards?

WHEN ONE fully understands that moral action is God, however, the frame changes again in a surprising way. One's whole attitude changes. It is *"t'shuvah,"* a return. When God is in our hands, all distance and all halfheartedness disappear. The framing of religious stories as "special" or "true in a certain way," which they certainly are, does not demote them; it promotes them. After all, when ideas work through acts, they have actuality. Beliefs that are acted upon *have a truth all their own* quite apart from the truth or falsity of what they picture or claim. Stories, hypotheticals, and beliefs that guide behavior become, themselves, agents in the world that are measurable as facts, that can be accepted for what they are, and honored (or disdained) for what they do. They can move us to joy and they can move us to tears.

---

76 *In fact, one might say that people who are prepared to act as if X is true, while knowing it is not, are taking an "as if" position with respect to the proposition itself—as in: "let's act as if Kant's Categorical Imperative was a good strategy, or as if Rawls' 'veil of ignorance' method would work...". Such people are committed to dutifulness and justice, and are interested in Kant's or Rawls' formulae only for the way they suggest operationalizing the commitment they have already made.*

The theology of theopraxy holds that the stories put forward by traditional religions, *in so far as they bring people to goodness*, are preliminary to the God who is actualized when we do good. The paradox is that this God, which our theology holds to be the one and only true God, is not like the God described by the very stories that help bring God about... except that God is wholly good. In our view, stories involving God create something higher and truer than what those stories entertain us with. They create a way of life in which striving to preserve, honor, and promote all forms and instances of life is an individual's highest aim.

If the theology of theopraxy were just a meta-religion, then it might as well meld with Unitarian Universalism, Ethical Culture, Baha'i, or Sea of Faith (to name a few would-be-universal creeds), bracketing God-talk all but completely and focusing instead on virtue and general "spirituality" as supported by readings from the world's wisdom traditions. But theopraxy is something other than that. It offers a unique theology and a unique poetics. It leaves us to choose whether to do good and be silent, which is perfectly fine, or to do good and engage in theological reflection also, knowing that true religion grows from roots not to be scorned, roots to which we must indeed attach ourselves, each to his or her own, without condescension. Whether in church, synagogue, mosque, temple, classroom, or library, we commit not just our lips and our hands to doing God's will, but our minds. For God is a work-in-progress, one to which we may all apply ourselves and, in so doing, help create peace and happiness, more freedom and more life, right where we are.

For many, the path to this understanding cannot be a straight one. There is a famous Zen saying about the path to enlightenment: "First there is a mountain; then there is no mountain; then there is." One might say something similar about the path to theopraxy: First there is a God; then there is no God; then there is. This last God is not the same as the first. This last God is no "as if" God. This last God is the good we do, and this God is as real—as actual—as your smile.

Bibliography

Adler, Felix (1887) *Creed and Deed,* New York: G. P. Putnam.

Adler, Felix (1905) *The Essentials of Spirituality,* New York: James Pott & Co.

Ajzenstat, Oona (2001) *Driven Back to the Text,* Pittsburgh: Duquesne University Press.

Alexander, Samuel (1950 [1920]) *Space, Time, and Deity,* New York: The Humanities Press.

Allen, Brooke (2005) "Our Godless Constitution," *The Nation,* February 21.

Alston, William P. (1967) "Religious Language," in Edwards, Paul, ed., *Encyclopedia of Philosophy,* Volume 7, New York: Macmillan and The Free Press.

Anon. (1941), "Science, Philosophy, and Religion, A Symposium," *Conference on Science, Philosophy and Religion in Their Relation to the Democratic Way of Life, Inc.,* New York.

Armstrong, Karen (1993) *A History of God: The 4000-Year Quest of Judaism, Christianity, and Islam,* New York: Knopf.

Arnold, Matthew (1924 [1873]) *Literature and Dogma: an essay towards better apprehension of the Bible,* London: Murray.

Arthur, Joyce (1990) "Believe It Or Not: Mensa's Religious Quotient," *MC²* (the magazine of Mensa Canada) Vol. 23, #3, available at *mypage.direct.ca/w/writer/mensagod.html.*

Bauman, Zygmunt (2000 [1989]) *Modernity and the Holocaust,* Ithaca: Cornell University Press.

Benedikt, Michael (2007) *God, Creativity, and Evolution: The Argument from Design(ers),* Austin, Texas: Centerline Books.

Block, Gay, and Drucker, Malka (1992) *Rescuers: Portraits of Moral Courage in the Holocaust,* Teaneck, New Jersey: Holmes & Meier Publishers, Inc.

Boyd, Gregory (2000) *God of the Possible: A Biblical Introduction to the Open View of God,* Grand Rapids, Michigan: Baker Book House.

Boyer, Pascal (2002) *Religion Explained: The Evolutionary Origins of Religious Thought,* New York: Basic Books.

Bruni, Frank (2002) "Pope Says Modern Mankind Is Usurping 'God's Place'" *The New York Times,* August 19.

Buber, Martin (1958) *Hasidism and Modern Man,* New York: Horizon Press.

Buber, Martin (1970 [1937, 1923]) *I and Thou,* transl. Walter Kaufman, New York: Charles Scribner's Sons.

Calvin, William H. (1996) *The Cerebral Code,* Cambridge: MIT Press.

Closson, Don (2006) "Islam and the Sword," *www.probe.org/content/ view/720/65/.*

Cupitt, Don (1988) *The Sea of Faith,* London: Cambridge University Press.

Dan, Joseph (1986) *Jewish Mysticism and Jewish Ethics,* Seattle: University of Washington Press.

Dawkins, Richard (2006) *The God Delusion,* New York: Houghton Mifflin.

Debray, Régis (2004) *God: An Itinerary,* London: Verso.

Dennett, Daniel (1978) *Brainstorms,* Cambridge: MIT Press.

Dewey, John (1934) *A Common Faith,* New Haven: Yale University Press.

Dukas, Helen and Hoffman, Banesh, eds. (1979) *Albert Einstein: The Human Side,* Princeton: Princeton University Press.

Dyson, Freeman (2004 [1989]) *Infinite in All Directions,* New York: HarperCollins.

Easterbrook, Gregg (1999) *Beside Still Waters,* New York: Wm. Morrow.

Edelman, Gerald (1987) *Neural Darwinism,* New York: Basic Books.

Epstein, Joseph (2003) "The Intimate Abstraction of Paul Valéry," *The New Criterion,* March, *www.newcriterion.com/archive/21/mar03/ valery2.htm.*

Feuerbach, Ludwig (1986 [1843]) *Principles of the Philosophy of the Future,* transl. Manfred Vogel, Indianapolis: Hackett Publishing.

Finkielkraut, Alain (1997) *The Wisdom of Love,* transl. Kevin O'Neill and David Suchoff, Lincoln: University of Nebraska Press.

Fogelman, Eva (1994) *Conscience and Courage: Rescuers of Jews during the Holocaust,* New York: Anchor Books.

Fox, Everett (1995), transl., *The Five Books of Moses,* New York: Schocken Books.

Freud, Sigmund (1961 [1927]) *The Future of an Illusion,* New York: W. W. Norton & Co.

Friedman, Maurice (1987) *Abraham Joshua Heschel and Elie Wiesel: You Are My Witnesses,* New York: Farrar, Straus and Giroux.

Geering, Lloyd (2002) *Christianity Without God,* Los Angeles: Polebridge Press.

Gibson, J. J. (1966) *The Senses Considered as Perceptual Systems,* Boston: Houghton Mifflin.

Gilbert, Sir Martin (2003) *The Righteous: The Unsung Heroes of the Holocaust*, New York: Henry Holt and Company.

Glanz, James (2000) "Scientist at Work: Steven Weinberg: Physicist Ponders God, Truth and 'Final Theory,'" *New York Times*, January 25, *www10.nytimes.com/library/national/science /012500sci-scientist. weinberg.html*.

Guth, Alan (1997) *The Inflationary Universe*, New York: Perseus Publishing.

Halbertal, Moshe, and Margalit, Avishai (1992) *Idolatry*, Cambridge: Harvard University Press.

Hamilton, Virginia (1988) *In the Beginning: Creation Stories from Around the World*, New York: Harcourt Brace Jovanovich.

Harris, Sam (2004) *The End of Faith: Religion, Terror, and the Future of Reason*, New York: W. W. Norton & Company.

Hartshorne, Charles (1965) *Anselm's Discovery*, La Salle, Illinois: Open Court.

Hassaballa, Hesham A. (2002) "What the Qur'an Really Says About Violence," on Beliefnet : *http://www.beliefnet.com/story/111/story_11172.html*

Haught, John F. (2001) *God After Darwin*, Boulder, Colorado: Westview Press, Perseus Books.

Hawking, Stephen (1988) *A Brief History of Time*, New York: Bantam.

Hegel, G. W. F. (1966 [1876]) *Begriff der Religion*, Hamburg: Felix Meiner.

Heschel, Abraham Joshua (1997 [1978]) *God in Search of Man*, New York: Farrar, Straus and Giroux/Noonday Press.

Hick, John (1989) *An Interpretation of Religion*, London: Macmillan Press.

Hitchens, Christopher (2007) *God Is Not Great: How Religion Poisons Everything*, New York: Hachette Book Group.

Horgan, John (2002) "Between Science and Spirituality," *The Chronicle Review*, Volume 49, Issue 14, p. B7; *http://chronicle.com/free/v49/i14/14b00701.htm*.

Hornstein, Gail (2000) *To Redeem One Person is to Redeem the World: The Life of Frieda Fromm-Reichmann*, New York: The Free Press.

Jacobs, Alan (2000) "George Eliot: Good Without God," *First Things* 102 April: pp. 50-53, available at *www.firstthings.com/article.php3? id_article=2006*.

James, William (1985 [1929]) *The Varieties of Religious Experience*, Cambridge: Harvard University Press.

Jamros, Daniel P. (1994) *The Human Shape of God: Religion in Hegel's Phenomenology of Spirit,* New York: Paragon House.

Kapleau, Philip (1967) *The Three Pillars of Zen,* Boston: Beacon Press.

Kaufman, Gordon D. (1993) *In the Face of Mystery: A Constructive Theology,* Cambridge: Harvard University Press.

Kaufman, Gordon D. (2004) *In the Beginning...Creativity,* Minneapolis: Fortress Press.

Kimball, Charles (2002) *When Religions Become Evil: Five Warning Signs,* San Francisco: HarperCollins Publishers.

King, Jr., Martin Luther (1956) "Paul's Letter to American Christians," speech delivered November 4, available online at *www.mlkonline.net.*

Konvitz, Milton R. (1978) *Judaism and the American Idea,* Ithaca, NY: Cornell University Press.

Kushner, Harold (1992) *Who Needs God,* New York: Summit Books.

Kushner, Lawrence (1994) *God was in this Place & I, i did not know,* Vermont: Jewish Lights Publishing.

Lakoff, George (1980) *Metaphors We Live By,* Chicago: University of Chicago Press.

Lang, Bernhard (2002) *The Hebrew God: Portrait of an Ancient Deity,* New Haven: Yale University Press.

Laughlin, Robert B. (2005) *A Different Universe: Reinventing Physics From the Bottom Down,* New York: Basic Books.

Lawrence, Raymond J. (2006) "Faith-Based Medicine," *The New York Times,* April 11.

Lewis, C. S. (1960) *Mere Christianity,* New York: Macmillan.

Mackie, J. L. (1982) *The Miracle of Theism,* London: Oxford University Press.

Magid, Barry (2002) *Ordinary Mind,* Somerville, Massachusetts: Wisdom Publications.

Maritain, Jacques (1951) "The Democratic Charter," in *Man and the State,* University of Chicago Press.

Masson, Jeffrey (1995) *When Elephants Weep,* New York: Delacorte.

Mawson, T. J. (2005) "Freedom, human and divine," *Religious Studies* 41, Cambridge: Cambridge University Press.

Miles, Jack (1995) *God: A Biography,* New York: Knopf.

Milgram, Stanley (1974) *Obedience to Authority,* New York: Harper and Row.

Miller, William (2003) *Faking It,* New York: Cambridge University Press.

Morowitz, Harold J. (2004) *The Emergence of Everything,* New York: Oxford University Press.

Morriston, Wes (2005) "Power, liability, and the free-will defence: reply to Mawson," *Religious Studies* 41, Cambridge: Cambridge University Press.

Moses, Jeffrey (1989) *Oneness: Great Principles Shared by All Religions,* New York: Fawcett Columbine Books.

Mumford, Lewis (1951) *The Conduct of Life,* New York: Harcourt Brace and Company.

Murphy, S. Gannon (2001) "Christology and the 'Chalcedonian Definition,'" *Minnesota Apologetics Project,* available online at *www.geocities.com/mnapologetics/Christology.htm.*

Neuhaus, Richard John (2002) "Remembering Martin Luther King, Jr." *First Things* 126 (October), available online at *http://www.firstthings.com/article.php3?id_article=2068.*

Niebuhr, Gustav (2000) "Interfaith Meeting Tries to Build on Shared Goals," *The New York Times,* September 2, p. B6.

Nieman, Susan (2002) *Evil in Modern Thought,* Princeton: Princeton University Press.

Nietzsche, Friedrich (1967 [1878]) *The Will to Power,* transl. Kaufman, W, Hollingdale, R. J., New York: Vintage Press.

Nietzsche, Friedrich (1974 [1882]) *The Gay Science,* transl. Kaufman, W., New York: Random House.

O'Keefe, Mark (1998) *The Oregonian,* December 25.

Pinker, Steven (2002) *The Blank Slate: The Modern Denial of Human Nature,* New York: Viking Press.

Pinnock, Clark, ed. (1994) *The Openness of God,* Downers Grove, Illinois: Intervarsity Press.

Podhoretz, Norman (1999) "Was Bach Jewish?" *Prospect Magazine,* December, available at *http://www.prospect-magazine.co.uk/article_details.php?id=3757.*

Prothero, Stephen (2003) *American Jesus: How the Son of God Became a National Icon,* New York: Farrar, Straus and Giroux.

Rawls, John (1971) *A Theory of Justice,* Cambridge: Belknap Press of Harvard University Press.

Ridley, Matt (1998) *The Origins of Virtue: Human Instincts and the Evolution of Cooperation,* New York: Penguin USA.

Rosenzweig, Franz (1970 [1930]) *The Star of Redemption,* transl. W. W. Hallo, New York: Holt, Rinehart and Winston.

Rubinstein, Richard L. (1992 [1966]) *After Auschwitz,* Baltimore: Johns Hopkins University Press.

Rue, Loyal D. (2005) *Religion Is Not About God,* New Jersey: Rutgers University Press.

Russell, Bertrand (1967) *The Autobiography of Bertrand Russell,* Vol. 1, London: Allen & Unwin.

Sack, Robert (2003) *A Geographical Guide to the Real and the Good,* New York: Routledge.

Sanders, John (1998) *The God Who Risks: A Theology of Providence,* Downers Grove, Illinois: InterVarsity Press.

Sartre, Jean-Paul (1956) *Being and Nothingness,* excerpted in Guignon, Charles, and Pereboom, Derk, eds. (1995) *Existentialism: Basic Writings,* Indianapolis: Hackett Publishing.

Schlagel, Richard H. (2002) *The Vanquished Gods: Science, Religion, and the Nature of Belief,* Amherst, New York: Prometheus Books.

Soloveichik, Meir Y. (2003) "The Virtue of Hate," *First Things* 129, January.

Sperber, Dan (1975) *Rethinking Symbolism,* London: Cambridge University Press.

Sperber, Dan (1982) "Apparently Irrational Beliefs," in Hollis, Martin and Lukes, Steven, eds. *Rationality and Relativism,* Cambridge: MIT Press.

Spong, John Shelby (2001) *A New Christianity for a New World,* HarperSanFrancisco.

Spong, John Shelby (2004) newsletter circulated February 11, from qna@johnshelbyspong.com.

Springsted, Eric O. (2002) *The Act of Faith: Christian Faith and the Moral Self,* Grand Rapids: Eerdmans.

Stackhouse, Max L. (2004) "A Christian Perspective on Human Rights," *Society,* Vol. 41, No. 2.

Stark, Rodney (2003) "Why Gods Should Matter in Social Science," *The Chronicle Review,* June 6, http://chronicle.com/free/v49/i39/39b00701.htm.

Suzuki, Daisetz T. (1986) *Essays in Zen Buddhism, First Series,* New York: Grove Press.

Thomas, Keith (1971) *Religion and the Decline of Magic,* New York: Charles Scribner's Sons.

Tillich, Paul (1955) *The New Being,* New York: Charles Scribner's Sons.

Tooley, Michael (2004) "The Problem of Evil," Edward N. Zalta, ed., *The Stanford Encyclopedia of Philosophy* at http://plato.stanford.edu/archives/win2004/entries/evil/.

van Cromphout, Gustaaf (1999) *Emerson's Ethics,* Columbia: University of Missouri Press.

van der Post, Laurens (1984) *Testament to the Bushmen,* New York: Viking.

Vermes, Geza (2000) *The Changing Faces of Jesus*, London: Penguin Press.

Visser, Margaret (2001) *The Geometry of Love*, New York: North Point Press.

Vitz, Paul C. (1999) *Faith of the Fatherless: The Psychology of Atheism*, Dallas: Spence Publishing Company.

von Kreisler, Kristin (2001) *Beauty in the Beasts: True Stories of Animals Who Choose to Do Good*, New York: Tarcher/Putnam.

Wall, John (2005) *Moral Creativity: Paul Ricoeur and the Poetics of Possibility*, New York: Oxford University Press.

Ware, Bruce (2001) *God's Lesser Glory: The Diminished God of Open Theism*, Wheaton, Illinois: Crossway Books.

Watts, Alan (1974a) *The Way of Zen*, New York: Vintage Books.

Watts, Alan (1974b) *Cloud-hidden, Whereabouts Unknown*, New York: Random House.

Weinberg, Stephen (1999) "A Designer Universe?" *New York Review of Books*, October 21; *www.stephenjaygould.org/ctrl/archive/design/weinberg_designer.html*.

Wielenberg, Erik J. (2005) *Value and Virtue in a Godless Universe*, New York: Cambridge University Press.

Wieman, Henry Nelson (1964 [1946]) *The Source of Human Good*, Carbondale: Southern Illinois University Press.

Williams, Robert (1997) *Hegel's Ethics of Recognition*, Berkeley and Los Angeles: University of California Press.

Wilson, David Sloan (2002) *Darwin's Cathedral: Evolution, Religion, and the Nature of Society*, Chicago: University of Chicago Press.

Wright, Robert (1995) *The Moral Animal: Why We Are the Way We Are: The New Science of Evolutionary Psychology*, New York: Vintage Books.

Zevin, S. Y. (2000) ed., *A Treasury of Chassidic Tales*, New York: Artscroll Mesorah.

Zimbardo, Philip (2004) "A Situationist Perspective on the Psychology of Evil," in Miller, A. G., ed., *The Social Psychology of Good and Evil*, New York: Guilford Press.